# Leisure and Life-style

# Leisure and Life-style

## A Comparative Analysis
## of Free Time

edited by
## Anna Olszewska and
## K. Roberts

SAGE Studies in International Sociology 38
sponsored by the International Sociological Association/ISA

First published 1989

SAGE Publications Ltd
28 Banner Street
London EC1Y 8QE

SAGE Publications Inc
2111 West Hillcrest Drive
Newbury Park, California 91320

SAGE Publications India Pvt Ltd
32, M–Block Market
Greater Kailash – I
New Delhi 110 048

**British Library Cataloguing in Publication data**

Olszewska, Anna
    Leisure and life-style: a comparative analysis of free time. –
    (Sage studies in international sociology; 38)
    1. Leisure, recreation & tourism
    I. Title
    306'.48

    ISBN 0–8039–8215–1

**Library of Congress catalog card number 89–062875**

Typeset by The Wordshop, Rossendale, Lancs

Printed in Great Britain by Billing and Sons Ltd, Worcester

# Contents

# Acknowledgements

This book is an international collaborative effort, and not merely in the sense of drawing together papers by eleven authors from nine different countries, for the project was originally conceived collectively in the course of discussions during the first half of the 1980s within the International Sociological Association (ISA) Research Committee on the Sociology of Leisure. There was then a consensus on the need for and, indeed, the urgency of an international assessment of the possibly momentous implications for everyday ways of life of the economic recession or restructuring (as the changes in process were variously described in different lands), the advent of new technology, and the weakening of many governments' commitment to social welfare policies. Apart from leisure being vulnerable to such broader trends, we believed that people's experiences of, and responses to, the changes might vary in significant ways depending on the ways of life to which they were already committed.

Leisure may still be among sociology's lesser specialisms in terms of its number of committed scholars. Yet over the last 25 years the sociology of leisure group has been among the ISA's more active and productive organs. As in most sociological forums, the membership has been constantly replenished, but certain individuals have been active throughout the committee's history. The first president, Joffre Dumazedier, is a contributor to this volume. And throughout the 1980s the sociology of leisure group met much more frequently than the four-yearly cycle of ISA conferences. Its members, though rarely exactly the same individuals, met several times each year for informal discussions, and held formally constituted meetings at conferences organised by national bodies such as the Leisure Studies Association in Britain, and at international events organised by the World Leisure and Recreation Association and the European Leisure and Recreation Association. Several cross-national projects have already been initiated and completed by study groups, including surveys of trends in the arts and sport.[1] The present book, however, is rather different and more ambitious, firstly in that all the contributors consider the totality of leisure and its relationships to broader economic, political and social trends in their societies, and secondly because the book is not addressed specifically to fellow sociologists of leisure but to the wider international sociological community.

At the time when this project was launched there was much uncertainty about exactly what was happening to leisure within specific countries, and enormous interest in whether developments that were known to be under way in given societies were part of an international trend. We felt that, if the necessary evidence and analyses could be assembled, we would have important things to say not just about leisure itself, but of much wider social relevance and sociological interest. These feelings and views were certainly not the exclusive property of the individuals who eventually wrote the chapters that follow. So we acknowledge the assistance of the numerous colleagues, apart from the authors of the following pages, who were involved in the discussions that gave birth to, then sustained the project to completion.

We are also grateful for the help received from the general editorial staff and special advisers to this series at Sage, especially Stephen Barr and Wilfried Dumon. Their support has been patient and constant. We would also like to acknowledge the helpful comments of the anonymous referees who appraised the initial drafts. We must also record our admiration for the efficient and rapid translations provided, when necessary, by the Merseyside Language Export Centre at Liverpool University. Finally, but certainly not least, we thank Patricia McMillan who was responsible for word-processing the successive drafts into the final manuscript.

**Anna Olszewska**
**Ken Roberts**
*October 1988*

## Reference

1.L. Hantrais and T.J. Kamphorst (eds) (1987) *Trends in the Arts: a Multinational Perspective.*The Netherlands: Giordano Bruno Amersfoort; T.J. Kamphorst and K. Roberts (eds) (1989) *Trends in Sport.* The Netherlands: Giordano Bruno Amersfoort.

# 1

# Introduction

## K. Roberts and Anna Olszewska

### The leisure problem

Sociologists of leisure have a long-standing grudge: we feel unjustly marginalised. Modern sociology, we believe, restricts its ability to understand where the world is heading by uncritically absorbing the everyday view of leisure as too trivial to merit serious attention. It is true that the founding fathers rarely referred to leisure. Even so, their works contained implicit leisure theories (Rojek, 1985). And we have no doubt that had Durkheim, Marx and Weber been late-twentieth-century sociologists they would certainly have addressed the growth and role of leisure. During this century there have been quite dramatic surges, in every industrial society and in most developing countries, in the quantity of work-free time, and in the amounts of money spent of sport, tourism, and other forms of recreation and entertainment. The leisure industries have become major business sectors in most countries. This is now widely recognised by governments and economists. Why not by sociologists also?

One reason why sociology needs to grapple with ordinary, everyday life, which nowadays contains so much leisure, is to better understand what it means to be male or female, middle or working class, white or black, young or old, employed or not employed, in a capitalist or a socialist country. The following chapters illustrate time and again the sensitivity of leisure to wider trends and divisions. They show that leisure is an extraordinarily useful indicator of the human significance of the political, economic and broader social changes that have been unfolding since the 1970s.

There is another, even more important, reason for present-day mainstream sociologists paying close attention to trends in leisure. This reason arises from the role that leisure has acquired during its long-term growth. It is not merely in quantitative terms that leisure has become more important than in the past. The inversion that has occurred in all the advanced industrial societies, whereby even the typical full-time employee's leisure time now exceeds his or her paid working time, is just the start, not the end of the story. The more leisure time, money and activities that people enjoy, the greater the likelihood of these becoming sources of values, relationships and identities which are then able to permeate other spheres, including work. This is not to claim leisure as the new social 'base', or that so-called leisure values such as choice, pleasure and expressivity are destined to govern life in general. The production and reproduction of leisure continue to rest on economic performance. Societies create leisure only in so far as their economies produce in excess of more 'basic' requirements. And the growth of leisure in the modern world continues to rest on the relentless application of science and technology. Collectively, as for most individuals, we can never be free of the need to earn our leisure. Paradoxically, the more committed and successful they are as workers, the greater will be any group's leisure opportunities. Leisure can never replace either work or the values that underlie economic success without undermining its own vitality. Hence the threatening contradiction inherent in capitalism, and maybe in all industrial societies, between the values of the economy and the ethos of free time (Bell, 1976). Production and consumption are an inseparable couplet: each presumes the other. The more that is produced, the more there is to consume. The greater the labour-efficiency of production, the greater the time available for leisure. The more people value leisure, the greater will be their incentive to earn these opportunities. Yet, simultaneously, the hedonistic values and identities derived from, and sometimes required in, leisure activities, may undermine individuals' labour power. Conversely, a powerful work ethic, producing workaholism when taken to extremes, may render individuals incapable of enjoying leisure. Max Weber regarded such an ethic, which abhorred consuming all the fruits of one's labour in immediate pleasure, as a prerequisite for societies to break with tradition and allow capitalism to take off. However, the classical protestant ethic seems less necessary, and arguably dysfunctional in advanced industrial societies whose economies depend on buoyant consumer markets.

There are solutions to most social and cultural contradictions. Groups tend to develop norms which define appropriate levels and forms of commitment to paid employment, family life, leisure, and so on. The work–leisure package, with all its potential contradictions, is not a historically novel product of very recent trends. The modern package was forged during industrialisation when work was wrenched from its former family, community and moral contexts. The promise of leisure was then used as a means of habituating otherwise ill-disciplined industrial workforces (Bailey, 1978). From the start it was necessary to define proper times for leisure activities, and proper uses of these times. Leisure had to be kept within bounds. What has happened subsequently is that expectations of both work and leisure have risen. So have levels of economic output and leisure activity. Simultaneously, work time has been reduced and leisure time has expanded. The work–leisure balance has had to be continuously renegotiated with higher demands and, therefore, greater pressure from each side. Harmonious balance has certainly not been set beyond the bounds of possibility. But the heavier the demands from each side of the equation, the more dramatic the likely implications of forced or voluntary changes in production or consumption. Also, establishing and maintaining agreed norms and balances inevitably becomes more difficult in turbulent technological, economic and cultural conditions.

This book was originally planned with *Leisure and the Crisis* as the provisional title. This was between 1983 and 1985, when it was uncertain whether the world economy would pull out and stay out of the deepest recession in postwar history. Unemployment had risen steeply in most advanced capitalist nations. Even if microelectronics were not wholly to blame, it seemed likely that this new technological revolution, with its immense labour-saving properties, would prevent employment recovering, certainly in the short term. Hence the crisis scenario of the world economy being unable to generate the employment necessary to sustain the spending power, access to leisure goods and services, and the life-styles that people had once led, or had learnt to expect. It seemed likely that former links and balances between production, employment and consumption would disintegrate and thereby fuel mass discontent with modern technology, business organisations and political systems.

We always knew that the trends and their impact would vary between and within countries. Some national economies were much stronger than others. Governments' policies differed in the extent to which they aimed to dissipate or focus, and thereby distribute the force of economic trends among different sections of their populations. Within capitalist countries, whatever the governments' priorities, some groups of workers were proving more able than others to attune to economic trends. Some regions remained buoyant while others were sinking into depression. Individuals with up-to-date qualifications were invariably faring better than those whose skills and industries were in decline. Moreover, there are historically rooted international variations in ways of life, and certain life-styles seemed likely to prove more capable than others of withstanding the vicissitudes of the 1980s. Even so, we believed that substantial sections of the populations in most countries would be affected in some way or another by certain global trends – the end of the 30 glorious years in which economic growth and full employment had come to be taken for granted, the new technological revolution, tougher competition in world markets, the shift of manufacturing from developed to less developed lands, and the trend towards service sector employment in the more advanced countries. Hence the idea of inviting an international group of sociologists to analyse and explain the effects of these trends on leisure in their own countries.

When the book was first planned we envisaged most chapters explaining how economic changes had undermined former leisure patterns and aspirations, albeit to different extents and in different ways, and with numerous exceptions. We envisaged discontents being expressed in different ways in different countries, but amounting to worldwide pressure for such changes as would make political and economic systems, and technology, respect and defend instead of riding roughshod over people's preferred ways of life. In the event the 1980s did not become the decade of global economic crisis that seemed likely, or at least possible at the outset. Nevertheless, the following chapters suggest that the economic problems of many countries were solved largely at the expense of their people's leisure. Most people's ways of life seem to have adapted so as to allow their national economies to stabilise and recover, at least in the short term. However, the evidence that follows indicates that, in the not too very long term, these adaptations could pose their own threats to economic stability and progress. The mounting crises of the early 1980s were not really solved so much as displaced into leisure and thereby rendered invisible in so far as leisure, and any problems therein, are still generally regarded as trivial. This book challenges such complacency.

All the authors embarked upon their chapters with an agreed definition of the problems to be addressed. This agreement was reached through regular discussions in the International Sociological Association's leisure research committee during the early 1980s. The initial idea was for each contributor to explain how his or her country, and its people's leisure, had fared amidst the global economic crisis. They were asked to begin with an overview of economic trends – whether the national economy had expanded or contracted in terms of output and employment, what had happened to the level of unemployment, and to the distribution of jobs between occupations and business sectors. They were then invited to explain how their governments had responded to these economic trends, paying particular attention to any efforts to preserve or improve the standards and styles of living of different groups, whether through taxation or social security policies, or by the provision of leisure and related services. Authors were then asked to describe and account for overall changes in leisure activity and spending, and in the life-styles of different sections of the populations in their countries, with regard not only to economic and political conditions, but also to the possible influence of broader socio-cultural movements – women's rights, ecology, health and fitness, or whatever. In the event the authors followed these guidelines to varying extents. Perhaps it would be more honest to say that some ignored the guidelines completely and no one was wholly faithful. Maybe this was only to be expected from an international group of sociologists. Each writer has emphasised trends and issues that, in his or her view, have been particularly significant in the country in question.

We never intended the book to offer statistical comparisons. This was not an option because although most governments assemble data on leisure activities and spending, they categorise this information in different ways. There have been previous cross-national studies that have collected their own evidence using standardised methods and measurements, most notably time-budgets (Szalai et al., 1972). Such investigations can produce findings that are highly significant statistically but sociologically meaningless. Carefully selected facts are rarely comprehensible when extracted from their contexts. This book is strong on context, and though it may lack precise quantitative comparisons the chapters show clearly that many major trends in the 1980s, including the exclusion of substantial sections of the populations from any benefits of the economic recovery and growth, have been present in many countries.

The varied approaches adopted in the following chapters reflect not only the fact that the societies were always very different, and remained so throughout the 1980s, but also the authors' theoretical stances. We suspect that Joffre Dumazedier in Chapter 9 would have emphasised the same trends and offered broadly the same interpretations had he been asked to write about France in the 1960s rather than the 1980s or, for that matter, about the USA or Poland rather than France. In fact his chapter argues that the grassroots aspirations behind Poland's Solidarity movement have much the same sociological significance as recent social movements in France. There has been no attempt to eliminate author bias. After all, this book is supposed to be sociology. Readers will be accustomed to taking account of authors' theoretical, political and other predispositions.

The selection of countries was not arbitrary, though one criterion was the availability of authors. We wanted contributors who could analyse how leisure in their countries had been reshaped by broader economic and political trends, who could use leisure evidence to make socially relevant and sociologically significant statements about these developments, and who would thereby reinforce the case for drawing in leisure from the fringe towards the centre of sociological debates about the modern world. Also, we deliberately sought contributions from socialist and capitalist, occidental and oriental, and relatively prosperous and less developed lands. The selection is certainly not statistically representative, but it offers a global perspective, enables common trends to be identified, and draws attention to types and sources of international variation.

**Leisure during the 1980s**

A further reason, and undoubtedly the main reason, why most authors strayed from the originally agreed guidelines was that leisure did not become the centre of the kind of world crisis that seemed imminent in the early 1980s. The world economy recovered from recession. The main leisure trend of the decade in most countries was not a shattering of former life-styles and aspirations. Such a global trend in leisure, had it occurred, might have provoked worldwide pressure for equally dramatic economic and political restructuring. However, in the following pages it is only the case studies of socialist countries that sketch anything resembling this chain reaction. Ever since the Second World War, the East European economies have remained weaker than their Western neighbours. Since the mid-1970s their central planning apparatuses have proved incapable of the rapid adjustments required by fluctuating energy prices and world market forces. These economies have been equally slow to adopt new technology. So the socialist economies became even less competitive in the world markets of the early 1980s, and their workforces needed to work longer and harder merely to maintain former living standards. Opportunities for such increased effort were not provided by the authorities in all the socialist countries. Nor are such opportunities available for every-one, as yet, in East Europe's expanding alternative economies. Nevertheless, all the socialist regimes have maintained their historic commitment to full employment, though often at a severe price in terms of perpetuating economic inefficiencies (Lane, 1987).

In Chapter 2 Anna Olszewska explains how Poland's economic output and consumer spending fell by over a quarter at the beginning of the 1980s. Such a steep and rapid decline is unprecedented in the modern world except in times of war and following natural disasters. The Polish crisis that Olszewska describes is more severe than the depression of the 1930s in the all-round drop in living standards being deeper and longer lasting. Most people's living standards have been not merely threatened but cut back savagely. Of course, there have been exceptions. Some Poles have prospered in the 'alternative economy', but the majority lack relevant skills and, in any case, their potential customers are impoverished.

In Chapter 3 Gyorgy Fukasz explains how Hungary, in the early 1980s, faced just as severe a crisis as Poland. Price fluctuations in world markets cost Hungary the equivalent of a year's national income. The economic impact in Hungary was as severe as that of the entire Second World War. But Hungary then became one of East Europe's economic success stories of the 1980s. Domestic output rose, more than compensating for the deterioration in the terms of international trade, so the population's living standards were maintained. However, Fukasz reveals some hidden costs. Hungary's economy has expanded not by adopting new technology or more efficient forms of work organisation so much as by persuading people to work longer. Official hours of work have been reduced, but overtime working has expanded more rapidly. Hungary's second economy has also grown. Some Hungarians, like some Poles, have made fortunes as entrepreneurs, but the second economies offer little to the majorities in both countries. Most Hungarians have simply worked longer in their main occupations to maintain and, sometimes, to gain marginal improvements in their living standards.

Certain effects on leisure of declining incomes in Poland, and longer working hours in Hungary, appear very similar. In both countries leisure has become more home centred. Holidays, participant sport and, indeed, most leisure activities that involve spending money or energy outside people's homes have been cut. Holiday facilities in both countries have become increasingly geared to international tourism. Olszewska likens the everyday ways of life that have spread in Poland during the 1980s to the life-styles of unemployed people in Western countries. Leisure is spent increasingly and mainly in the home, watching television, listening to the radio, and reading. The mass media have become more central than ever in most people's leisure even though, certainly in Poland, the public now has less choice of films and publications. Both Olszewska and Fukasz draw attention to the decline in the amounts of time that adults devote to education. They argue that life-styles have become less healthy since many people lack the time, energy or money to do other than just rest. These writers agree that the effects on non-working life of economic conditions in the 1980s can only jeopardise their countries' longer-term hopes of recovery. Leisure has adapted to and, in this sense, has borne the strain of economic trends. The downward spirals that threatened have thereby been arrested, but with alarmingly fragile props.

During the early 1980s both socialist and capitalist countries faced deepening contradictions between the aspirations and expectations that had been fostered to guarantee industrial and political acquiescence, and what their economies could deliver. A difference was that, in the socialist lands, the economic problems were shared by the vast majority of the people. In uncompetitive capitalist economies weaker firms can sink while others thrive. In Poland and Hungary all workers kept their jobs. Inequalities of work and leisure have remained narrower than in the West. Interest in the arts, for instance, is less strongly linked to socioeconomic status in Poland than in the USA. Socialism can ensure that the benefits of economic success are distributed to all citizens, and these same systems also guarantee that misery is widely shared. Hence the general discontent that has led to pressure for reform in Poland and elsewhere in Eastern Europe, and which has pushed the word *perestroika* into the international vocabulary.

The Western world spent the greater part of the 1980s pulling out of the recession with which the decade opened, then surpassing earlier levels of output. Needless to say, countries varied in their economic achievements. Chapters 4 and 5 on Great Britain and Belgium follow the socialist case studies with capitalist success stories, in economic terms at least. However, a cost of recovery in Britain and Belgium, and possibly a precondition, has been wider socioeconomic divisions. The majority of those in employment in these countries, especially workers with key skills, are now enjoying higher earnings and levels of consumption than ever before. But at the end of the 1980s these countries still faced massive unemployment problems. The growing numbers in the retirement age groups, at least those dependent on state benefits, were also becoming more impoverished than ever, in relative terms. Thrusting capitalist enterprises succeed, and their staffs are able to reap the rewards because they can off-load or ignore the less talented, or just less fortunate.

Talk of economic crisis has passed into recent history in Belgium and Britain. In Belgium recovery has assuaged earlier tensions between the country's different cultural and linguistic communities. Neither Britain nor Belgium has faced a political crisis. The 'haves' are now the majority in both countries, and government policies have allowed them to keep a greater proportion of their earnings. The deprivations of marginalised groups may be calamities for the individuals and families directly affected, but their predicaments have hardly become even a problem let alone a crisis for their wider societies. The retired, the unemployed and other disadvantaged groups have adapted and coped, as in Poland. Their leisure has been pared back to 'basic' activities in their homes and families, as in Eastern Europe. The life-styles and problems of the disadvantaged are mostly privatised. On balance, in Britain and Belgium their situations have been aggravated rather than alleviated by the governments' economic, taxation and spending priorities. The gap between media-flaunted life-styles and these groups' circumstances is huge. But why should there be any general alarm unless or until these groups thrust their frustrations on to the public stage? The chapter on Great Britain draws attention to the rising crime rates in disadvantaged areas, and the seemingly intractable problem of unrest among socially marginal young adults. Even so, there may be no crisis while the better-off remain content to pay the costs of social control by working as long or longer, and often harder than ever, often more from fear of losing their positions than because of any real enthusiasm for their ways of life. Among the prosperous, as among the disadvantaged, leisure tends to be home centred, but based on higher levels of consumption. In Chapter 5 Govaerts draws attention to the rise in spending on electronic home-entertainment equipment in Belgium. When the better-off venture for out-of-home recreation it is often in short bursts of conspicuous consumption, as during holidays, or to maintain their health by escaping and recovering from the stress and oppressiveness of work.

Polarisation of rich and poor is familiar in the world's less developed countries. Brazil, discussed by Renato Requixa and Luiz Camargo in Chapter 6, is a rapidly developing country. The 1980s became yet another growth decade in terms of economic output and leisure activity. Yet Brazil is also a country where just 36 percent of the population works in, and supports the remainder from the formal economy. And, among those available for employment in Brazil, Requixa and Camargo estimate that as many as 40 percent are either unemployed or casually employed. They argue that Brazilians are not work shy. Those in employment work long hours by present-day international standards – over 50 per week on average when commuting time is included. Requixa and Camargo envisage a general reduction in work hours, thereby spreading Brazil's workload, alongside the gradual spread of a leisure ethic. Yet the evidence in other chapters indicates that the trend in most market economies since the 1970s has been towards greater polarisation. It seems that developed countries such as Britain and Belgium are becoming more like Brazil in their contours of stratification, rather than vice versa. The forms of welfare capitalism and social democracy that were ascendant in the 1950s and 1960s may have ceased to be an option. The 'haves' seem less willing than formerly to share their work and salaries. Their self-perceived interests, and possibly the economies in which they operate, appear to require them to earn as much as possible, by working as long and as hard as is compatible with the reproduction of their labour power.

Puerto Rico is another developing country. It shares Brazil's unemployment rate of 40 percent or thereabouts. But a significant difference is that Puerto Ricans have never subscribed to a work ethic. Nelson Melendez, in Chapter 7, explains how their colonial history fostered entirely different attitudes towards work. And for many Puerto Ricans work has never become even a financial necessity. Melendez argues that many of the island's unemployed can live as well on welfare as from the low-paid and insecure jobs that are open to the less qualified and unskilled. The typical Puerto Rican life-style is modern. It is characterised by heavy spending, in excess of income, whether from welfare or employment. Puerto Rican life-styles are based on debt. Consumption outstrips production. The entire country is heavily indebted, which is a common predicament in the present-day Third World. The USA plays banker for Puerto Rico, and benefits from access to the consumer market. US corporations advertise and market goods that equate leisure with consumption. Everyday leisure in Puerto Rico, as in all the countries discussed in this book, is now dominated by television which, in Puerto Rico, is full of adverts which surround the purchase of commercial products and services with promises of fulfilment. When Puerto Ricans go out for leisure, shopping is among their most common activities. In Puerto Rico, and probably elsewhere, shopping centres account for much more space, and many more leisure trips, than urban parks. There was no manifest economic or political crisis in Puerto Rico during the 1980s, yet it has immediately been apparent to all forward thinkers, including the island's government, that the imbalance between consumption and production cannot continue for ever. The more prosperous nations are unlikely to underwrite Third World life-styles indefinitely, especially when growing sections of their own populations, like the aged and the unemployed, are becoming trapped in relative poverty.

Japan is surely Puerto Rico's diametric opposite – the twentieth century's leading example of a work ethic in action. Sampei Koseki, in Chapter 8, describes his country as an enigma. It is probably this century's greatest economic success story. Japan's economic growth barely fluctuated during the energy price spirals and recessions of the 1970s and 1980s. However, Japanese living standards still lag behind other advanced capitalist countries'. There is a huge gulf, in Japan, between employees in the primary economy of large, usually high-technology firms, and the much larger numbers in small businesses who generally work longer, for lower pay, and with less security. Even so, unemployment in Japan has remained extremely low by 1980s standards. There is still work for all who want it, and the Japanese very evidently want to work. They work harder and longer than in any equally advanced industrial society. The two-day weekend is still the exception, not the norm in Japan. The enigma is that the 'worker bees', as Sampei Koseki describes his compatriots, do not seem to want to ease up. When official holidays are lengthened, workers fail to take their entitlement. During the 1980s some Japanese have been made to feel that maybe they ought to become more leisure conscious. Foreign governments have urged the Japanese to produce fewer, and to buy more goods, especially imports. Japanese governments have felt obliged to reflect international opinion. But most of the 'worker bees' seem content with their staple 'narcotics' from the mass media and sex industries. These 'bread and circuses' preserve political apathy. So there is little pressure for change let alone a political crisis, and the Japanese economy and currency remain among the world's strongest. Sampei Koseki sees the 1980s as an opportune time for reassessment. He believes that the Japanese need to consider what they have gained from economic growth and just where they wish to head. He detects signs of young people preferring enjoyment to hard work, and of housewives developing leisure-based life-styles. However, the majority of Japan's male, adult workers are continuing to behave in their customary ways. Japan's economic performance has earned much admiration overseas, but it is difficult to parade Japanese life-styles as models for international emulation. Since the 1970s Hungary seems to have been embracing the Japanese answer to recession – harder work for longer hours. But it is simply impossible for every country to run a surplus on its balance of trade, and to win a growing share of world markets.

Joffre Dumazedier believes that in France (and other advanced industrial societies) the most significant changes during the 1980s have not been new, but rather a continuation of longer-running trends – the growth in economic output, the expansion of work-free time, and the rise of leisure activity and spending. Dumazedier's chapter restates, updates and consolidates an argument with which he has become associated during the last quarter-century. He argues that understanding the significance of the above trends requires a new sociological theory, and Dumazedier's own life-project has been towards its production; Chapter 9 is the latest version. The central argument is that we underestimate the role of contemporary leisure if we judge its importance solely in terms of the amount of time that it now accounts for. There has been a 'historical inversion': leisure time now exceeds paid working time. Then, in addition, leisure activities are said to have become a source of values and styles of sociability which cannot replace, but enter into a dialectical relationship with, employment values and structures. Dumazedier argues that the growth of leisure is slowly changing the character of present-day work, family life, education, politics and religion in ways that familiar sociological theories are simply unable to grasp.

Phillip Bosserman's analysis of leisure in the USA is partly congruent with Dumazedier's arguments. They agree that the most important changes in the 1980s have been the much longer-running trends towards a larger and stronger role for leisure which, Bosserman argues, has brought the most advanced industrial societies, including the USA, to the verge of a major historical transformation which he likens to the earlier transition from mechanical to organic solidarity. But rather than these trends having already created new life-styles that sociology, hidebound in its traditional theories, fails to understand, Bosserman argues that his fellow citizens have not yet learnt to translate economic growth into a higher quality of life. He envisages, hopefully, the advent of a 'personal communalism' in which work and leisure will be combined within small-scale communities in which individuals will choose to live freely for their personal satisfactions.

**The invisible crisis**

Taking issue with contributors is not a proper editorial function, but this book's preceding chapters offer few glimpses of the developments that Bosserman anticipates. The search for alternative ways of life was more evident in the 1960s than the 1980s. The most communal societies examined in this book, the communist states of Eastern Europe, seem the least able to generate the wealth to satisfy more basic aspirations, let alone to pioneer prosperous but leisurely ways of life. In the capitalist countries the general trend since the 1970s has been away from, rather than towards, a more equal sharing of work, income and leisure opportunities. In these countries there are wider than ever divisions between the haves and have-nots, the prospering and the poor, those working long hours and those without any paid employment.

The growth of leisure that was studied in the 1960s, 1970s and before arose from technological advances which enabled working time to be trimmed while incomes and leisure spending rose. This was an era when welfare programmes ensured that the benefits of growth reached all citizens. At any rate, this was most governments' stated aim. The growth of work-free time and leisure spending have continued during the 1980s in most countries, but governments have retreated from redistributive policies, and time released from work and higher incomes tend to have gone to entirely different groups. Weaker would-be workers – the oldest, the youngest, the least qualified and the least skilled – have often been driven out of employment altogether. Meanwhile, the financial benefits of economic growth have been monopolised by groups with the capital or skills on which thriving businesses depend.

The kind of crisis which appeared to be threatening in the early 1980s did not become a reality. We can only speculate on the likely implications had the world economy remained in recession, if unemployment had continued to rise throughout the decade, and if most people in most countries had been forced to relinquish cherished leisure possessions, habits or hopes. Mass discontent with economic trends and governments' inability to control them might then have led to new social movements pioneering new ways of life. In the event, the 1980s did not become a decade of this kind of mounting crisis. On the surface, by the end of the decade, there seemed little reason for any major change of course. Even the Polish crisis appeared capable of solution by suppressing or incorporating reform movements, and by restoring growth through some combination of absorbing new technology and persuading and enabling people to work harder and longer.

Our contention is that, in most countries, the economic and political troubles of the early 1980s have been resolved largely at the expense of leisure, as we suspected would be the case, though we did not foresee the specific adaptations that have in fact occurred. Up to now most of the costs of change have been contained within leisure, but we do not believe that this containment will last indefinitely. In every country discussed in this book, with the single exception of Hungary, there are substantial and often growing sections of the populations enduring relative impoverishment, lagging far behind living standards that are normal among citizens in regular paid employment, to say nothing of the life-styles that the media flaunt daily and invite all to emulate. The leisure of deprived groups has been ground back towards 'basics'. It is mostly spent in and around their homes, with family members and close friends. Their entertainment is mainly from television. For the families and individuals concerned, their predicaments may be crises, but up to now most of their problems have been privatised. In every country examined in this book, except Poland, the deprived groups are a minority. During the 1980s they have coped, even in Poland. They have been able to fall back on a basic infrastructure of family relationships and home comforts where they receive the 'bread and circuses' that their societies broadcast. Health-promoting life-styles became trendy during the 1980s, but only within certain strata. Not everyone began playing more sport, taking other forms of regular exercise, or patronising health-food stores. Alcohol consumption has increased in many countries, particularly among marginalised groups, including the young. The use of other drugs has reached epidemic proportions in some places. Crime rates have risen, especially in high unemployment areas. These areas seem to breed above-average proportions of criminals, at least of those who are caught, but these same populations are also crime's most common victims.

During the 1980s many of the world's strongest economies did not need the labour power of the old, unqualified or unskilled members of their populations. Governments were able to survive without these groups' votes. Their wider societies required only the passive acquiescence of the deprived. But what happens when their deprivations begin to corrode the infrastructure that has so far cushioned the vulnerable groups? What happens as neighbourhoods become dangerous and unhealthy places, as families break up, and as homelessness increases? These trends are real, not hypothetical. What happens if and when some combination of demographic and economic trends creates labour shortages that cannot be met without drawing from the new underclasses? Retirement could be delayed, but the groups that have been marginalised during the 1980s include many young adults who have now begun rearing further generations of heavily disadvantaged children. This is how underclasses reproduce themselves down the generations. Is there any prospect of the new underclasses nurturing the kinds of vocational motivation and skill that modern economies require? Even passive acquiescence has a price. Their wider societies will have to bear the rising cost of social services, police, basic domestic and neighbourhood amenities, and 'bread and circuses'. Will the 'haves' remain willing to pay?

The USA still subsidises Puerto Rico. Will Hungary share its relative prosperity with Poland? Will those prospering in Britain, Belgium, Brazil, Japan and elsewhere make sacrifices for their own countries' retired and unemployed? The trends during the 1980s were towards the 'winners' holding on to more of their gains. Today they are working as long and often harder than ever. They are also spending more than ever before on leisure. But much of this leisure seems to be spent displaying wealth conspicuously while recovering from the stresses of earning it, and protecting the individuals' well-being by ensuring that they take enough exercise, consume some healthy foods, and control their drug use which has spread among yuppies as well as the unemployed.

This book's final chapter deals with no specific country, but with a truly cross-national form of leisure, international tourism, which in many ways encapsulates and highlights all the main trends and contradictions of the 1980s. The tourist industry has remained on its steeply rising trajectory. In Chapter 11 Marie-Françoise Lanfant explains how, between 1950 and 1985, the number of people crossing national frontiers rose from 40 million to 310 million, and a further rise to almost 500 million by 1990 was confidently predicted. Fuel crises and economic recessions have resulted in minor pauses, but there has been no halting the upward surge. Of course, international tourists remain a small minority of the world's people. They are minorities even in the richest countries. Tourism has become the internationally recognised trademark of the prosperous – a manner of expressing richness that is understood in all lands. Trips to tourist resorts and sites – the further away and the more exotic the better – are now the favoured way of spending holiday time among those of all nationalities who can afford to pay. Holidays are now among the more expensive single items, occasions for orgies of consumption, in the leisure budgets of the rich.

The tourist industry has surrounded itself with propaganda that envisages all manner of benefits flowing to all categories of people. Tourism is supposed to foster links between countries, promote international understanding, and reduce tensions. It is claimed that the employment generated helps to spread the international tide of prosperity. But the reality that Lanfant exposes often involves locals being cleared from sites, or required to participate in the manufacture of traditions, heritages, cultures, identities and even nature. These products are then 'worshipped' in tourist rites – the rituals of the latest world religion. International tourism provides many stark illustrations of the fragile and often illusory foundations of successful life-styles. It is not so much the rewards of success in the 1980s that have kept many on the treadmill as the fear of slipping down, losing their positions and, maybe eventually, falling into the underclasses. Working a little less in terms of hours, or at a more leisurely pace, do not appear to be options given current forms of business and career organisation. It is understandable if the prosperous do not feel unduly rewarded for their efforts. So why should they be generous towards those who, voluntarily or involuntarily, avoid the pressures of business life? We doubt whether this state of affairs is any more likely to endure indefinitely than the kind of crisis that seemed to be looming at the beginning of the 1980s, but which was averted. If talk of crisis has been swept to the margins of economic and political agendas, this is not because genuine internal and international equilibrium have been restored. The stresses have simply been displaced into people's leisure – most people's leisure, that of the haves as well as the have-nots. This book's, like sociology's, historic purpose is to alert the world to the true facts of its predicament.

## References

Bailey, P. (1978) *Leisure and Class in Victorian England*. London:Routledge.
Bell, D. (1976) *The Cultural Contradictions of Capitalism*. London: Heinemann.
Lane, D. (1987) *Soviet Labour and the Ethic of Communism*. Brighton: Wheatsheaf.
Rojek, C. (1985) *Capitalism and Leisure Theory*. London: Tavistock.
Szalai, A. et al. (1972) *The Use of Time*. The Hague: Mouton.

# 2

# Poland: The Impact of the Crisis on Leisure Patterns

*Anna Olszewska*

The rest of the world has many good reasons for paying close attention to Poland's crisis. During the years preceding the crisis of the 1980s Poland became linked to more developed Western economies through a system of credits amounting to billions of dollars, and through the export of raw materials and goods. Then Poland became insolvent, production declined and exports dwindled, as did the country's ability to repay foreign creditors. However, interest with an economic motivation has been accompanied, and probably overshadowed, by political concerns. Poland is perceived, rightly, as a country shaken by political events which could vibrate in other socialist lands and thus, indirectly, throughout the world system of power. So world opinion has followed closely the recent social movements which have been striving for a comprehensive democratisation of life in Poland.

The country lost its independence in the mid-eighteenth century. Its territory and population were then divided between three states – Prussia, Austria and Russia. Yet the Polish people preserved their language, culture and national consciousness. Their persistent yearning for independence inspired a series of uprisings. Poland became independent again in 1918, and the following years saw a rapid development of the economy and culture. Compared with other European countries which had undergone rapid economic development in the eighteenth and nineteenth centuries, Poland remained relatively backward. Even so, the levels and styles of life of the population were greatly improved and diversified. Economic growth continued after the great crisis of the early 1930s, but was interrupted by the outbreak of the Second World War when Germany invaded Poland. During this war Poland suffered 6 million casualties, and 70 percent of the nation's property was destroyed.

The state established in 1944–5 had an entirely different, socialist character, and the new authorities embarked upon a total reconstruction of the economy, social and political life. The ruined economy and low living standards were gradually improved during the 1950s and 1960s, but the period of greatest economic advance was between 1970 and 1975. Substantial foreign credits, an increase in exports, and a liberalisation of social and political life brought marked improvements. The everyday life of the people changed, and their aspirations rose to even greater heights. They expected their standards of living to become similar, eventually, to those in highly developed Western countries, and the administration kept claiming that these aspirations would be realised. Then in the late 1970s Poland's economy ran into increasingly acute difficulties. Today politicians and social scientists generally agree that, in the 1940s and 1950s, many errors were made in the economy and politics. With hindsight it is perhaps easy to see that these errors were almost bound to produce the successive crises of 1956, 1968, 1970, 1976 and 1980–82.

**The crisis**

The latest crisis has been the most acute in the history of postwar Poland. It has economic, political and social dimensions. Economic growth ground to a halt in 1980. Indeed, the gross national product (GNP) actually declined. Between 1981 and 1986 inflation reached several hundred percent, levelled out at 27 percent in 1987, but was expected to rise again to 45 percent in 1988. Most people experienced a steep fall in their real incomes. Standards of living dropped. A minority was able to take advantage of the situation to make huge profits, and grow richer and richer, but for most people the economic reversal meant shortages of many basic products. Rationing of food, petrol and cigarettes was introduced. By 1987 the foreign debt had reached $36 million.

The problems of Poland's economy in the early 1980s were part of a world crisis. Its course in Poland, however, was rather distinctive. Firstly, the economic crisis in Poland meant shortages of many basic, everyday commodities, including foodstuffs. Secondly, in Poland there was no spread of unemployment. All workers kept their jobs. Thirdly, Poland's crisis was intensified by the introduction of restrictions by creditor countries. Their aims were primarily political, but the direct effects were economic. This is among the few cases in history where creditors have intentionally made it more difficult for a debtor to repay.

In 1981 the administration began to reform Poland's economy, but the first years' efforts yielded disappointing results. The reforms were blocked or blunted by opponents who felt threatened. Hence, by 1985, the economy was lagging further than ever behind those of other European countries. Among the 20 main European countries in a 1985 survey, Poland occupied the last but one place as regards GNP per person. The last place was held by Turkey. Twelve countries had levels of production per capita twice as high as Poland's, and five had levels more than three times higher. In that year, 1985, Poland had the lowest level of consumption per person in the whole of Europe. Even other relatively poor countries such as Jugoslavia and Hungary had levels of consumption exceeding Poland's by more than 40 percent.

Poland's crisis produced not just stagnation, but regression in the infrastructure of leisure, culture, sport and holiday-making. For example, during 1981 and 1982 more than 500 trade union clubs were closed, the number of cinemas decreased, fewer books and magazines were published, and production of certain types of sporting equipment including skis was simply discontinued. This was due to shortages of basic raw materials, the disruption of trade with other countries, and to Poland exporting whatever foreign countries would buy to the disadvantage of the home market. For a time there was a black market for books. As a result of limited production on the one hand, and galloping inflation on the other, books, along with certain other leisure goods, became investment items. Since 1985 production of books has increased considerably but their prices have been raised, sometimes tenfold, which has decreased sales. So books remain luxuries in Poland, which can only hinder the democratisation of culture.

The political crisis has surfaced in several forms. Perhaps the most glaring indication of crisis is that the authorities – the government and the ruling party – have clearly lost their society's trust. The people have voiced fundamental criticisms of their country's political institutions and have demanded changes, backed by strikes and the establishment of new trade unions. Poland's politicians and scientists may agree on the extent of the crisis of the 1980s, but their views on solutions vary. This debate has been in motion for some time in scientific publications, political documents and newspaper articles. The crisis has been variously attributed to an over-centralised economy, the inefficiency of the administration and its agencies, bad investments of Poland's huge foreign credits, neglecting the basic laws of economics, and wasting raw materials and products.

Stefan Nowak described the crisis at the sixth Polish Sociological Meeting, held in 1981, as follows:

> The Polish crisis is an acute economic, social, and political one. Its economic character was determined both by the rate of production

decrease, growth of international debt, and drastic shortages of
commodities. Thus, this crisis was also an acute social one which
occurred when the social system did not provide its members with
expected living conditions. The extent of the crisis was determined both
by the strength and mass scale of deprivation of basic human needs, and
by the fact that people considered these needs basic and found the
source of their frustration to lie in the operation and structure of the
system which had promised an increasing level of satisfaction of
ever-increasing financial needs.

The depth of Poland's crisis can be measured by the discrepancy
between people's felt needs and values, and the performance of the
system as regards their satisfaction. A widening gap between
people's aspirations and their satisfaction has opened not only in the
realm of basic needs, but also in other values – those expressing the
ideals of equality and social justice, and those referring to freedom
and democracy. 'The outcome of deprivation of values connected
with equality and justice is a critique of the social system from the
point of view of its own ideology' (Nowak, 1981). The denial of
aspirations to freedom and democracy resulted, at the beginning of
the 1980s, in a withdrawal from organised structures, and a
preoccupation with personal aims, aspirations and problems. This
produced a social vacuum, and actual social disintegration at certain
levels. Social atomisation and the associated decrease in the
efficiency and effectiveness of the entire socioeconomic system had
various socio-psychological repercussions. Some people experienced a loss of dignity. Others felt powerless and helpless. The mass
threatening of people's sense of personal value has been among the
covert elements in Poland's crisis.

No one claims that Poland's political structures and administrative practices were actually intended to negate the principles of
equality and justice, to deprive citizens of the necessities of life, or
to retard the economy. Everyone in Poland is well aware that it was
at least the intention of the authorities to produce the opposite
results. Yet by the end of the 1970s Poland was in the grip of a
covert crisis syndrome with ever-deepening economic and political
problems. The events of August 1980 marked the passage from a
covert to an overt crisis. The explosion was triggered by financial
needs and demands. At this juncture, however, many additional
demands were raised, including a shortening of the working week
and a lengthening of leisure time. Many groups felt a sense of deep
inequality in access to leisure. There was also a sense of restriction
on how this time could be spent, and thus a lack of freedom in
everyday life, both family and personal.

## The reform of the working week

The events of August 1980 resulted in the negotiation and, later on, the signing of the 'Gdansk, Jastrzebie, Szczecin Agreement' between the striking workers and their government. These three towns were the main centres of the strike movement, and in the discussions leading to this so-called August agreement, the workers expressed a number of demands. Proposals to shorten the working week, to introduce work-free Saturdays, and to lower the retirement age for women to 55 and for men to 60 accompanied more widely publicised demands for the right to strike, freedom of speech and publications, more openness in public life, increased wages and their indexation, and abolition of the privileges of elite groups.

Having signed the agreement, the government did not rush to implement all its clauses, including the reform of the working week. Only when Solidarity threatened a further general strike was the 42-hour week introduced in February 1981. The majority of enterprises then introduced a five-day working week, retaining the eight-hour day. Three Saturdays a month were free, but the fourth remained a working day. Despite prolonged negotiations, the lowering of the retirement age proved impossible to realise. However, the reform of the working week embraced the majority of Poland's working people in industry and services. It was also introduced in trade, which contributed to making everyday life more difficult for consumers. However, the reform did not include farm workers, who still comprise 26 percent of employees in Poland. There were varied responses to the changes. The employees who benefited directly called the reforms a 'blessing'. Most people regarded the reforms as 'long overdue'. The government, economists and many journalists, in contrast, viewed the reforms less favourably. They argued that the changes had been 'enforced' in an unfavourable situation, thereby adding to the country's economic difficulties.

The basic working week in Poland had previously amounted, officially, to 48 hours. However, in many branches of industry, including some where work is particularly hard, actual hours of work were as high as 56 per week. People undertaking work on Sundays and holidays did so in answer to the government's appeals to their patriotism, asking them to work for the good of the country, under pressure from managements in their enterprises, and also because work on these days was better paid. The 48-hour working week was introduced in Poland in 1918 in adherence to the Washington Convention. At that time Poland belonged to the not too numerous group of countries which observed this agreement.

The 48-hour working week then remained in force until after the Second World War and into the 1970s, though it was often exceeded in practice. The 1970s saw preparations for the reform of the working week. One free Saturday a month was introduced, then two. However, the right to these free Saturdays was conditional: enterprises had to maintain production at previous levels. The late 1970s was a period when experts prepared for further stages in the shortening of the working week, but the reality remained unchanged. Thus, the 1981 reform can be regarded as a change which could and would have been introduced earlier, had Poland's economy been sufficiently strong.

The thwarting of the 1981 reforms had many causes. These included a further deterioration in Poland's economy and fears that the lack of facilities for leisure and holiday-making would make it impossible for people to use the time beneficially. However, one factor behind the slow progress was the decision-makers' ignorance about the living conditions and aspirations of workers and their families. The living conditions of the majority were growing worse and worse, and the long working week was experienced as exploitation. Sheer ignorance and indifference towards workers' conditions and feelings were common among the intellectual and scientific strata, who tended to regard the workers as a nameless, colourless mass. Changes in workers' consciousness often passed unnoticed. Decision-makers and intellectuals rarely appreciated the extent to which, in the consciousness of workers, leisure time had gradually become an important value. The adoption of leisure time as a central value was partly a result of greater knowledge of how people in other countries were living and working. The 1970s saw the opening of Poland to contacts with more highly developed countries, which led to an inflow of new cultural patterns and aspirations. The facilities for travelling abroad that were introduced by the government after a long period of isolation also helped to change people's consciousness and values.

**Social revolt**

The 1970s brought an increase in leisure time due to the partial introduction of Saturdays off. The result was that trends in uses of daily and holiday leisure time, which had begun earlier, were reinforced. These trends were towards ways of spending leisure that, in Poland, were previously rare and available only in narrow social groups, though the 'new' patterns were already well established in more highly developed countries. There were increases in the numbers of people watching television, and visiting cinemas and theatres. Tennis, skiing and jogging became popular. Weekend trips to the countryside became widespread among the urban population. More people went abroad as tourists. The car was increasingly adopted as a means of transport for weekend and holiday trips. The leisure aspirations of the entire society increased; the possibility of making life better through a good holiday, or seeing the world as a tourist, appeared to be moving within everyone's reach. The government fostered the propaganda of success, did not reveal the true state of the economy, and thereby created the appearance that it would be possible, before long, to realise all the people's aspirations. Gradually, however, due to shortages of basic agricultural products, people found themselves having to spend more and more time on shopping and household chores, and their real leisure time became shorter and shorter.

The revolutionary events of 1980 occurred at a time when a dramatic slump in production was creating acute shortages of many goods. During this period of revolt, 'leisure time' was devoted mainly to shopping. Waiting in lines and looking for commodities became the main free-time activities of working people. Another time-consuming activity for many was participation in the new forms of political and public life, namely, strikes and protests.

As a result of the legal shortening of the working week in February 1981, mean work time became, for the first time in Poland's history, shorter than mean leisure time. Leisure time increased, but the period of actual rest and enjoyment became very little longer. Shortages of commodities and foodstuffs, as well as the inflation, made it necessary for people to produce things for their own use in their own households. Many people ceased buying services and developed 'do-it-yourself' activities. Time devoted to activities that can be described as 'semi-leisure' increased. Participation in culture and sport actually declined. In 1981 fewer people went on holiday than in the preceding years. Economic conditions were the main limiting factor, but people were also inhibited by the tensions between the authorities and various social groups, and the troubled relationships between Poland and its allies.

However, this same period witnessed a spontaneous development of new forms of cultural life among college and secondary school students, and young working people. Poetry and music were written and performed. Cabarets and street theatres were set up. Protest songs and political pamphlets circulated. The society appeared to be developing a new solidarity. In the same period there was also a growth in religious participation.

**Martial law**

Martial law was imposed on 13 December 1981 and lasted two years. Its toughest limitations were in force for the first two months, then, as time went by, these were gradually relaxed. This period of martial law was an exceptional situation in Poland's history. Apart from the psychological shock, people found themselves with increased amounts of leisure time due to the introduction of non-working Saturdays, while simultaneously martial law limited the opportunities for its use. There was a curfew from 11 p.m. to 5 a.m. (from 8 p.m. for schoolchildren), the country's borders were closed to incoming and outgoing traffic, travel inside the country required special permits, and most newspapers, periodicals and publishing houses were closed. Cultural institutions such as cinemas, theatres, museums and concert halls were also shut. The same applied to restaurants, cafés, schools and universities. People were not allowed to use private cars, and telephones were disconnected. Mail for domestic and foreign destinations was suspended. A single programme was broadcast on the radio, limited to political news and classical music. Television broadcasts were also limited to a single short programme devoted to political events. Only a few official journals appeared. All meetings and assemblies were outlawed. Major factories and enterprises were militarised. This meant that, under the threat of punishment, employees had to report for work at every call of management, even on supposedly non-working Saturdays and Sundays. Many sport stadiums were closed, and were then used for stationing troops.

All the evidence points to a fall-back towards leisure patterns of the past. There was an increase in direct, face-to-face contacts, as well as reading books from home libraries. Social visits became mainly for conversation. Having meals with members of other households became rare because of food shortages. Listening to records and tapes became more prominent in people's leisure. The radio (tuned to foreign stations) was the main source of information about world events. The home became the main site of leisure and recreation. Only two forms of leisure continued to be practised widely outside the home: walking, and forms of cultural life that shifted into churches. These included theatrical performances and concerts. The ban on assemblies and meetings did not apply to churches and religious institutions. Their activities reflected the gravity of the people's situation, and helped to define an emergent social mood – a combination of defeat and hope. This period of martial law saw another increase in religious practice among many social groups. Both trends – the increase in home-centred leisure, and in religious practice – have occurred in other societies, and perhaps would have emerged in Poland even under different economic and political conditions. However, the crisis undoubtedly intensified both trends. Martial law eliminated some forms of play and entertainment since they did not conform to the prevailing atmosphere of extreme gravity and sense of menace. Even jogging, which did not require any special equipment, all but disappeared from streets and parks. Then the gradual lifting of the restrictions allowed renewed access to various forms of leisure that had been popular in the late 1970s.

**Reform**

In 1982 the administration began a reform of the economy, and of social and political life. Officials, experts and politicians themselves now acknowledge that, in the early years, the reforms were ineffective and indecisive, and did not bring the expected results. So in 1987 the administration began introducing the second stage in Poland's economic reforms. The aim was to achieve a balance between the demand and supply of commodities, and to satisfy basic needs firstly as regards food, accommodation and health care. These goals, according to supporters of the reforms, will be realised by making production more responsive to the market, increasing individual incentives, changing the principles of operation for state-owned enterprises, and introducing profit-making. Part of the reform programme has meant steep price rises for nearly all commodities and services. The sharpest rises were in February 1982, and in the spring of 1988. These were accompanied by pay increases, but not at anything like the same pace as prices.

An autumn 1982 survey by the Institute of Philosophy and Sociology into a sample of 5325 respondents' living conditions proved that, in order to protect their existing levels of consumption, households were resorting to strategies such as spending savings, procuring loans, selling valuables and producing at home all that was possible. Food processing, making clothes and household implements including furniture, redecorating flats, and repairs to cars were being undertaken on a do-it-yourself basis. The crisis had led to a spread of 'prosumption' – production at home by consumers in order to satisfy their own needs (Toffler, 1970). This was accompanied by reductions in spending on culture and holidays – inevitable when funds did not cover even food and other basic items.

**Daily leisure**

The daily leisure of Poles was studied in detail in a time-budget survey conducted in 1984 by the Central Statistical Office. This survey embraced 45,087 respondents from 5400 households, and the results (see Table 2.1) are representative of more than 90 percent of the Polish population aged 18 and over. Seven groups of activities were distinguished: physiological needs, work, commuting, outside-household activities, household activities, studying, and leisure, which was subdivided into twenty pastimes. The mean time devoted to the investigated activities, calculated for all respondents, indicated that in the average citizen's 24-hour time-budget the largest block of time was devoted to physiological needs (10 hours 15 minutes), followed by leisure time (4 hours 30 minutes). Work-time amounted to 3 hours 55 minutes, household activities to 3 hours, and studying to just 10 minutes. For the first time in the history of Polish society, leisure time was longer than time spent working. This was a result of the introduction of Saturdays off, as well as a decrease in the number of occupationally active persons. It was also due to the fact that in 1982 and 1983 more than half a million people took the new opportunity provided by the law for two years paid child-care leave.

Paid work was performed by 54.3 percent of the respondents and lasted, on average, for 7 hours 12 minutes. Leisure time was enjoyed by 95.6 percent and amounted, on average, to 4 hours 42 minutes. Studying was pursued by only 3.2 percent, but lasted, on average, for more than five hours a day. There were great differences between women and men. The length of paid work time for women was shorter than for men. However, women's leisure time was also 1.5 hours shorter because the former's household activities accounted for 3 hours more.

The most popular forms of spending leisure time were watching television (80.3 percent of respondents), passive rest (38.0 percent), reading newspapers and magazines (32.5 percent), and casual social interaction (24.1 percent). On a typical day, 18.8 percent of respondents were devoting some leisure time to religious practices, 15.4 percent were going for walks, and 12.4 percent were reading books. Only a very small percentage of respondents were going to the theatre, the cinema, or on excursions. Active participation in sports and cultural events was also very exceptional, and only a small percentage of respondents were doing any voluntary or political community work. Time spent watching television amounted, on average, to 2 hours 15 minutes. The amount of time devoted to social interaction was similar. Time spent on hobbies

Table 2.1   *Time budgets by sex*

|  | Mean time devoted to different activities (in hours and minutes) | | |
|---|---|---|---|
|  | Total | Men | Women |
| Total | 24.00 | 24.00 | 24.00 |
| Physiological needs | 10.45 | 10.11 | 10.18 |
| Work | 3.55 | 5.09 | 2.55 |
| Commuting (to work) | 0.44 | 0.53 | 0.38 |
| Activities outside the household | 1.04 | 1.01 | 1.07 |
| Activities in the household | 3.22 | 1.23 | 4.59 |
| Studying | 0.10 | 0.10 | 0.10 |
| Leisure | 4.30 | 5.14 | 3.54 |
|  | Percentages of persons performing different activities | | |
| Physiological needs | 100.0 | 100.0 | 100.0 |
| Work | 54.3 | 64.7 | 46.0 |
| Commuting (to work) | 61.2 | 68.2 | 55.5 |
| Activities outside the household | 50.3 | 41.6 | 57.4 |
| Activities in the household | 81.9 | 63.7 | 96.6 |
| Studying | 3.2 | 3.1 | 3.3 |
| Leisure | 95.6 | 97.5 | 94.0 |
|  | Average time devoted to each kind of activity (in hours and minutes) | | |
| Physiological needs | 10.15 | 10.11 | 10.18 |
| Work | 7.12 | 7.57 | 6.21 |
| Commuting (to work) | 1.12 | 1.17 | 1.08 |
| Activities outside the household | 2.07 | 2.26 | 1.57 |
| Activities in the household | 4.07 | 2.10 | 5.09 |
| Studying | 5.09 | 5.23 | 4.48 |
| Leisure | 4.42 | 5.22 | 4.09 |

*Source: Analiza budzetu czasu ludnosci Polski w latach 1976 i 1984 (Analysis of the leisure time of the Polish people in the years 1976–84), GUS, 1987: 27*

amounted, on average, to 1 hour 45 minutes, while passive rest amounted to 1 hour 20 minutes.

The main factors associated with different uses of leisure were age, sex, education, family status, occupation, income and place of residence. However, watching television occupied the first place among all groups of respondents. Listening to the radio, in contrast, was most widespread among pensioners and women. Listening to and playing music were most common among young adults, and likewise going to the cinema, playing sports, and making excursions. Religious practices were pursued mainly by women and the rural population. Political and community work were most wide-spread among teachers and persons in managerial posts. Passive rest accounted for relatively high proportions of time among pensioners, the rural population and men as opposed to women.

## Changes in daily leisure between 1976 and 1984

Ways of spending leisure time in the evenings had changed compared with preceding years. These changes can be measured by comparing the results of the 1984 survey with a time-budget enquiry in 1976 (see Table 2.2). The 1976 survey was also carried out by the CSO with a smaller, but still representative, sample comprising 21,819 respondents aged 18 and over.

Table 2.2    *Leisure in 1976 and 1984*

| | Percentages of persons performing the activities | | | | | |
| | Total | | Men | | Women | |
| | 1976 | 1984 | 1976 | 1984 | 1976 | 1984 |
|---|---|---|---|---|---|---|
| Total | 93.1 | 95.6 | 96.1 | 97.5 | 90.7 | 94.0 |
| Watching TV | 67.2 | 80.3 | 72.9 | 84.6 | 62.8 | 76.8 |
| Reading newspapers and magazines | 31.1 | 32.5 | 42.3 | 45.7 | 22.5 | 21.9 |
| Reading books | 12.7 | 12.4 | 11.5 | 11.8 | 13.6 | 13.0 |
| Listening to the radio | 7.9 | 10.7 | 10.9 | 14.6 | 5.7 | 7.6 |
| Listening to music, making music | 1.6 | 2.8 | 2.2 | 4.0 | 1.2 | 1.9 |
| Theatre | 0.5 | 0.3 | 0.5 | 0.4 | 0.5 | 0.5 |
| Cinema | 2.0 | 1.4 | 2.2 | 1.7 | 1.8 | 1.2 |
| Sports | 1.1 | 0.6 | 1.7 | 1.0 | 0.6 | 0.3 |
| Walks | 12.3 | 15.4 | 13.1 | 15.9 | 11.6 | 15.0 |
| Hobbies | 3.7 | 4.4 | 6.2 | 6.8 | 1.8 | 2.5 |
| Passive rest | 33.6 | 33.8 | 39.5 | 47.3 | 29.2 | 32.0 |
| Social life | 24.6 | 24.1 | 23.9 | 23.8 | 25.2 | 24.3 |
| Religious practices | 16.4 | 18.1 | 11.6 | 14.3 | 20.0 | 21.0 |
| Chatting with the family | 20.1 | 26.4 | 22.9 | 29.1 | 18.0 | 24.3 |
| Chatting with other persons | 12.0 | 13.2 | 12.0 | 13.4 | 12.0 | 13.1 |
| Social work and activities | 2.6 | 1.0 | 3.7 | 1.5 | 1.7 | 0.6 |
| Studying | 6.9 | 3.2 | 7.4 | 3.1 | 6.6 | 3.3 |

*Source: Analiza budzetu czasu ludnosci Polski w latach 1976 i 1984 (Analysis of the leisure time of the Polish people in the years 1976–84), GUS, 1987: 64*

By 1984 there had been increases in the numbers of people watching television, listening to the radio, and going for walks. There were also greater numbers spending their leisure chatting with their families, and a slight increase in those spending time talking with other people. There were more people taking passive rest, especially among men, performing religious practices, and listening to music at home. In contrast, between 1976 and 1984 the numbers going to the theatre and cinema declined. The proportion spending some leisure time on sport declined by nearly a half, and the numbers studying or broadening their education were also greatly reduced. In addition, fewer people were taking part in community work or political activities. The main overall trends can therefore be summarised as follows. Firstly, there had been increases in those forms of spending leisure time which were available at home and did not require constant financial outlay or effort. These conditions were fulfilled mainly by television, available regardless of weather, health conditions or financial status. The second prominent tendency had been for people to give up forms of leisure that required not only time but also effort or money on the part of the individual or household. People had been giving up activities which demanded a financial outlay, preparation, equipment or a means of transportation. Examples included sports such as tennis and skiing.

When an economy is disorganised and there exists considerable political tension, and when to organise life at the lower average level requires a lot of time and energy, people find that their resources will simply not stretch beyond the requirements of basic everyday existence and easily accessible pastimes. The concentration of leisure within the household enforced by Poland's crisis encouraged people to adopt new, or to revive older, values. There was more striving to make homes better and more comfortable. People began attempting to improve their appearances by making their own clothes. Home-centredness acted as a means of escape from an external world experienced as posing problems which individuals themselves could not solve, and on which they could have little influence. It was also a means of escaping the conflicts and aggressiveness, as well as the very milieu of work, where many unpleasant changes were occurring.

### Leisure during weekends

Did non-working Saturdays contribute to new and lasting weekend patterns of leisure? Answering this question is not easy. Despite its numerous advantages, time-budget research suffers from a major drawback – too general information. A full answer to the above question would require reference to other types of research such as surveys asking somewhat different questions, observation with or without participation, and biographies. Very little research of these types has been conducted in Poland during the crisis. This section, therefore, simply describes the main tendencies which characterise weekends.

For most Poles in the 1980s Saturday has become a day for numerous occupations. Some people work on Saturdays partly because, as in the 1970s, this 'overtime' is relatively well paid. Some do odd jobs. There has been a growth in the number of women who, despite family obligations, work on Saturdays to increase their incomes and maintain the living standards of their households. Researchers have linked this trend to a breakdown in child care, and disruption of normal household rhythms. Work on officially non-working Saturdays for the higher remuneration has become a source of new conflicts between the authorities and workers. The latter have resorted to strikes to claim higher wages for their work from Monday to Friday in order not to need to work during weekends. When people are not involved in paid work, Saturday has become first and foremost a day for household chores in Poland: cleaning and shopping. Only Sundays and, occasionally, Saturday nights, are times of true leisure. Most Poles spend their Saturdays and Sundays at home, when they are not doing paid work. However, in summer the weather permits some outdoor activities in city parks, playgrounds and forests. In the 1960s and 1970s Sunday leisure centres were created in a number of Polish cities. These usually contained zones for walking, sports centres, restaurants, cafes and fast-food stalls, and stage platforms for concerts. Due to the crisis and the resulting lack of funds for repair and maintenance during the 1980s, the condition of these centres has deteriorated.

A form of leisure characteristic of Saturdays and Sundays, and which has expanded during Poland's crisis, is gardening on small plots of land, or in family gardens. Not counting families with gardens adjacent to their dwellings, some one million Polish households cultivate small plots located up to a dozen miles from their homes. Some 1.5 million households are waiting to be awarded such plots, the area of which is generally 200 square metres. These plots are usually planted with vegetables, flowers, fruit trees or bushes. They may also feature a small weekend cottage or bower. Their cultivation has become a common way of passing weekends, and they have also become sites for social and family gatherings. They are an inexpensive way of obtaining regular supplies of vegetables and fruit. However, their importance extends further. They provide city dwellers with opportunities for manual labour and contact with nature, to transform their environments and to be creative. The plots also meet people's aesthetic needs through observation of nature's charms, and provide some owners with additional income from the sale of crops. However, the importance of gardening plots in Poland does not rest on the opportunity to actually own a small tract of land since, unlike most other socialist countries where most land belongs to the state, over 80 percent of the land in Poland is in private hands.

A small proportion of Poles own somewhat grander summer houses. The spread of summer houses began in the 1970s and has since expanded, but only within the middle- and high-income groups. The growth rate has slowed during the 1980s. Nevertheless, weekends at the summer house continue to be an element in the leisure of part of the population.

For most Poles, Sunday is a day of leisure which is usually spent at home. Uses of Sunday leisure are much as ever, but changes are apparent with respect to the proportions of time, and also the meanings attached to different activities. This applies particularly to the time spent watching TV, and to social and family gatherings. All of these activities have taken on a different character. They are now celebrated in a mood which sets them apart from everyday events. Such meetings generally take place on Sundays, but occasionally also on Saturdays, and often involve alcoholic beverages. For many people the celebration of Sundays is linked with religious participation. Over 80 percent of Poland's population declares its adherence to the Catholic church.

Another feature that distinguishes Sunday leisure (and sometimes Saturday leisure) from everyday life is travel for purposes other than work. Weekends are sometimes occasions for single or two-day excursions. Postwar Poland has seen large-scale migrations of the population, an outcome of urbanisation and industrialisation. Subsequently, weekend travel has played an important role in maintaining family bonds and friendships among people separated by these movements.

The time-budget evidence on ways of passing Saturdays and Sundays in 1984 is summarised in Table 2.3. Weekend travel was most common among young people, and least common among persons aged over 70. It was clearly linked to education and income. The higher the level of education, the more were people likely to travel at weekends. People who did not travel at weekends pointed to the following barriers: 27 percent stressed financial problems and the excessive costs of travel, family obligations were named by 21 percent, and poor state of health by 14 percent, while only 15 percent declared a lack of interest in weekend travel.

Most of those travelling at weekends spent some nights away at the homes of relatives or friends (some 75 percent). The majority used buses and trains as their means of travel: only 11 percent used cars. Poland's economic crisis has halted the growth in the use of private cars which took off rapidly in the 1970s. The use of the car has been restricted by petrol rationing, for the typical monthly allocation is just 24–36 litres. The crisis has also slowed down the expansion of the necessary infrastructure, such as roads and highways, as well as many other services related to cars and tourism.

Table 2.3    *Percentages involved in various uses of time on non-working Saturdays and Sundays in 1984*

|  |  | Total | Men | Women |
|---|---|---|---|---|
| Leisure at home | Saturdays | 47.3 | 49.5 | 44.8 |
|  | Sundays | 76.0 | 77.1 | 74.8 |
| Household chores | Saturdays | 55.3 | 44.1 | 68.4 |
|  | Sundays | 15.6 | 10.3 | 21.8 |
| Obligations outside home | Saturdays | 10.2 | 14.2 | 5.6 |
|  | Sundays | 1.1 | 1.5 | 0.7 |
| Receiving visits or visiting | Saturdays | 10.0 | 9.5 | 10.5 |
|  | Sundays | 25.2 | 23.8 | 26.8 |
| Shopping, use of services | Saturdays | 8.0 | 5.1 | 12.8 |
|  | Sundays | 0.2 | 0.2 | 0.3 |
| Additional paid work | Saturdays | 4.9 | 7.2 | 2.2 |
|  | Sundays | 0.9 | 1.2 | 0.5 |
| Cinema, theatre, entertainment | Saturdays | 3.4 | 3.7 | 3.0 |
|  | Sundays | 4.3 | 4.3 | 4.2 |
| Travel to visit family | Saturdays | 7.9 | 8.2 | 7.6 |
|  | Sundays | 11.7 | 11.7 | 11.7 |
| Organised weekend tours | Saturdays | 1.3 | 1.2 | 1.5 |
|  | Sundays | 1.8 | 1.8 | 1.9 |
| Individual weekend travel | Saturdays | 3.9 | 4.3 | 3.6 |
|  | Sundays | 3.7 | 3.6 | 3.7 |

*Source:* see Table 2.1

## Leisure on holidays

The democratisation of holiday entitlement in Poland dates only from 1974 when a resolution of the Diet gave the right to 26 days paid leave to all persons with ten years or more in the workforce. A small section of the population previously enjoyed, and continues to enjoy, even longer vacations. These are given to people in so-called high-risk jobs, and to teachers and scientists.

Given the conditions of existence in Poland, it is easy to understand why holidays are used for both leisure and household tasks. The time is often used for house repairs and renovations, new furnishings, and so on. Some holiday time is used to take on additional paid jobs. Spending holiday time on household obligations is a long-standing phenomenon which can be traced to the beginning of the century. Using holiday time for leisure and travel was rare until after the Second World War. Travel during holidays, once reserved for the privileged and middle classes, then became widespread, promoted by the socialist state, enterprises and trade unions. At first the working class responded to this promotion hesitantly (Dobrowolska, 1963; Olszewska, 1969). Some time had to pass before travel during holidays became common. However, in the 1970s travel to domestic resorts, and foreign travel also, came to be seen as desirable ways of spending holidays, and became more frequent. However, the crisis of the 1980s halted and reversed these trends. Holiday travel declined, especially during the years of martial law, and the following period of economic and political reforms has not restored the situation that existed in the late 1970s. Conditions of holiday leisure have worsened. Leisure travel has again become inaccessible to many groups. There is a growing gap between those who can afford expensive journeys and those who cannot afford even the least expensive holidays. Leisure during holiday time is an unresolved social problem in present-day Poland.

In 1986 the Central Statistical Office surveyed a representative sample of 24,405 persons aged over 15. During that year only 25.6 percent of the sample were taking the opportunity to leave home for one week or more. The age of the respondents seemed to be an important influence. Young adults were the most likely to travel. In the 70-plus age group, the proportion travelling was under 10 percent. Education was also related to travel. The higher the level of education, the higher the percentage taking holidays away from home. Table 2.4 shows that the likelihood of taking holidays varied considerably between occupational groups.

While one in two white-collar workers were taking holidays, this was true of only one in three to five among different groups of

Table 2.4 *Percentages in different socio-professional groups leaving home for more than a week in 1986*

| | |
|---|---|
| Students | 62.8 |
| Engineers and technicians | 55.0 |
| Other specialists | 45.1 |
| Administrators, clerks | 43.3 |
| Farmers | 3.0 |
| Farm labourers | 10.3 |
| Construction workers | 22.7 |
| Industrial workers | 30.2 |
| Retired, pensioners | 15.9 |

*Source: Uczestnictwo w turystyce ludnosci Polski w 1986 roku, GUS, 1987: 19*

manual employees. The least privileged groups in terms of holidays were farmers, farm labourers and retired people. Only 12 percent of those from the lowest income group were leaving on holidays, against 33 percent in the higher groups.

This study provides a number of clues to the barriers to holiday travel. Many respondents pointed to the financial problems (44 percent), family obligations were the second most often stated barrier (by 22 percent), state of health came third (15 percent), followed by a declared lack of interest in holidays (9.6 percent).

Holiday travel generally takes place during summer in Poland. The sea coast and mountains are the most popular destinations, but travel to other cities is also common. Many (40 percent) of those who travel on holidays do so purely for leisure, but a substantial number (30 percent) take the opportunity to participate in household obligations and farm work. This is understandable given that over 40 percent of those who travel stay with their families or friends. Half of those who travelled on holidays did so by rail. The bus ranked as the second most popular means of holiday transport, while cars were used by just 23 percent.

The 1980s have brought many threats to holiday leisure in Poland. Pollution and deterioration of the natural environment have restricted the regenerative function of holidays. At many resorts it is now impossible to use beaches, or to swim in the sea, rivers or lakes, or to walk in the forests. Many mountain resorts lack clean air. The deterioration of the natural environment is largely a consequence of the economic crisis. Lack of adequate technical equipment, obsolete production techniques, and the absence of sanctions against producers who pollute the environment have all contributed to worsening conditions for holiday and weekend leisure.

In 1986 foreign travel was enjoyed by a very small proportion of Poles, just 3.5 percent. Travelling abroad for leisure and tourist purposes was most common among the urban population (5 percent against 1.8 percent from rural areas). Those who travelled abroad were mostly young people with higher education, and from the high-income groups. Besides students, the groups most likely to go abroad were engineers and technicians. They travelled mainly to the neighbouring countries: Hungary (20.3 percent), the German Democratic Republic (16.6 percent), Czechoslovakia (12 percent), and Bulgaria (9.4 percent). This type of travel was often related to family links abroad. The number of Poles who have emigrated (both recently and in the more distant past) is now estimated at 10 million. Some 24 percent of those who travelled abroad in 1986 went on guided tours, while the rest organised their own travel or were assisted by their firms (16 percent).

Finance was the main barrier to foreign travel – 37 percent of respondents pointed to travel and living costs abroad, while general financial problems were mentioned by another 27 percent. Family obligations were much less of a barrier (mentioned by 15 percent), while state of health was quoted by 13 percent. Lack of interest in foreign tourism was admitted by only 14 percent of respondents; this group consisted mainly of older people.

A comparison between the results of the 1986 study and a similar investigation in 1973 points to major changes. The number of people travelling within Poland on holiday had declined, and the same was true of travel abroad. The number taking holidays in Poland had nearly halved, while travelling abroad had fallen even more steeply (see Table 2.5).

Table 2.5    *Percentages of people engaging in holiday travel*

| Year | Domestic | Abroad |
|------|----------|--------|
| 1973 | 41.6 | 8.5 |
| 1986 | 25.6 | 3.5 |

*Sources:* 'Wykorzystanie urlopow pracowniczych' (*How workers' holidays are spent*), GUS, 1974, CSO and *Uczestnictwo w turystyce ludnosci Polski w 1986 roku*, GUS, 1987: 21

### Leisure in the social consciousness

In the minds of workers, the most numerous class in Poland, as well as within other social strata, leisure and free time have become major values. Notions of a decent life now comprise not just non-injurious work and good remuneration, but also access to leisure and culture, political freedom, freedom of conscience and the freedom to form associations.

It is not enough to describe *behaviour* in leisure time: it is equally important to establish how leisure is *seen* and *experienced*. Some clues as to popular aspirations in Poland are offered by a study of social inequality conducted in 1983 and 1984. This study was based on a representative sample of 2375 persons, plus special samples from selected socio-professional groups – workers and engineers from large industrial enterprises (samples of 394 and 399 respectively). Most surveyed persons stated that in the years 1982–3 their conditions for leisure had deteriorated (58 percent of the engineers and 48 percent of the workers). Only small proportions (6 percent of both groups) felt that their leisure had improved. Asked about the outlook up to 1986, 28 percent of the engineers and 32 percent of the workers expected their leisure to deteriorate even further. Only 20 percent of the engineers and 18 percent of the workers envisaged any improvement. As far as cultural participation was concerned, 19 percent of the engineers and 20 percent of the workers expected it to decrease, while similar proportions, 20 and 18 percent, expected an upturn.

In its analysis of daily life, this chapter has pointed to the low and declining rates of participation in some forms of leisure in Poland, especially in sports, theatre attendance and education. However, all the evidence indicates that, in the social consciousness, these forms of leisure continue to be regarded as very important and, indeed, as almost essential needs. Education and hobbies were named by 74 percent of the engineers and by 43 percent of the workers in the 1983–4 survey as important or very important. The percentages for theatre attendance were 37 and 17. Participation in sports was considered important or very important by 27 percent of the engineers and by 25 percent of the workers, and reading books by 81 and 57 percent respectively. Some 41 percent of both the engineers and the workers regarded listening to or playing music as important or very important, and 30 and 31 percent in the case of the cinema. Only 30 percent of both groups regarded watching TV as an important or very important activity, though nearly all respondents were involved in this use of leisure. Comparing the results of surveys on social *behaviour* and the social *mind* suggests that some activities are infrequent despite being highly valued, which raises the issue of deprivation of leisure needs.

### Crisis and disintegration of styles of leisure

'Style' of spending leisure is used here with a special meaning. The notion of 'style' is borrowed from art and architecture, and means choosing a broad trend characterised by distinctive features. It may mean a specific mode of behaviour which entails posing as 'something' or 'someone'. A style of spending leisure time is thus an outcome of an individual or group consciously choosing activities, aiming to shape and develop them in a certain manner. A total style of leisure is something rather different than merely the sum of the ways in which people spend their time. The notion of a leisure style incorporates individuals striving to achieve a certain state, and all that accompanies this striving.

Let us take an example from the sphere of sport. A sporting style of spending leisure can mean that an individual's time is dominated by sport, that the person wants to become proficient in the selected field, exerts himself or herself to achieve this by practising and buying the appropriate equipment and clothes, and subordinating to it his or her daily life, including other leisure interests. One may say that such an individual has adopted a sporting life-style. We may speak about an overall style of spending leisure when there exists an intention and a will, with individuals striving to take up given activities, and when external conditions allow for the realisation of these intentions and aspirations. Now shaping a style of leisure is possible only when individuals and groups can make choices. The opposite to having a general style is the accidental and occasionally chaotic spending of leisure time.

The main conclusion of this chapter is therefore as follows. The styles of spending leisure time that were being shaped during the 1970s were severely disrupted by Poland's crisis. Existing styles disintegrated. The years during and following the crisis were characterised by accidental leisure, with individuals restricted to what was possible, given the constraints of the crisis. Shaping general styles of leisure is possible only in reasonably stable societies, where individuals can know what conditions they can count on. Thus individuals have the chance to shape their life-styles and ways of spending leisure time. In societies disrupted by sudden changes for which preparation is impossible, people are denied such opportunities. Their leisure is characterised by grasping whatever happens to be available during a given day, month and year, often accompanied by a need to renounce true likes, intentions and aspirations. This is why their present leisure behaviour tells us not so much what Poles themselves are really like, as the circumstances under which they now have to exist.

**References**

*Analiza budzetu czasu ludnosci Polski* (1987)Warszawa: GUS.
Bedskid, L. (ed.) (1984) *Warunki zycia i potrzeby spoleczenstwa polskiego.* Warszawa: IFIS PAN.
Dobrowolska, D. (ed.) (1963) *Robotnicy na wczasach w pierwszych latach Polski Ludowej.* Wroclaw: Ossolineum.
Habermas, J. (1976) *Legitimation Crisis.* London: Heinemann.
*Kryzysy spoleczno-polityczne w Polsce Ludowej, praca zbiorowa* (1983) Warszawa: IPPML.
Milic-Czernak, R. (1985) *Zroznicowanie struktury dobowego budzetu czasu mieszkancow Polski 1982.* Warszawa: IFIS PAN.
Muller, A. (ed.) (1985) *Uzrodel polskiego kryzysu.* Warszawa: PWN.
Nowak, S. (1981) *Dylemat Wieznia.* Warszawa: Kultura No. 39.
Olszewska, A. (1969) *Wies uprzemyslowiona.* Wroclaw: Ossolineum.

*Protokoly porozumien Gdansk, Szczecin, Jastrzebie* (1980) Warszawa: Dokumenty, KAW.

Olszewska, A. (1979) 'Leisure in Poland', in H. Ibrahim and J. Shivers (eds) *Leisure: Emergence and Expansion*. Los Alamitos: Hwong.

Olszewska, A. (1985) *Czas wolny, wypoczynek i kultura w spoleczenstwie okresu kryzysu, maszynopis*. Warszawa: IFIS PAN.

*Raport o stanie kultury* (1986) Warszawa: Narodowa Rada Kultury, Maszynopis Powielony.

Skotnicka-Illasiewicz, E. (1987) 'Zmiany w sferze potrzeb czasu wolnego', in E. Wnuk-Lipinski (ed.) *Nierownosci i uposledzenia w swiadomosci spolecznej*. Warszawa: IFIS PAN.

Toffler, A. (1970) *Future Shock*. London: Bodley Head.

*Uczestnictwo w kulturze w 1985 roku* (1987) Warszawa: GUS.

*Uczestnictwo w turystyce ludnosci Polski w 1986 roku* (1987) Warszawa: GUS.

*Warunki zycia ludnosci, w 1986* (1987) Warszawa: GUS.

Wnuk-Lipinski, E. (1981) *Budzet czasu-struktura spoleczna-polityka spoleczna*. Warszawa: Ossolineum.

# 3
# Hungary: More Work, Less Leisure

*Gyorgy Fukasz*

## Hungary and the world economy

Hungary is a socialist country, but with relatively open borders which leave the economy highly sensitive to wider world markets. This is why the energy price spirals of the 1970s, the crisis in the international monetary system, the heavy credit conditions, the rise in interest rates, and less favourable terms of trade created especially severe difficulties for Hungary. Changes in world market prices destroyed the whole of one year's national income. The economic impact was more severe than the entire Second World War. Mounting international debts combined with strenuous efforts to preserve internal economic equilibrium in the 1980s have imposed heavy but unavoidable burdens on the Hungarian population. Pay rises have lagged behind price increases, which has made even conserving, let alone enhancing, living standards more difficult for most Hungarian workers.

## The Csepel project

It is possible to document the consequences for everyday life and leisure of these broader socioeconomic trends and conditions, together with national economic policies in Hungary, with evidence from the unique Csepel study. This project commenced in 1969 with a sample of 400 blue-collar workers, approximately a fifth of the total workforce, in one of Hungary's largest metal factories. This sample became a panel which was studied intensively throughout three periods: 1969–72, 1975–9 and 1979–82. Interviewing was the main method of enquiry, but time-budget data was also collected, and selected members of the panel were interviewed in depth and treated as case studies. A wealth of information was gathered on work habits, leisure activities and values, and the longitudinal nature of this enquiry enables us to chart in detail the changes associated with broader economic developments. In 1985, after the panel studies had ended, another interview survey was conducted with a 'simulation sample' from the same factory. Members of this sample were not the same individuals as in the earlier panel enquiry. On average, the simulation sample was younger, in 1985, than the members of the then ageing panel. This means that apparent changes in values and behaviour between 1982 and 1985 could, in some instances, be caused by the change of subjects. However, the follow-up study allows us to trace, albeit tentatively, the effects of continuing trends in economic conditions in the 1980s.

The Csepel project was a case study. Neither the factory nor its workers are representative of the larger Hungarian population in every respect. We cannot assume that uses of leisure within the sample are typical of the country as a whole. However, there are senses in which the Csepel findings are genuinely representative. Its workers have been subjected to the same pressures, and have responded in ways that are known to apply more widely. So the Csepel evidence is exceptionally useful for shedding light on the processes linking macroeconomic trends and policies to the life-styles of specific social groups.

The findings and methods of investigation in the Csepel study are reported in detail elsewhere (Fukasz, 1974, 1983, 1984). The following passages draw selectively on the evidence to illustrate, firstly, how leisure trends and problems never arise in an isolated, pure form, but are always embedded in the tissue of broader social relations and economic conditions. This will apply anywhere, at any time. Secondly, however, in the case of Hungary, the evidence illustrates how recent economic trends and policies have had contradictory implications for leisure. New possibilities for leisure have been created. Simultaneously, new barriers have been erected, and the still-evolving end-product could become a crisis in the development of leisure in Hungary.

**Work time and leisure time**

Over the period covered by the Csepel study, official hours of work in Hungary were progressively reduced. The basic working week was cut from 48 to 44 hours, then to 42.5, and then to 40. As a result, official work time today amounts to about 1800 hours per year, no more than in some of the world's most prosperous countries.

Reducing working time is a precondition for a growth of leisure, and this has been a declared objective. However, in Hungary the decrease in official working time has not been accompanied by any reduction in actual hours of work. Rather, it has created the conditions for a spread of overtime working in main occupations and, for many people, second jobs in addition. As a result, total working time has actually increased and leisure time has shrunk. Official and actual working time have never coincided in socialist Hungary. Only 5 percent of the Csepel workers had second jobs in 1969, but a much larger number, almost 30 percent, would have preferred to earn more money instead of enjoying free time on Saturdays (see Table 3.1). During the following years, as Hungary's economy developed, the prestige of leisure appears to have grown. Only 6.4 percent in 1976 and 3.9 percent in 1979 preferred work to leisure on Saturdays. During the second half of the 1970s economic conditions were deteriorating, but workers did not feel the consequences immediately. However, by 1982 the economic crisis was biting and 22.5 percent of the panel wanted Saturday work rather than leisure. The 1985 simulation sample also gave a much higher priority to working on Saturdays than was recorded in the 1970s.

Table 3.1    *Percentages of respondents who wanted to work on free Saturdays*

| | |
|---|---|
| 1969 | 29.8 |
| 1976 | 6.4 |
| 1979 | 3.9 |
| 1982 | 22.5 |
| 1985 | 15.2 |

Broader economic trends and conditions in Hungary in the 1980s have created fundamental barriers to the reductions in basic hours of work leading to a growth of leisure time and activity. People have found it necessary to increase their actual hours of work merely to maintain their conditions and standards of living. Since the mid-1970s second jobs have become increasingly common. The spread of this type of work between 1982 and 1985 among the Csepel employees was dramatic. There are two ways in which Hungarians can extend their working time beyond basic hours. Firstly, they can join so-called Factory Economical Teams (FETs) and other groups in which staff undertake productive tasks for extra pay in what would otherwise have been spare time. During the period covered by the Csepel study the proportion of all the factory's workers who belonged to economical teams rose to 53.3 percent. The second way in which individuals can extend their working time, and thereby enlarge their incomes, is by taking second jobs. In 1969 just 5 percent of the Csepel workers held such jobs. This figure had risen to 10 percent by 1979, and to 16 percent by 1982. In the 1985 simulation sample as many as 43 percent held second jobs.

Hungary's response to the wider economic crisis has involved enlarging its own productive capacity. Liberalisation has been one method. This has meant, among other things, greater use of economic incentives, and encouraging production and earning outside the official economy. These policies have been spectacularly successful in strictly economic senses, but the resulting increase in working time and the reduction in leisure time have been equally spectacular. More officially disposable time has meant less leisure time in Hungary in the 1980s.

**Value orientations**

Cuts in official work time may lead to a widening and enrichment of leisure activities and experiences, but only alongside other favourable conditions. *How* time is used when released from official work schedules inevitably depends on additional factors. Satisfying uses of leisure need a favourable conjunction of objective and subjective conditions. A leisure consciousness, or *Bewusstsein*, is probably among the most important. So have those Hungarian workers who have joined FETs and taken second jobs been bereft of this consciousness?

The evidence from the Csepel study suggests that the main obstacles to a growth and enrichment of leisure in Hungary are not rooted in inadequate leisure education, or in a weakening or absence of leisure values. Rather, the barriers have been erected by objective material and financial conditions. The latter have discouraged individuals from using reductions in official work time to enhance their leisure. We are not entitled to use the case for leisure and culture to condemn the Csepel workers for misspending their time. Orientations to leisure are always rooted in broader value systems. During the panel studies there was a clear trend towards workers placing a higher value on earning money at the expense of leisure activities, but this trend seems to have been a product more of mounting economic difficulties than of changes in basic values. Economic problems were leading to changes in immediate evaluations of free time and its possible uses rather than to any erosion of the basic value placed on leisure time and activities. Throughout the Csepel project work was given a far lower rank in the subjects' values than in their actual behaviour. The workers' leisure was constrained, often increasingly, by a lack of time, money and, in some cases, the energy to do more than just earn a living then recuperate. Many respondents would have liked to attend concerts and theatres more frequently, but explained that they lacked the necessary money and time. Families with young children were particularly constrained. Their need for income was especially acute, and the children restricted the parents' opportunities to go out. Poor housing was sometimes an additional constraint. Some respondents explained that they avoided inviting guests to their cramped flats. Others complained that their homes were too far from their places of work, as well as from theatres, cinemas and other cultural facilities. Interviewers repeatedly reported that workers seemed tired, exhausted and, in some cases, were being made ill by the sheer pressure of work.

In the 1980s Hungary's workers have been spending more time earning money not because they now place a greater intrinsic value on work than formerly. They have worked longer hours out of perceived necessity. In many cases they have been struggling to maintain former standards of life and, thereby, to preserve the conditions for realising leisure values. Paradoxical though it may seem, the enlargement of total working time in Hungary has been the free choice of people seeking to defend their leisure. Their behaviour has been rational in the short run, given the workers' own values, though, as will be argued presently, there could be harmful longer-term consequences for the very values that underlie the behaviour.

### Leisure activities

Hungary's second economy has helped to create a small super-rich elite. There has also been a growth in the ownership of second homes where families spend weekends and vacations. However, most of Hungary's new property owners are from the better-paid, white-collar strata (Dingsdale, 1986). The most spectacular growth of leisure activity in Hungary in the 1980s has been by visitors from other lands. Tourism has been promoted as a currency earner with the result that, by 1985, a country with a population of only 10.5 million was attracting 16 million foreign visitors annually.

The Csepel enquiry gives a better indication of trends in leisure activity among Hungary's own blue-collar workers. Table 3.2 lists the percentages engaging in various spare-time activities in different years. The sharpest increases between 1969 and 1985 were in paid activities. Work was expanding at the expense of conventional leisure interests. Increases in leisure activity were clustered in passive forms of recreation – watching television, and just relaxing.

Leisure in Hungary has not been entirely released from 'natural' rhythms. There are still important seasonal variations. Gardening

Table 3.2    *Percentages of workers participating in different leisure activities*

|                                | 1969 | 1976 | 1979 | 1982 | 1985 |
|--------------------------------|------|------|------|------|------|
| Television                     | 79   | 82   | 80   | 91   | 84   |
| Radio                          | 60   | 46   | 35   | 44   | 41   |
| Newspaper                      | 59   | 57   | 56   | 67   | 44   |
| Books                          | 45   | 41   | 43   | 46   | 47   |
| Family                         | 39   | 56   | 56   | 53   | 53   |
| Gardening                      | 36   | 47   | 46   | 48   | 37   |
| Household                      | 33   | 26   | 29   | 22   | 39   |
| Cinemas                        | 31   | 16   | 14   | 11   | 17   |
| Walks                          | 26   | 30   | 37   | 37   | 33   |
| Participation in sports events | 20   | 6    | 12   | 9    | 8    |
| Hobbies                        | 19   | 30   | 40   | 35   | 26   |
| Building                       | 19   | 23   | 19   | 25   | 17   |
| Parks                          | 11   | 11   | 19   | 17   | 17   |
| Rest                           | 10   | 0    | 11   | 13   | 22   |
| Theatre                        | 10   | 6    | 10   | 9    | 4    |
| Self-education                 | 9    | 15   | 15   | 7    | 10   |
| Handiwork                      | 8    | 12   | 10   | 8    | 16   |
| Cards                          | 8    | 4    | 5    | 4    | 5    |
| Sport                          | 7    | 3    | 3    | 7    | 6    |
| Second job                     | 5    | 6    | 10   | 16   | 43   |
| Social work                    | 5    | 2    | 2    | 7    | 11   |

and sports participation are most common when the weather is good. In winter leisure becomes focused around the home, television, radio, records and books. Even so, it is urban and work-based routines that structure and often dominate leisure in present-day Hungary. Television viewing has become the staple leisure activity. It is cheap and effortless. It is also multi-functional. The interviews with the Csepel workers distinguished various ways in which television was used – as family entertainment, for information and education, and sometimes just for background noise. Radio listening had declined alongside the spread of television, but the radio was still important. It was being used for music and information, and was particularly important at certain times of the day such as in the mornings, around breakfast time, while preparing to leave home for work.

Television and radio have contributed to the strengthening of home-centred life-styles in Hungary, and have led to a decline in cinema attendances: 'Nowadays we can watch pictures on televi-sion.' American films were most Csepel workers' favourites. Their factory had its own workers' centre where concerts, film shows and quizzes were held regularly, and from which excursions to theatres and exhibitions were organised. Most workers took part in some of these activities, but their homes were their main leisure centres. Earnings from main and second jobs were being invested in 'private' leisure equipment – second and third television sets, video-recorders, and on portable and car radios in addition to household receivers. Paradoxically, investment in leisure equipment can sometimes generate more work. One respondent's favourite leisure activity was motor repairs: 'Not for money, but just so as to use it.' Second jobs can also make the home an additional work-base.

This is not the place to delve into all the psychological and health implications of Hungary's second economy, but complaints of fatigue rose among the Csepel workers. In certain respects their leisure was deteriorating qualitatively as well as quantitatively. Individuals had less time and energy for traditional cultural and social leisure activities after prolonged and often exhausting paid work. Between 1969 and 1985 use of the radio and cinema declined. So did sports participation and self-education. The proportion involved in the latter activities never rose above 15 percent. It had dropped to 7 percent by 1982, and only 10 percent of the younger respondents were involved in 1985.

### Reform or deformation?

Hungary's recent history illustrates how leisure orientations and activity patterns can only be properly understood when set in their surrounding socioeconomic context. And once placed in this context the study of leisure can clarify the significance of broader economic, political and cultural trends for everyday ways of life. Leisure in Hungary in the 1980s has been reshaped primarily by trends in the material context, including economic reforms. Relationships between leisure and other areas of life have changed and, in the process, the character of leisure itself has been modified – generally towards less activity and greater passivity. In certain senses these changes amount to a deformation of leisure.

So-called 'liberalisation', the introduction of some market mechanisms in what remains basically a planned economy, has been an outstanding success in Hungary, the envy of some other socialist countries, on certain counts. The strains created by developments in wider world markets have been absorbed. The buoyancy of the second economy has led to increased output overall, and has helped to maintain living standards. It has kept Hungary in internal economic equilibrium, and in balance with wider economic markets. However, there are glaring contradictions in the implications for leisure. Reductions in official hours of work, which were originally planned to facilitate an enrichment of culture, have actually led to people working longer and enjoying less leisure time. Defending their standards of living has obliged workers to sacrifice the very time and energy on which their preferred life-styles are based.

There can be no denying the objective contradiction between the current restructuring of time use on the one hand, and on the other, the higher erudition, education and skill requirements on which future economic growth and therefore leisure must depend. The low and declining levels of participation in continuing training and instruction among the Csepel workers, and their reduced inclination to engage in these activities, should be read as warning signals. Shorter hours of work and greater leisure are among the conditions for permanent, lifelong education. Nevertheless, despite reductions in official work time, broader economic trends and policies in Hungary have been forcing workers to dissipate and sacrifice the future for momentary gratifications or, in some cases, merely to hang on to existing standards of living. These trends are bound to make economic modernisation increasingly difficult and, indeed, could strangle the goose that would otherwise lay golden eggs.

## References

Dingsdale, A. (1986) 'Ideology and Leisure under Socialism: the Geography of Second Homes in Hungary', *Leisure Studies*, 5: 35–55.

Fukasz, G. (1974) 'Effects Produced by the Introduction of Saturdays off in the Weekend Activities of Hungarian Workers', *Society and Leisure*, 3: 59–71.

Fukasz, G. (1983) 'Les Changements dans les Loisirs des Ouvriers Hongrois 1969–1979', *Society and Leisure*, 5: 307–20.

Fukasz, G. (1984) 'Basic Features of Leisure Habits of Workers at the Hungarian Csepel Factory over the Years 1969–1982', *Leisure Newsletter*, 11: 29–33.

# 4

# Great Britain: Socioeconomic Polarisation and the Implications for Leisure

## K. Roberts

### The economy: breakthrough or breakup?

In 1987 the Thatcher government sought and achieved re-election claiming a record of proven economic success. Britain was then in her sixth year of continuous economic growth. The rate of inflation had been lowered from over 20 percent in the 1970s to 4 percent in 1987. The number of workers in employment had risen steadily since 1983. Wages and salaries had risen well ahead of inflation. Taxes on incomes had been lowered. Company profits were at historically high levels. The stock market had broken through former ceilings. The Conservative Party claimed that, until 1979, Britain was over-taxed, many firms were over-subsidised, and even more were overmanned. Too many were said to be controlled by indifferent managers who were intimidated by over-powerful trade unions. Hence the severe impact of the 1979–81 world recession, the deepest in postwar history. 'Lame ducks' had to be allowed to sink. Excess labour had to be shaken out to give firms any chance of survival. The medicine was admittedly unpleasant. It meant a dramatic rise in unemployment between 1979 and 1982. Subsequently, the government could claim, the leaner and fitter firms that survived the recession, together with new companies, had begun winning larger shares of domestic and overseas markets. On all these counts the Thatcher administration could claim a breakthrough, and could present Britain's economy as a success story of the 1980s.

The opposition parties spread different 1987 election messages. They insisted that the 1980s had seen Britain sinking into an ever-deeper economic crisis. They deplored the seemingly permanent loss of manufacturing capacity that had occurred between 1979 and 1982 when many firms disappeared completely. In 1987 Britain's manufacturing output was still beneath its 1979 level. During the 1980s, for the first time in its industrial history, Britain was carrying a trade deficit in manufactured goods. In 1987 unemployment was still above 3 million, approximately 13 percent of the workforce. There had been no significant decline in these figures since 1982. The numbers living in poverty had increased substantially since 1979. The consumer boom of the 1980s was said to be based on credit and imports, the latter funded by the country's diminishing reserves of North Sea oil. By 1987 many families, communities and entire regions had already experienced years of crisis which, government critics claimed, would grip the entire nation eventually unless there was a radical change in economic management. Britain's economic base was judged in danger of total disintegration.

The health of the British economy has varied according to the observers' politics, but all parties have agreed on certain points, such as that the country has felt the full weight of recent worldwide trends. Unemployment in Britain rose following the 1973–4 oil price spiral. The level of joblessness subsequently declined, but lurched upwards again even more sharply during the 1979–81 recession. Firms and jobs were particularly hard hit in manufacturing sectors where the impact of recession was aggravated by the advent of micro-electronic technology. After 1982, despite the recovery of Britain's manufacturing output, employment in manufacturing continued to decline. Recent job creation has been mainly in private services – in financial and business services, hotels and catering, and sport and recreation.

Employment in Britain has shifted from manufacturing to services, and from manual to non-manual occupations. The proportions and absolute numbers of jobs at the professional, management and technician levels have increased. This is partly a product of the decline in manufacturing employment, but occupational restructuring within firms, especially by manufacturing companies, has also contributed. New technologies have generally meant fewer operatives, and more jobs in the design and management of the new systems. Britain's blue-collar jobs have declined in number, and changed in character. In the past male employees in manufacturing were rightly treated as the backbone of the manual working class. They are now outnumbered by a new working class based in service industries. Not all service sector jobs are white collar. These businesses employ thousands of sales assistants, cooks, cleaners and security staff. Many of these jobs are part time, and a high proportion are filled by women.

The destruction of old jobs and the generation of new employment have tended to occur in entirely different parts of Britain. Regional inequalities have widened. New jobs tend to be based in the south-east, the seat of government and where most of Britain's high-technology manufacturers and corporation headquarters are located. Industry no longer needs to be located close to coalfields. It makes better sense to locate amidst the largest domestic market, in the south-east, and close to Britain's main trading partners in continental Europe. Britain's provinces have suffered a net decline in employment, especially blue-collar employment. Hence the talk of two nations. However, there are equally dramatic inequalities within regions. The majority of would-be workers are still in employment even in Britain's most depressed areas, and many have good jobs in the public sector, or in successful manufacturing and private service companies. Conversely, there are pockets of high unemployment within the generally prosperous south-east. The unqualified and unskilled, and Britain's ethnic minorities, are heavily over-represented within these pockets.

Most people are inevitably concerned less about the performance of the economy in general than about trends in their own conditions and prospects, which have varied considerably. Britain in the 1980s has become a more polarised society. People's experiences have depended on the parts of the country they inhabit, their skills and qualifications, and the industries in which their experience and careers have been based. Over 3 million were unemployed in 1987. More people than ever were dependent on state benefits, and their standards of living were lagging further behind the average than in previous decades. Simultaneously, more people than ever were prospering. Some had made fortunes, while far greater numbers had simply seen their incomes and standards of living forging well ahead of price rises. Which of Britain's politicians appeared to be telling the truth in 1987 varied with the experiences of their audiences.

**Government policies**

Making sense of political responses to economic trends in Britain in the 1980s depends on recognising that the country's Conservative governments subscribed to the 'breakthrough', not the 'crisis' definition of the situation. Ministers acknowledged that the economy was severely battered by the 1979–81 recession. It was then government policy to expose firms and workers to the full rigours of market forces, thereby motivating all sections of the population to surmount their own problems. This meant ensuring that success was rewarded handsomely, and allowing failure to be penalised. The government endeavoured to revive enterprise by encouraging firms and individuals to stand on their own feet, and to accept responsibility for shaping their own prospects. Part of this strategy involved releasing businesses from political control, most spectacularly in the series of transfers of nationalised industries to the private sector – oil, telecommunications, gas, and Britain's main airline. Reducing taxes on earnings was a complementary strategy. The standard rate of income tax was cut in a series of stages from 33 percent in 1979 to 25 percent in 1988. Higher rates of taxation on top incomes were cut even more sharply and dramatically, from over 80 percent to 60 percent immediately following the 1979 election, then to 40 percent in the first budget after the 1987 election.

The government aimed to reduce its own spending, as a proportion of the gross national product, if not absolutely. However, the same government regarded the national interest as requiring higher spending on defence and policing. Circumstances forced increased spending in certain other areas – mainly on state pensions alongside the growth of the population in the retirement age group, and on unemployment benefits. This meant cut-backs in other programmes in order to prevent the rise of total government spending. The victims included most sections of the public dependent on state welfare. Britain's state earnings-related pensions scheme was dismantled. In the future the retired will receive only basic, flat-rate state pensions. New restrictions were imposed on the benefit entitlements of certain unemployed groups, including young people. Public housing subsidies were slashed. Homelessness increased. Even so, the government needed to raise other taxes in order to create scope for reductions in taxes on earnings. There were sharp increases in VAT, Britain's main sales tax, and in 'the rates', the property taxes imposed by local authorities. Rather than counterbalancing, these government taxation and spending policies tended to widen the inequalities arising from economic trends. As a result Britain's rich grew much richer in the 1980s, while the poor became relatively poorer. Critics accused the government of being uncaring and heartless. Ministers replied that their policies guaranteed a safety net for the weakest, while creating incentives for everyone to earn self-respect by supporting themselves in employment, even those who could obtain only low-paid jobs. Moreover, the government argued that its policies were building the incentives necessary to stimulate the enterprise which, given time, would generate higher living standards for all.

Spending on public leisure services was not actually cut by the Thatcher administrations. Grants to the main national agencies – the Sports Council and the Arts Council – did not decline, but any expectation that these agencies' incomes would rise inexorably was shattered. Sport and the arts were advised to tap other sources of sponsorship, meaning commercial advertisers. Central government experienced only limited success in its efforts to curb spending by Britain's local authorities. The latter's spending on leisure services continued to rise in the 1980s, though at a more modest rate than in the 1970s when new public sports and leisure centres were built throughout the land. 'Consolidation' became a keyword in the 1980s. 'Community recreation' also became fashionable. This meant greater reliance on voluntary associations to deliver leisure services, and using existing premises – schools, church halls or whatever – instead of planning new purpose-designed leisure buildings.

The government claimed agnosticism on the proper length of the working day, week, year and life. Efforts to reduce unemployment by work-sharing were minimal. A job release scheme allowed over 60-year-old males to retire on state pensions in order to free their occupations for younger workers. A job splitting scheme offered cash bonuses to employers who divided full-time jobs, thereby removing someone from unemployment. However, these measures made little impact on the level of joblessness. There was no general encouragement towards shorter hours of work all round. The government's view was that hours of work and rates of pay were best left to free bargaining, preferably between individual workers and employers, but otherwise by collective agreement. Average hours actually worked did not decline among Britain's manual or non-manual workers. By the mid-1970s, in Britain, the latter were working more hours per week, on average. Britain's professions have long ceased to be refuges for leisurely gentlemen.

The 1980s governments have not broken with British traditions in refusing to plan comprehensively for a growth of leisure. Britain has never hosted a domestic political debate on 'the leisure problem'. There has never been a central government ministry with overall responsibility for leisure or culture. Different government departments continue to support the arts, sport, broadcasting, tourism, services for young people, and so on, but without co-ordinating these efforts into overall leisure policies. Most local authorities now have departments providing leisure or recreation services. In the main, however, these departments simply deliver services that have historically been defined as their province. Once again, all this has happened without any conception of an overall way of life that might be desirable, or to which all citizens are entitled. Other countries' governments have formed definite views on the proper length of the working week, and amounts of free time in the form of annual holidays to which citizens are entitled. Britain has never had such a government. In some lands leisure time and opportunities to enjoy it have been defined as rights of citizenship, and the enjoyment of leisure may even have been elevated into a civic duty. Some governments have made no secret of their views that certain life-styles deserve public promotion. Some have sought to democratise culture so as to spread elite heritages, or to nurture and enhance the status of alternative arts and their publics. All these ideas remain foreign in Britain, where people's leisure is still treated as essentially a private, not a public, issue.

Of course, British governments have proscribed or discouraged particular pastimes, ranging from the use of certain drugs to enjoyment of sex movies. Other leisure activities, especially sport and the traditional arts, have benefited enormously from state support. But all this has been achieved without any overarching leisure or cultural policies, and without any conceptions of the overall ways of living that the state should encourage. Governments have intervened in leisure in the course of addressing a variety of health, crime and educational issues, and in their efforts to promote the well-being of children, young people, the disabled, the retired and so on. Despite all these efforts, the concept of leisure has never been politicised. Keeping politics out of leisure is one of the few stances on which Britain retains a broad political consensus.

## Leisure

The significance of trends in leisure behaviour in Britain in the 1980s can be fully appreciated only when set in the above economic and political contexts. Many tastes and habits forged in previous years, including the popularity of television, have continued to flourish. A great deal of leisure in Britain throughout the 1980s has amounted to neither more nor less than 'business as usual'. Some of the main developments have been extensions of longer-running trends. For instance, work-free time and spending on leisure have continued to grow. However, even the same behaviour and trends can yield different experiences when surrounded by new economic and political conditions.

It is possible to distinguish four broad trends in British leisure in the 1980s.

### Home-centredness
The privatisation of leisure is a long-term trend in Britain. It is a product of a more mobile population, the decline of local neighbourhood communities, and the rise of the relatively independent nuclear family. The spread of car ownership has accentuated privatisation: families with cars can even go out in private. Radio

and television have strengthened the home's position as most people's main leisure centre. In recent decades home-centred life-styles have been further strengthened by the spread of home-ownership. Two-thirds of Britain's dwellings are now owner-occupied. This has helped to promote the various forms of do-it-yourself. Home repairs, decorating, car maintenance and gardening are now the nation's main hobbies.

In the 1980s more time than ever is being spent at home, partly as a result of the declining proportion of lifetime claimed by employment. In addition, however, more money is being spent on in-home recreation, and this spending is mainly by the employed sections of the population. Britain's main growth areas in leisure spending in the 1980s have been on sound and vision reproducing equipment, telecommunications, and computer technology (Martin and Mason, 1986).

The proportion of employment in service sectors has increased, but much of this employment is in producer services such as banking and insurance. The proportion of consumer spending on services has actually declined. There has been a trend towards purchasing goods which are then used for self-servicing (Gershuny, 1978). Transport is a prime example. We are buying more motor cars to transport ourselves instead of purchasing bus and train journeys. For entertainment we are purchasing televisions, videos and music centres instead of attending live performances.

Participation has declined in most forms of out-of-home recreation that can be replicated or closely substituted by in-home entertainment. Cinema and theatre audiences, and paid admissions at spectator sports events are in long-term and continuing decline. In Britain they have now been joined by out-of-home drinking. We are consuming more alcohol per capita than during any previous period in twentieth-century history, but there is less drinking in public houses and more off-sales for home consumption. Drink, film and sports producers have survived by gearing to increasingly home-centred markets. Most films are now made for television and video distribution rather than cinema performances. Live sport is played to tele-viewing audiences. Commercially successful sports promotion now depends on television coverage. The presence of the media attracts sponsors, and attracting the media requires top-level performers. Hence the changing structure of professional sports occupations (Whannel, 1986). Stars command astronomical fees while the rank and file must be motivated primarily by the slender prospect of joining the elite.

Life-styles are generally home centred in all social strata, but homes vary tremendously in their comforts. Individuals in employment, who spend least time at home, can best afford large and well-equipped dwellings. Home has different connotations for most of the unemployed and retired, many of whom have become trapped in home-based life-styles by poverty, and as a result of local community facilities – cinemas, sports teams and pubs – either declining or disappearing completely.

### Out-of-home recreation

During the 1980s out-of-home recreation in Britain has grown in just two main areas. Participant sport is one. The spread of sports participation has been facilitated by new provisions, especially for public sector indoor sport, that have opened since the 1960s. However, this trend in supply largely reflects an independent growth in demand. The public has become more concerned with health and fitness. Hence the decline in cigarette smoking, and the popularity of health foods and diets, the development of jogging, and the transformation of marathon runs into mass participation events.

Tourism is the second main growth area in out-of-home recreation. More people are taking more holidays away from home. Overseas holidays have become more common, with Greece and Spain as the most popular destinations. There are also more main and second holidays being spent inside Britain. In addition, more day trips are being made to coastal and countryside destinations, and to visit historic buildings. Theme parks have been launched on the growing demand for places to go and things to do.

But it is necessary to stress that not everyone has been part of the growth of sports participation and tourism. Two-thirds of British adults do not take part in any sport, unless long walks and swimming during seaside holidays are counted. Two-fifths of households do not take a holiday involving even one night away from home. A fifth of British adults never visit the countryside from year to year. Non-participants in these different activities tend to be the same individuals. Households without motor cars, approximately two out of every five in Britain, suffer general recreational disadvantages. The decline of public transport has led to enforced home-centredness among these groups. The old and the infirm, together with the poor and the unemployed, are sharing neither in the enrichment of home-based leisure, nor in the growth areas in out-of-home recreation.

### Connoisseur leisure

The expert and committed minorities that are surrounded by much larger numbers of less frequent, often voyeuristic, participants in most leisure activities are growing in size. It is impossible to measure this trend precisely. Participation data rarely permit a clear distinction between the dedicated and the casual. However, sales of specialist magazines have risen, while membership of leisure-based voluntary associations is also growing (Bishop and Hoggett, 1986). More people are seeking special-interest holidays in preference to mass-marketed packages.

In virtually all leisure activities, whether pursued at home or outside, there are minorities of enthusiasts with finely tuned skills and exceptional knowledge who commit considerable cash, time and energy to their pastimes. Among the mass of sports participants there are dedicated minorities who make cultivating peak performance into a serious occupation. Most spectator sports attract core groups of dedicated fans. The arts, the countryside, wines and home improvements are further bases for minority enthusiasms. Collectively these leisure connoisseurs have little in common. Their interests are highly specialised. At the connoisseur level leisure tastes are fragmented. Nevertheless, it is possible to discern a general bifurcation in Britain's leisure markets, with the experts, who are growing in number, demanding a different standard of service to the larger armies of dabblers who are content with mass-marketed goods and packaged experiences (Darton, 1986).

Serious or committed leisure appears capable of performing some socio-psychological functions normally associated with employment such as structuring time, providing interests and social relationships, status and identity (Haworth, 1986). Yet the unemployed are rarely leisure connoisseurs. Committed leisure seems most common among sections of the population whose current, past or future occupations provide the income, economic security and status on which to build leisure careers. Students in post-compulsory education are one section of the population where committed leisure is common. Early retirees, and some individuals who begin withdrawing from employment psychologically prior to officially terminating their working lives, often become connoisseurs in their chosen fields of leisure interest. Many middle-aged citizens in the post-parental life-stage for whom compulsory retirement is imminent, or earlier as an option, remain physically fit and active, and mentally alert. Their current or former occupations supply the status and economic security from which to build entire life-styles around leisure enthusiasms.

## The threat of the mob
Other sections of the population, including the unemployed and those financially impoverished for other reasons, have far less

opportunity to become leisure connoisseurs. The leisure of impoverished adults and the ageing, however deprived, rarely surfaces
as a public issue in Britain. Their life-styles and problems are
usually privatised. Unemployment accentuates privatisation. Lack
of income and loss of work-based social networks conspire to
confine the victims indoors.

Young people are different. They are less likely than other age
groups to become trapped in domesticity through lack of employment. Young people are an exceptional age group in so far as their
life-styles are not normally home-based: the majority have no
homes of their own. This is one reason why their peer groups and
friendships tend to survive unemployment. Young people usually
spend more time with friends when out of work than when in jobs.
This is one reason, possibly the main reason, why *youth* unemployment in Britain has been defined as a particularly urgent problem.
The young unemployed tend to be visible, on the streets and in
other public places. Fears of the uncouth mob and of the devil
making work for idle hands that have flickered throughout urban
history have been rekindled and are settling on the young
unemployed.

Unemployment among young adults in Britain has risen to well
above average levels. In some neighbourhoods, especially within
Britain's depressed regions, youth unemployment has become more
common than youth employment. Yet while so many young
people's job prospects have been receding, their education has
become more, not less, vocational. The threat of unemployment
prompts young people and parents to demand the kinds of
education that seem most likely to boost their job chances. Young
people are still being schooled to expect employment. Simultaneously, overt and hidden persuaders are continuing to train them
to become consumers. The attractions of spending are flaunted
daily in television adverts and shop displays. Hence the multiple
frustrations of unemployed youth.

Of course there are plenty of recreational programmes aimed at
young people, especially at the young unemployed. The twin aims
of policing the age group and offering satisfying life-styles are
usually uncomfortably interwoven, and equally unfulfilled.
Wagelessness restricts young people's access to leisure while
joblessness makes them more dependent than otherwise on leisure
activities to establish independence and adult identities (Roberts,
1983). Officially sponsored, socially hygienic recreation seems less
likely to supply the satisfactions that socially excluded young people
seek than symbolic and sometimes physical warfare to claim space
on streets and soccer terraces, among other places. Efforts to

marshal and contain these young people are constantly liable to provoke outbursts of hooliganism, even riots. These are highlights in some young lives, and are currently contributing to a breakdown of law and order in some of Britain's high unemployment inner-city areas. The young unemployed are over-represented among the officially recorded perpetrators of crime; they are also crime's most frequent victims (Kinsey et al., 1986). Lawlessness is currently exacerbating the deterioration in the quality of life in many of Britain's high unemployment neighbourhoods. Policing is one of the few public services in Britain on which expenditure has risen sharply in the 1980s. The country has more police than ever. They are also better equipped, and better paid than formerly. Yet the country also has a record crime rate. Hence the decline in public satisfaction with, and confidence in, the police. Certain sections of the public, especially the young, have grown increasingly hostile towards the police and the society they represent. This is just one instance of the benefits of economic growth being consumed by the costs of handling the attendant problems.

## A less leisurely society

The 1980s trends in leisure become intelligible only when set in their political and economic contexts. The British government has defined economic trends as the 'real world' to which people should adjust, and has therefore allowed these trends to threaten or undermine many adults' former ways of life. These same economic trends have been allowed to thwart many young people's routes to the jobs, wages and consumer life-styles to which they aspire. The victims have certainly not welcomed their predicament, yet it has inspired neither demands that the government should protect, nor widespread communal efforts to defend, leisure opportunities *despite* economic conditions. Britain's unemployed have marched for the right to work, not a right to leisure. They have protested at the government's failure to protect their livelihoods, not their life-styles. Conditions in the 1980s have not undermined Britain's consensus that life-styles are private, not public, issues. The two parties that have dominated British politics since the 1920s have been challenged by a centre alliance of Liberals and Social Democrats, but this new political force has joined the debates on familiar political issues – the rate of economic growth, the level of unemployment, the gap between rich and poor, and the condition of public education, health and housing services. Leisure has not been promoted towards the head of Britain's political agenda.

Some of the unemployed have responded pro-actively and

devised satisfying uses of their spare time (Fryer and Payne, 1984). A minority have experienced gains in physical and psychological well-being on being released from the pressures of employment (Walter, 1985). However, the most common adaptations to unemployment in the 1980s are the same as in the 1930s and involve resignation and apathy, not self-fulfilment (Jahoda, 1982; Kelvin et al., 1984). Intellectuals have debated the possibility of compensating for lack of jobs and wages by promoting leisure-based life-styles. Public service leisure professions have been anxious to 'do something' for the disadvantaged, and have pioneered special programmes for the unemployed and other low participation target groups. However, these efforts have struck few chords, certainly among Britain's unemployed. The latter have sought escapes from, rather than means of adjustment to, the predicament.

Industrial capitalism has in-built contradictions. Hence the century of debate about alienation and anomie, the almost incessant talk of crisis and prophecies of collapse in the absence of some *fundamental* reform. The system has consistently defied these predictions and has demonstrated an enormous capacity to absorb tensions. People whose preferred ways of life are endangered may or may not experience personal crises. They can resort to a variety of socio-psychological games which modify their goals or definitions of reality. Some such games, especially young people's confrontations with authority, inflict penalties on the wider society, but these costs are spread widely: private troubles are not automatically translated into public issues. Britain's political and economic systems have not descended into crisis during the 1980s. Certain contradictions identified in previous decades have actually lessened. For instance, it used to be argued that the costs of meeting their political demands and thereby integrating the economically disadvantaged into capitalist societies would become mounting and eventually crippling burdens for the wealth-generating systems (Offe, 1984). During the 1980s, in Britain, the tendency has been to roll back the frontiers of legitimate demands on state welfare.

Neither the kind nor the severity of the threats to preferred ways of life in the 1980s are unprecedented. Most victims of economic restructuring and unemployment have been from Britain's working class, not the middle classes, and the former have a history of coping with fluctuating earnings and other misfortunes. Blocked goals are traditional frustrations for working-class youth. The literature on their deviant and 'magical' responses began to accumulate long before the 1980s (Merton, 1938; Cohen, 1976). Even during the long postwar boom, working-class life-styles endured repeated assaults – from rehousing, especially in high-rise flats, from the breakup of neighbourhood communities, and from the influx of ethnic minorities. The part of the United Kingdom where people feel that their ways of life are in the gravest danger in the 1980s is not mainland Britain, but Northern Ireland, where the majority fear that their protestant culture could be overwhelmed by Roman Catholicism and Irish nationalism.

In the long run Britain's middle classes could prove the more effective cultural revolutionaries. New and growing social movements in the 1980s have mainly middle-class activists. The Social Democratic and Liberal parties have overwhelmingly middle-class memberships. So does the Campaign for Nuclear Disarmament which, in Britain, plays the umbrella role of green parties in other countries, drawing together a variety of crusades against threats to the environment and peace. The women's movements with their opposition to patriarchy in families and labour markets, and to the stereotyped treatment of women solely on grounds of their biological sex, offer further examples of collective efforts to change ways of life independently of underlying economic conditions. These movements are also, as yet, the work of mainly middle-class women.

In the 1970s Daniel Bell drew attention to the contradiction between the rational values of capitalist enterprises with their necessary stress on efficiency and disciplined toil, and the relatively expressive, even hedonistic, values of the surrounding cultural systems (Bell, 1976). People are expected to derive their main rewards for occupational success through consumption, in leisure time. Yet the stresses of earning success can poison its enjoyment. In Britain in the 1980s more people than ever have good jobs which support rising standards of living. These people are working as long and probably harder than ever. Membership of the 'harried leisure class' (Linder, 1970) is growing, and the predicament is becoming more acute. The people who possess the money to afford consumer goods and services often lack the time to enjoy and, in some cases, even to use them. Leisure is becoming more home centred. Prosperous sections of the population in particular are spending more money than ever in purchasing and equipping their dwellings. Yet family life is less stable than formerly. A third of recent marriages in Britain will end in divorce if current rates continue. Many white-collar occupations are being proletarianised in terms of the conditions of work, career prospects and salaries. In some cases this is a straightforward consequence of the decline in blue-collar jobs, and the increased proportion of employment in non-manual occupations. This makes it impossible to reward the majority of white-collar employees with status and incomes that set them well ahead of the national average. Individuals who desire real success can no longer be content with simply getting into, but must climb career ladders within, management, education and other public services. During the 1980s this seems to have been the most common middle-class response to economic trends. Dropping out and experimenting with alternative life-styles look less attractive as the risks increase of being unable to scramble back.

Even so, there are contrary indicators. Connoisseur leisure is most common among the middle classes, especially among young people in post-compulsory education, and among individuals who are enjoying or anticipating retirement. These groups could lead a pincer movement strengthening the role of leisure throughout the life cycle. The middle classes make the greater use of commercial and public leisure services. They derive the greatest benefit from access to the countryside, provisions for sport and support for the arts. There could be a cross-fertilisation, or alliances with environmentalist, feminist and other broader social movements. Slowly the benefits should filter into the working classes who, in the 1980s, have become more preoccupied than ever with simply holding on to or regaining employment and wages, and making the best of home-centred life-styles.

All the trends contributing to the growth of leisure during earlier periods in industrial history have continued in Britain in the 1980s. Work-free time and leisure spending have continued to grow. If life has not become more leisurely for most people this will be due entirely to the trends' separation. Time released from employment has been given to the poorest sections of the population, while spending power has increased mainly for those with the least leisure time. A change of government could lead to a quick redistribution of leisure time and spending. Even without political intervention, working-class pressure for jobs and a more generous share of the nation's prosperity, combined with middle-class concerns that improvements in standards of living are not being matched in the quality of everyday life, could become major forces governing the development of leisure during the remainder of the twentieth century.

## References

Bell, D. (1976) *The Cultural Contradictions of Capitalism*. London: Heinemann.
Bishop, J. and P. Hoggett (1986) *Organizing Around Enthusiasms*, London: Comedia.
Cohen, P. (1976) 'Subcultural Conflicts and Working Class Community', in M. Hammersley and P. Woods (eds) *The Process of Schooling*. London: Routledge.

Darton, D. (1986) 'Leisure Forecast 1986: the Leisured Society', *Leisure Management*, 6(January): 7–8.

Fryer, D. and R. Payne (1984) 'Proactive Behaviour in Unemployment: Findings and Implications', *Leisure Studies*, 3: 273–95.

Gershuny, J. (1978) *After Industrial Society?* London: Macmillan.

Haworth, J.T. (1986) 'Meaningful Activity and Psychological Models of Non-employment', *Leisure Studies*, 5: 281–97.

Jahoda, M. (1982) *Employment and Unemployment: a Social-Psychological Analysis.* Cambridge: Cambridge University Press.

Kelvin, P., C. Dewberry and N. Morley-Bunker (1984) *Unemployment and Leisure*, unpublished manuscript, University College, London.

Kinsey, R., J. Lea and J. Young (1986) *Losing the Fight Against Crime.* Oxford: Blackwell.

Linder, S. (1970) *The Harried Leisure Class.* New York: Columbia University Press.

Martin, B. and S. Mason (1986) 'Spending Patterns Show New Leisure Priorities', *Leisure Studies*, 5: 233–6.

Merton, R.K. (1938) 'Social Structure and Anomie', *American Sociological Review*, 3: 672–82.

Offe, C. (1984) *Contradictions of the Welfare State.* London: Hutchinson.

Roberts, K. (1983) *Youth and Leisure.* London: Allen and Unwin.

Walter, T. (1985) *Hope on the Dole.* London: SPCK.

Whannel, G. (1986) 'The Unholy Alliance: Notes on Television and the Remaking of British Sport 1965–85', *Leisure Studies*, 5: 129–45.

# 5

# Belgium: Old Trends, New Contradictions

## *France Govaerts*

The world crisis of the 1980s is not only economic and financial, but also political, technological, cultural, organisational and environmental (Cahiers, 1984). In few European countries have the many aspects been so thoroughly interwoven as in Belgium, and yet so difficult to capture and interpret because of the country-specific economic, political and cultural dimensions.

Belgium is a small country of 9.858 million inhabitants, 323 per square kilometre, with an area of 30,519 square kilometres, set between the North Sea, the Netherlands, Luxembourg, the Federal Republic of Germany and France. The kingdom of Belgium is divided into three regions: Flanders with 5.67 million inhabitants, Wallonia with 3.208 million inhabitants (to which must be added 60,000 German-speaking people), and the Brussels region with just under one million inhabitants (INS, 1985a, 1986a). Two main languages are spoken: Flemish and French.

Belgium is one of the twelve member countries of the European Economic Community (EEC). As an independent political state it is relatively young. The kingdom was established only in 1830 when Belgium seceded from Holland, to which it had been joined after the Congress of Vienna. French was the official language for several decades: in the courts until 1892, for employment in public administration until 1878, in the school system until 1883, and for legal documents until 1898 (Mabille, 1986). Belgium's main sources of industrial wealth – the coal and steel industries – are located mainly in Wallonia. After the Second World War, parallel to the beginning of decline in these industries, French-speaking cultural and political dominance started to diminish. A period of bitter linguistic feuds then tore the country's intellectual, political, economic and cultural life. Fortunately these feuds are largely appeased today.

Coal mines began to close in Wallonia in the late 1950s. While the steel crisis became acute only in the early 1980s, some consider that already in 1961 the conditions were present for Flanders to become economically dominant (Mabille, 1986). The constitution was revised in 1970, establishing the existence of the three regions, as well as the principle of cultural autonomy for each linguistic community. The special law of 8 August and the ordinary law of 9 August 1980 on constitutional reform, defined the means and scope of the new regional institutions corresponding to a territorial definition, and of the new cultural communities' institutions corresponding to linguistic groups. Thus were created the 'French Community' and the 'Flemish Community'. Regional and community institutions were to have both executive and legislative organs. The reality, however, is more complex than this suggests, for there is no precise parallel between the institutions. The first oil shock in 1972 exacerbated the structural tensions which were already present in Belgium including the various linguistic, religious, philosophical, political and economic divisions associated with regional, national and cultural identity issues.

### Changes in the occupational structure and the decrease in work time

Belgium shares a number of employment trends with other European countries. There has been a substantial movement into the tertiary sector. The economically active population in 1985 consisted of 106,000 in agriculture, 1.073 million in industry and 2.458 million in the service or tertiary sector, compared to 1970 levels – 174,000 in agriculture, 1.537 million in industry, 1.987 million in the tertiary sector (INS, 1985a, 1986a). As in virtually all industrial countries, the technological revolution has affected not only the nature of work and its duration – including housekeeping through the provision of time-saving home appliances – but also the supply of leisure equipment, which in turn has influenced leisure activities and life-styles.

Work time for the economically active population in Belgium has been reduced, as elsewhere, through technological change and social pressures. The reduction of working hours and the corresponding growth of free or non-work time have been unequally distributed. Time-budget studies have demonstrated the significance of adding commuting time between home and work to actual working hours. In some sectors and professions working hours have not decreased at all, but have remained frozen for years or have even increased. Married women with children, especially those who are also earning a living, also have much less free time than most other groups: their actual work week often continues to exceed 60 hours, and their leisure time even during holidays is limited. Equal housework sharing between members of the family, to reduce women's burden, is still not widespread even among the younger generation with higher education levels.

The economic crisis has increased non-work time in Belgium, possibly more than in most other industrial countries, through unemployment. However, this imposed non-work time cannot be equated with leisure. For the past 15 years Belgium has had one of the highest unemployment rates in the EEC. When levels first began to rise, unemployment affected the high-risk social groups in economically depressed areas: youth with little education or diplomas in subject areas for which a demand no longer existed, unskilled workers, and women. Unemployment was highest in the older industrial region of Wallonia in 1971, and it has remained higher there than in the two other regions (INS, 1985b). In 1971 unemployment was 4.5 percent in Wallonia, 2.5 percent in Flanders and 1.8 percent in the Brussels region. By 1980 the respective figures had grown to 14.5, 11.9 and 11.7 percent. As the recession set in, other social groups increasingly became threatened by unemployment – middle-level managers aged over 45, young engineers and doctors, then even more successful top managers, old and young, because the firms which employed them went bankrupt or adopted so-called retrenchment policies. In 1970 there were 71,000 unemployed people. In June 1985 477,000 were unemployed, representing 13.1 percent of the economically active population. Unemployment certainly cannot be equated with free time since the loss of employment is not free at all but is rather a crisis for underprivileged people. In Belgium until June 1987 the unemployed worker was a victim of an absolute legal prohibition on occasional work – sometimes including even repainting his own home. In some cases he was allowed to receive specialised training. That is not leisure time either, but education time, although self-development could be said to constitute a free-time activity. Administrative measures in Belgium still constrain the unemployed: every day they have to check in to receive their unemployment allowance, which is issued on a daily basis. The hours are different every day and communicated only the day before. Illegal work is thus meant to be difficult, but this also hinders the planning of leisure time before 5 p.m. Overall, unemployment must clearly force a drastic change in life-style.

Retirees are a second category of population with imposed non-work time. This category is increasing in two ways. First, there is considerable pressure, accompanied by economic incentives, towards 'voluntary' early retirement. Second, as in most advanced industrial societies, the size of the over-65-year-old population is growing. In 1900 the Belgian population aged 65 years and over represented 6.2 percent of the total, whereas in 1987 they represented 14.4 percent and, according to statistical projections, the figure will rise to 15.2 percent by the year 2000 (INS, 1975, 1980, 1982).

Ageing, as stated in an ILO study (Beckerman et al., 1979), is by far the major cause of poverty in industrial societies despite improvements in pension schemes. To summarise a recent study on old age and poverty in Belgium, three-quarters of the poorest among the poor are elderly, and three-quarters of the poorest among the elderly are women (Govaerts and Marques-Pereira, 1986). This study examined three indicators of poverty – isolation, housing and income. For the majority, retirement was associated with a reduction of disposable income, a substantial decrease in social contacts, and a general process of marginalisation, all of which exacerbated the gradual loss of physical autonomy. There are obviously older persons who live comfortably on either the interest from capital or their pensions, or both. However, they are only a small minority within their age group.

## Decreasing disposable income and reductions in social benefits

As early as 1976 the Belgian government began to introduce austerity policies, meaning budget cuts. By 1982 a turning point had been reached in the social philosophy of the state. Special powers were given to the government to rule by decree, with the aim of limiting public expenditure, balancing the social security budget, and reducing the global amount of salary expenditure. This was related to broader changes in economic thinking. One of the aims of the austerity measures was to increase Belgium's competitiveness vis-a-vis other industrial economies by reducing the cost of labour – a supply-side strategy adopted after the failure of demand stimulation.

The concept of social security in which benefits had previously been considered an individual right was modified by the government in order to take total family income into account and thus reduce payments. Other rules, regulations and fiscal laws resulted in substantial cut-backs in the incomes of the unemployed and the elderly. The rules of eligibility for payment of unemployment allowances, as well as the amounts, were revised. New fiscal laws increased the tax on social benefits. The life-styles of young people were further constrained by the fact that the income of domestic companions was taken into account in computing their unemployment allowances. The income of other population categories was also affected. Social security benefits in general, especially health and disability payments, were reduced.

For four years (1982–6) the salary index was frozen in both the public and private sectors. At a point when salaries had again come to reflect increases in the cost of living, a quarterly index was established which resulted in a time lag in salary adjustments. Those living below the official poverty line, formerly 5 percent of the population, rose to 10 percent, while nearly all social groups suffered cut-backs in purchasing power. Hence the creation of the 'new poor'. They are concentrated mainly in urban areas, and some have been thrust into the predicament through sudden loss of employment or through disability. The change in life-style is, of course, particularly acute for those whose consumption patterns have been based on instalment plans. An indication of the rate of increase in the new poor can be gained from the increase in electricity cut-offs when electricity bills are overdue, since such an important claim on a household's budget is usually the very last one not to be paid. The increase in electricity cut-offs during the winter of 1983 was such that special measures had to be introduced by the social welfare sector.

Social groups not affected by the crisis – the wealthy who have become even richer, and the new rich – are more difficult to identify in official statistics. In Belgium, as elsewhere, a minority has increased its wealth. Firms that have adapted through changed management techniques (requiring to some extent a new set of values) are among those that have prospered. Though precise data are not available, the income disparity between rich and poor has widened.

### The perception of a crisis here to stay

The crisis in Belgium did not immediately affect life-styles and behaviour in a dramatic way. Behaviour is modified only marginally at the beginning of any crisis. Cut-backs, whether at the government or the family level, affect only the least significant expenditure so long as a feeling prevails that the situation is temporary. It may take five to ten years, and the repeated failure of all standard remedies (from both the political Right and Left), for the realisation to take hold that a crisis has structural causes and that no short-term remedies are possible, but only a slow and difficult adaptation to emerging structures and different value systems.

By the 1980s a new vocabulary had become commonplace in the Belgian media: 'adjustment', 'restructuring' and 'retrenchment' to characterise painful processes of salary cut-backs, wage and pension freezes, loss of acquired social rights and the decline in purchasing power. As in most other European countries, the crisis in Belgium was at first treated as temporary. Until 1982, especially on the eve of elections, governments claimed that 'the end of the tunnel was in sight' and asserted that, thanks to their new measures, economic growth could be resumed, income would grow again and unemployment recede through creation of jobs (Lebaube, 1986). The awareness of an economic crisis with no end in sight, from which few could claim to remain forever safe, probably entered into the national awareness only when, in an increasing number of families, a son or a daughter could not get a first job, or when a relative or neighbour, however successful, was suddenly fired and joined the long line of the unemployed, and when various acquired rights were suddenly taken away by employers or governments, with no successful legal challenge. Job security had formerly been associated with work performance, over which one had some control. Thus the impact of job insecurity associated with economic factors outside one's own control (mergers, bankruptcies, restructuring and retrenchment policies) may have had a more profound impact in Belgium than in countries where occupational mobility has been accepted as normal.

### Tensions between media-promoted life-styles and disposable income

The necessity to produce more, to consume more, and to export more – from different sectors than in the past – has resulted in new practices of knowledge and work, marked by changes and hesitations about life models within a framework of economic recession and attempts to improve the quality of life. For a large part of Belgium's population, a value conflict is arising between media-promoted life-styles and reduced disposable income. For a growing minority – particularly among the unemployed and the elderly – the life-styles being promoted are even less affordable than in the past. Values and hierarchies in leisure activities are therefore being reorganised in many social groups. This also means increasing commercial competition among the different leisure industries.

Although not directly linked, electronic media and various communication techniques have developed in parallel with the crisis. In Belgium, as in other advanced industrial countries, the leisure industries and media have built up a virtual cultural hegemony, particularly during the last ten years (Mattelart and Piemme, 1980). They introduce new life-styles not only during leisure time, but also in the interacting domains of education, self-development, employment, unemployment and retirement. Social values are presented in advertising as inherent characteristics of the consumer goods being sold. These goods then become sources of social and cultural prestige leading to increasing social differentiation, especially in times of crisis. Advertising has expanded dramatically with the expansion of television networks. This has been one reason for the decline in movie-going. In 1971 a total of 29.38 million people went to the movies, while by 1982 their number had dropped by nearly one-third, to 20.526 million, and this decline has continued (INS, 1985a). Advertisements in times of crisis tend to schematise cultural values and to reduce them to the affirmation of a reality portrayed as desirable for all, but which, in practice, is accessible only to some. Advertisers claim, rightly, that they do not sell products alone, but also dreams. The greater the economic recession, the less this commercial dream has a chance to be realised by the majority.

Leisure industries and advertisements have segmented the life-styles of various social groups in terms of consumer markets. The linkage of leisure ideologies with the economic system masks the privileges of certain groups, by presenting them as life-styles desired by all while hiding the plight and exclusion of others from these same life-styles. These leisure ideologies serve as a support to economic production, especially in times of crisis. Since leisure activities may become a compensation for, and an escape from, a depressing daily life, some advertisements increasingly capitalise on feelings of insecurity, associating the concept of security with the product being marketed, and playing on the felt precariousness of daily life. An ongoing analysis of advertisements in Belgium, which began in 1972, indicates that there has been a subtle change in the contents over the past ten years; the risk of some kind of failure is nowadays more often associated with the non-purchase of the product, thus transferring on to the consumer the risk properly borne by the firm itself if it cannot achieve a sufficient number of sales (Govaerts, 1979). This dimension has grown in importance compared to the association of a sexy young woman with any type of product, although the youth element implicit in the latter continues to be reinforced in one form or another with possible negative social consequences for the status of the elderly in industrialised societies (Govaerts, 1975).

The increasing importance of disposable income for commercial leisure activities is suggested by comparisons of leisure activities in 1980 and 1983 in Flanders (Naeyaert and Claeys, 1984). Over the years, leisure has become a highly profitable economic sector. Partly as a result of policies promoting the democratisation of culture and sport, a number of previously expensive leisure activities (tourism, tennis, skiing, golf and so on), which were once associated with higher income groups and the life-styles of the rich, have become more affordable by the population in general. At the same time, a large number of new leisure activities have appeared, replacing less expensive ones which have fallen out of fashion (card playing, for instance). Many of the new popular activities require not only an initial capital investment to purchase equipment, but involve recurrent costs of participation, and also repeated capital expenditure due to technological and fashion obsolescence. Even for old-time activities such as walking, special shoes and clothes are now widely promoted. Decreases in disposable income result in re-prioritising expenditures, thus altering life-styles and leisure activities, though not always in the same way.

## Changes in the perception of leisure and of the relationship between leisure and work time

Until the 1950s most definitions of leisure were derived from the meaning of work. Then, during the period of sustained economic growth, when some people dreamed of a civilisation of leisure, the centrality of work was questioned (Dumazedier, 1974). Many sociologists argued that leisure was assuming a life of its own, and that leisure values were permeating other spheres including workplaces. Leisure values and life-styles were seen to be growing increasingly important. To illustrate the point, a number of surveys in the 1970s suggested that, if given the choice, the majority preference would be for a decrease in working hours rather than a salary increase (Best, 1980; Fukasz, 1982). This was said to be a strong trend in all industrialised countries (Samuel and Romer, 1984).

There is no doubt as to the social reality of leisure values. Nor that in the 1980s the value of leisure is persisting, and may even be growing from strength to strength despite the leisure civilisation looking more remote. Leisure values today in Belgium have run into conflict with other values associated with the crisis and present-day economic needs. Work and leisure, and their interrelationship, have to be re-examined in this new socioeconomic and cultural context. The nature of work has changed for many with the new technological revolution – hard physical labour is a concern for decreasing numbers of people. Moreover, for many groups work traditionally had a value in itself and for itself. In times of general unemployment, however, a different value is associated with work, derived from the scarcity of jobs. This scarcity value has begun to change the hitherto dominant work–leisure relationship, and to overshadow the competition between work time and leisure time. One visible result of the crisis in Belgium has been a drop in absenteeism during recent years, as employers must note with satisfaction. For the expanding groups at risk of unemployment, employment – any kind of employment – is becoming a central value, and is overshadowing the notion of work either as a transcendental value or as a source of alienation. The fear of losing one's job and not finding a new one is strengthening values of competition, productivity and efficiency in the workplace.

Leisure within work time seems to be diminishing, and overtime – among professional categories as well as among manual workers – is tending to increase. Today, in many sectors, whenever a job becomes vacant either through early retirement or for any other reason, the tendency is not to fill it but to redistribute the tasks. Middle- and high-level executives who worked overtime during the period of growth were defined (negatively) as 'workaholics', whereas in Belgium today an increasing number of executives as well as lower-level employees are becoming workaholics through no volition of their own, but in order to meet assigned production targets if they are not to risk losing their jobs. Thus a double process is taking place. On the one hand, legal working hours are decreasing at the macro-level, while at the micro-level overtime is increasing, thus reducing the amount of non-work time, which is in direct conflict with people's leisure aspirations.

In addition, the perceived need to hold a second job, declared or non-declared, has increased. In Flanders a 1983 survey indicated that 14.3 percent of those with a monthly income of less than 30,000 BF (approximately US$810) had declared second jobs, as did 12.8 percent of those in the higher income bracket of 60–69,000 BF, probably reflecting the greater survival needs of the former group, and the need to maintain a minimum accustomed life-style among the latter. Precise figures are not available on moonlighting or undeclared second jobs in the evening and at weekends. The numbers must be considerable in some social groups, though it is doubtful whether the total exceeds 25 percent of the working population (Samuel and Romer, 1984). Thus, not only may income affect the choice of leisure activities more than in the past, but for an increasing number, leisure time, which had become so valued, has had to be cut back through working more hours and moonlighting in order to supplement regular incomes.

Perceptions of leisure seem to be changing in present-day Belgium. Studies during the last 25 years have defined leisure as time free of constraints, that is, of obligations linked to social roles.

However, another paradigm now seems to be emerging: one of stress leisure. The word stress, so commonly used today, reflects the psycho-physiological effects of constraints which are exacerbated by the many aspects of the crisis: apprehension as to what role one is expected to play, fears for the future, and tensions due to value conflicts and insecurity in the workplace, at home, in the family and in any other life situations where traditional values are no longer recognised or rewarded. In such a context leisure can be appropriately defined as 'absence of stress'. Indeed, many leisure pastimes today, more than in the past, may be identified as activities chosen to avoid stress or to reduce its effects. The rest, recuperation and relaxation often assigned to leisure are no longer needed to recover from physically hard labour, but from stress in daily life, at home and in the workplace. In the USA several hundred companies now offer stress management programmes to their employees (Freudenheim, 1987).

**An added dimension: leisure and health**

A number of new leisure activities are now explicitly promoted as preventive health measures. The health movement, which started in the USA two decades ago and has more recently reached Belgium, has many dimensions, and seems related to the economic crisis as well as to the crisis in values. This concern for health takes many forms ranging from anti-smoking movements to the fitness and exercise boom (aerobics, jogging, health foods and so on). Individuals with knowledge and know-how are taking preventive health action by physical exercise, healthy living and healthy food habits, by breaking the smoking habit, controlling alcohol consumption, by learning about stress management, and by having regular physical examinations. An effect should be to lower social security and health insurance costs through improvements in people's health, and because of the increasing reluctance of insurance companies and social security to pay for the treatment of illnesses which could have been prevented.

From a social perspective, the fitness boom involves mainly the active age groups. It reflects another facet of the ideology of youth, and reinforces the messages conveyed by many advertisements. From the perspective of sociology of leisure and changes in life-styles, it is a phenomenon which seems to be gaining attention, in terms both of the shifting expenditure patterns of leisure industries and of the increasing amount of leisure time now being devoted to health-associated activities at the expense of other pastimes such as alcohol, smoking and conviviality around heavy meals. Some leisure activities are explicitly promoted and sold as stress relief measures and as a form of stress prevention – playing on the fear, especially among the middle class, of cancer and cardiovascular diseases. The media have played a mediating role in bringing about this change.

Similar effects are being observed with another health-threatening phenomenon, namely the recent spread of AIDS and its coverage in the media. Though not addressed in this chapter, the increasing public awareness of the threat of AIDS is already modifying life-styles and the sexual revolution in a manner that is likely to have profound effects in coming years.

### Changes affecting the supply of leisure

During the 1960s and early 1970s, the Belgian government increased its efforts towards the democratisation of education, culture and sports. Cultural infrastructures were enlarged throughout the country. The creation of the new regional and linguistic community institutions reinforced these efforts, and contributed to both increasing and further widening the supply of leisure opportunities. The emphasis on cultural identity in a period of international and national socioeconomic changes may thus form the implicit basis of a development strategy. As far as Brussels is concerned, the increase in leisure supply of arts exhibitions, concerts, films and other cultural events, meetings, clubs, outings and so forth, announced every Thursday in the daily newspaper, *Le Soir*, is immediately apparent if one compares these listings today with those in the 1970s.

As a result of the decentralisation process, policies and related measures to promote leisure and cultural activities, including tourism, have become the responsibility of a wide range of administrative structures at all levels (Ministry, 1984; Govaerts, 1986). Thus leisure supply appears to respond readily to demand in Belgium, especially as far as sports clubs and associations are concerned. This holds notably for provincial cities which are growth points, and also for many small communes, even if the share of their budgets allocated to sports and cultural activities has been reduced due to economic difficulties. Different classifications of public expenditure were used over the period 1972–85 by the various levels of government involved (Drumeaux, 1986), which makes it difficult to draw exact comparisons to ascertain whether there has been an overall decrease or increase in public expenditure related to specific leisure and cultural practices. Overall, however, such expenditure has risen.

**Evidence on changes in leisure patterns**

Identifying changes in leisure patterns raises a number of methodological difficulties. Since the 1965 international study there has been no further nationwide time-budget survey in Belgium which would allow an analysis of shifts in time use. Instead, three principal data sources can be used. At the macro-level expenditure trends can be examined from 1970 to 1985 as reflected in national accounts (INS, 1986b, 1986c). At the regional level, there are two major recent studies; one undertaken in Flanders in 1983 by Daniel Naeyaert and Urbain Claeys (1984), and the other in the Francophone community in 1984 by two research teams, one from the Free University of Brussels and the other from the Catholic University of Leuwen (Institut de Sociologie, 1986; Institut de Sociologie ULB, 1985). Unfortunately, comparison is difficult between the Flanders and Francophone findings because the surveys used different conceptual frameworks and analytical categories.

The Flemish survey of 1983 among a representative sample systematically sought to compare participation in various leisure activities with the findings from a 1980 investigation, taking the economic crisis explicitly into account. The changes identified highlight the impact of the crisis. The cumulative character of the changes observed between 1980 and 1983 supports the hypothesis that the observed developments amount to genuine trends rather than mere fluctuations in leisure activities. Given their growth in importance, the unemployed and half-time workers were distinguished in the analysis. However, as is still often the case, groups over the age of 64 were not considered, thus excluding from observation an important though marginalised section of the population.

The 1984 survey in Belgium's Francophone community, based on a sample of 3059 persons, did not examine the unemployed or part-time employed, but this investigation did consider two older age groups, 55–65 year olds, and those aged 65 and over. However, within the 55–65 group the economically active were aggregated with retirees, two very different income groups with different social roles in terms of work and leisure. Furthermore, the Francophone survey did not introduce the economic crisis into its problematic. Because the economic crisis is more acute in Wallonia than in Flanders, it may be assumed that the differences and increasing inequalities in leisure participation directly linked to income, to part-time employment and to unemployment would be even stronger in the former, but no comparative data are available.

In both Flanders and the French-speaking community, new

activities like aerobics and jogging have appeared within broad categories such as sports (Bouillin-Dartevelle, 1986). These developments reflect changes in life-style that were not identified quantitatively in the above surveys. Also, with the dissemination of new technologies such as the 'Walkman', some activities are now emerging which these surveys could not record.

At the macroeconomic level, the share of leisure within private consumption reveals some interesting trends. Notwithstanding the economic crisis, expenditures on leisure have increased slightly overall, reflecting the success of certain commercial leisure industries. The growth rate of expenditure has been uneven, ranging from negative growth in certain years and areas to strong positive growth in others. More significant are the shifts and the trends in expenditure for specific categories of leisure activity, as given in the unpublished tables of the national accounts (INS, 1986c). All prices and indexes cited below use 1980 prices as a standardised basis for comparison.

The pattern of leisure expenditure has changed substantially, with the most dramatic increase being recorded by cable television. The rate of its growth – more than a hundredfold – has been partly at the expense of other leisure activities. In Belgium cable allows the reception of programmes from neighbouring countries. Payment of the subscription price, added to the taxes collected by the state, suggests that for many households, television ownership – there is one in virtually every home – represents a recurrent monthly cost which must limit other entertainment expenditures independently of the number of hours spent actually viewing and the total amount of available free time. Spending on television grew from 67 million BF in 1970 to 3971 million BF in 1976, and to 8219 million BF in 1985. The taxes paid on radio and television were 6875 million BF in 1970, 9000 million BF in 1976, and some 11,219 million BF by 1985. Thus cable television, plus radio and TV taxes, amounted to nearly 19,500 million BF in 1985. During the preceding years expenditure decreased on other forms of entertainment such as movies and the theatre – from above 6000 million BF until 1975 to just over 4000 million BF in 1985.

However, expenditure on games, betting, horse racing and casinos has increased substantially – reflecting as elsewhere the willingness of even low-income groups to accept risk for the prospect of a potential major financial gain. Spending on sport fees and equipment has also grown steadily from 1970 onwards (67 million BF in 1970 to 121 million BF in 1985). Expenditure on books, newspapers and magazines has increased overall, from 13,712 million BF in 1970 to 16,700 million BF in 1976, and 20,869 in 1985. Disaggregation indicates that expenditure increased mainly on imported newspapers and magazines, that expenditure on books began to decline in 1982, and that a slight decline in expediture on Belgian newspapers started in 1981.

In general, for most categories which do not present steady long-term trends, a decline in expenditure seems to have set in since 1982 or 1983. This is the case, for instance, with photography which reached its peak in 1982 (10,037 million BF) and then declined to 6034 million BF in 1985. Expenditure on private flying and yachting increased steadily from 1970 (223 million BF) to 1980 (395 million BF), then began a decline to 315 million BF in 1985.

Total expenditure on hotels and cafes has remained relatively constant, but it is impossible to disaggregate this area so as to distinguish, for example, holidays and going out for dinner from non-leisure spending to ascertain whether leisure spending has remained the same, increased or decreased.

**Vacations – tourism**

For many years, even alongside decreases in purchasing power, the holiday has remained many people's almost sacred leisure value. Holidays (if possible twice a year) have remained an ultimate goal, and for many they are still the *raison d'être* for working year-round in uninspiring jobs. Many people seem prepared to cut all other expenses, including other leisure expenses, and even to draw from their savings in order to continue to go away on holidays. This has become a 'felt right'. People believe that they 'need' recuperation, to relax in different environments. Nevertheless, Belgians are now taking vacations less far away, less often, and for less time (Weisgerber, 1986). An analysis of expenditures and shifts among types of accommodation also indicates that, in order to continue to be able to afford vacations, many have modified their styles of holiday-making by finding cheaper places to stay (OECD, 1986). Yet, for vacations as in other leisure sectors, some citizens are spending more than in the past, thereby demonstrating that they are the 'winners'. It would appear that conspicuous consumption, class differentiation by spending patterns and luxury symbols, is again increasing. The gap between the life-styles of the upper income groups and the rest is becoming wider. Advertising and the media reflect and reinforce this trend. As has been widely noted, extravagant consumption in the USA was more commonly reported in the media in 1929–30 than during other periods.

In Flanders, the proportion of people going on holidays declined from 57 percent in 1981 to 53 percent in 1983. The decline in one-day excursions was even sharper – from 76 percent in 1980 to 63 percent in 1983. In 1985 a survey on holidays away from home was carried out for the EEC in member countries (Commission, 1987). During their holidays, 59 percent of Belgians stayed at home and only 41 percent went away, placing the country near the bottom of the European list, just above Ireland (39 percent) and Portugal (31 percent). In contrast, 65 percent of the Dutch went away on holidays. The main reason given by Belgians for not going away, by 40 percent, was lack of finance. The finding that a much higher proportion of people in the upper than in the lower income groups went on holiday was common in all countries, but was more marked in Belgium than in other EEC states such as the Netherlands and the United Kingdom.

Among the main findings concerning the holidays of Belgians in 1985 was that over two-thirds of those who went away did so during July and August. Thirty percent stayed in a hotel or a boarding house, 21 percent rented a bungalow or chalet, 17 percent stayed in a camping ground, 16 percent with relations or friends, 5 percent in a youth hostel, and 2 percent in a weekend home. As to the method of transport, 77 percent used their cars, 10 percent went by plane, 7 percent by coach, 6 percent by train, 2 percent by bicycle or motorbike and 1 percent by boat. Some 55 percent went to the seaside. Out of the 56 percent who went abroad, 47 percent went to another EEC country, 6 percent to some other European country, and 3 percent went outside Europe to America, Asia or Africa. The most attractive points when choosing somewhere to go on holiday for Belgians were unspoilt countryside (43 percent), marvels of nature (42 percent), the desire to be in a totally different country (30 percent), the cost of living not being too high (25 percent), comfortable hotels (25 percent), entertainment facilities (22 percent), monuments, museums and galleries (16 percent), and opportunities to take part in sports (14 percent).

**Movies and television**

As already indicated, in Belgium fewer people are going to movies. In Flanders, 50 percent went to the movies in 1980, but only 32 percent in 1983. This decline was common across all population groups, but as in other countries, the highest movie-going rate is among 15–19 year olds (73 percent). After students, the unemployed have the next highest attendance rate (56 percent). In terms of education the highest movie-going rate (53 percent) is among the best educated. In the 1984 survey of the Francophone community, the highest movie attendance was also found among the young. It was also the most educated – 68 percent of them in Wallonia, and 73 percent in Brussels – who went to the movies most often. Retirees both in Flanders and in the Francophone community were going to the movies less often than any other groups.

Nearly everyone in Belgium watches television, but not for the same amount of time, nor necessarily the same programmes. Overall, in Belgium as elsewhere, it is the working class who spend the most time viewing TV. In the Francophone community, 34 percent of manual workers spend over 20 hours weekly with TV, compared with 22 percent in the lower middle class, 15 percent of the upper middle class, and 14 percent of the upper class. The opposite ranking appears for spending less than 10 hours per week viewing TV; 52 percent of the upper class and only 28 percent among manual workers. In general, more time is spent watching television in Wallonia than in Brussels. In terms of age, the young and the retirees do most viewing: over 60 percent of the under-25s view TV at least 10 hours per week, and 80 percent of those aged 65 and older.

**Reading books, magazines and newspapers**

With the economic crisis in Belgium, people are buying fewer books than before. Students and those in the upper middle class are the most active readers. They are the most likely to buy books and to use public libraries. In the Francophone community, 31 percent of workers had not read a single book in 1983, against only 9 percent in the upper class. Twelve percent of the upper middle class read over 50 books in 1983 (the highest of any group). For the total Francophone sample, when asked to rank their favourite leisure activities, reading was cited first, followed by sports, walking, meeting friends, listening to radio and watching TV.

Some 76–8 percent in the Francophone community read at least one newspaper a week, ranging from 63 percent among workers to 90 percent in the upper class in Brussels. The young read newspapers the least. Overall, some 75 percent of the population read at least one magazine per week, with the choice of magazine predictably associated with age, sex, income and education. In Flanders, some 55 percent of women and 51 percent of men read a book at least occasionally. The strongest readers are the under 20-year-olds; 70 percent of them are book readers. In terms of occupation, those who read books the most are students (76 percent), the part-time employed (71.5 percent), who are mostly women, and the unemployed (64.8 percent). In Flanders also, students and the most educated in the higher income brackets read the most books. These groups also have the largest percentages who use public libraries. Compared with other leisure activities, there were no marked changes in book-reading patterns between 1980 and 1983.

## Sports

In 1970 only a minority practised sports, but the figures have subsequently increased to approximately 50 percent of the population. The survey in Flanders made a distinction between 'active' sports (38 percent of the population) and 'hobby' sports such as walking and biking. If the latter are included, more than 53 percent of the population practise a sport and 35 percent are spectators at sports matches. By age group, active sports are practised most by the young – 60 percent of 15–19 year-olds, and 49 percent of 20–29 year-olds. The percentage steadily decreases with age, to 8.6 percent of 60–64 year-olds. 'Hobby' sports are practised by 43 percent of the elderly and 62.8 of 15–19 year-olds, with the highest overall percentage found among the better educated (70.2 percent). Active sport participation increases steadily with levels of education and income. In general, attendance at matches decreased substantially between 1980 (46 percent) and 1983 (35 percent), especially among retirees (from 35 percent to 18 percent), and among those with the least schooling (to 23 percent). Increases in match attendance were found in only two groups: the unemployed (from 36 to 42 percent) and the 55–9 age group (28 to 31 percent).

In the French-speaking community, slightly more than half of the upper class practise a sport, compared with 42 percent in Wallonia. In Brussels 46 percent of the lower middle class do so. Among workers, participation is 32 percent in Wallonia and 38 percent in Brussels. By age group, 63 percent practise sports among those aged under 25 and this percentage steadily decreases with age, dropping to 13 percent among over-65 year-olds in Wallonia and 19 percent in Brussels. Attendance at matches is higher among all social groups in Wallonia (just over one-third in all social groups) than in Brussels (25 percent).

## Social relations: meeting family, relatives and friends

Social relations constitute a traditional and valued leisure activity for virtually all the population (90 percent or more in all social groups). However, analysis of social contacts across age groups indicates changes which might be occurring in value systems surrounding family relationships. After the age of 45, contacts with relatives and neighbours start slowly to decrease, reflecting the social isolation accompanying ageing in industrial societies. The lowest and the highest income groups both have fewer contacts with neighbours than the middle-income groups. However, none of the existing surveys permits analysis of the qualitative changes which may be taking place because of modifications in value systems, social roles and survival strategies brought about by the crisis.

**Going to 'cultural' venues (theatre, concerts, opera, museums)**

Traditional cultural activities such as opera (2.8 percent), ballet (3.9 percent), and classical music (6.2 percent) have always been associated with education and income, and thus restricted to a minority, and these elites are now changing their patterns. While 36 percent in Flanders went to the theatre in 1980, only 21.5 percent did so in 1983. Participation diminished in all social categories, among all age groups, income groups and educational levels, though the least affected were those with the highest education. Visits to museums and exhibitions dropped from 47 percent in 1980 to 32 percent in 1983. The percentages attending traditional cultural activities are higher in Brussels, where the opportunities offered are greater, than in Wallonia. Participation tends to increase with age until 55 years.

**Going out to cafes, restaurants and dancing**

Some 71 percent in Flanders went to cafes in 1983, 62 percent to restaurants, and 47 percent went dancing. As elsewhere, more men (80 percent) were going to cafes than women (63 percent), but more women went to restaurants (66.6 percent) than men (58 percent). The highest proportion going to cafes was found among 20–24 year-olds (88 percent), while the highest percentage for restaurants was among 30–34 year-olds (76 percent). Dancing was mostly an activity of those between the ages of 15 and 24 (76 percent overall). Visits to cafes and restaurants increase in direct relation to income. This pattern is particularly significant for restaurants: only 45 percent of the lowest income group go to restaurants compared with 81 percent in the highest income group. The association with level of education is similar.

These patterns are also found in the Francophone community, where more than 80 percent of the upper class and the upper middle class go to restaurants, compared with 53 percent of workers in Wallonia and 60 percent in Brussels. Going to cafes and restaurants decreases after the age of 45.

**Hobbies**

The Flanders survey lists hobbies under six main categories. The most frequently practised are technical hobbies including car repairs, metal and woodwork (32 percent). The other categories are hobbies associated with nature such as gardening, raising plants and animals, then artistic hobbies including photography and playing music (5 percent overall), plastic arts (3.1 percent), scientific hobbies (3 percent) and collecting (7.3 percent). Except among students and the unemployed, the most popular single hobby is gardening, which is practised by 40 percent of the Flemish population. Immediately after gardening are do-it-yourself activities in the home (28 percent), and knitting and sewing (35 percent).

Participation in nearly all hobbies decreased between 1980 and 1983, with gardening being the main exception. Overall, the decrease was least marked for utilitarian hobbies such as car repairs (only 11 to 10 percent), and knitting and sewing (38 to 35 percent), two hobbies clearly associated with sex roles. Hobbies which involve recurrent expenditure dropped sharply: photography and home movies from 23 to 13 percent and 'collecting' from 19 to 7 percent. Playing a musical instrument decreased only slightly from 6 to 5 percent. This practice does not seem to be strongly associated with either income or economic activity.

Also noteworthy is the clear economic confirmation that philatelists in Belgium are a fairly stable group. Philatelic expenditure, roughly 150 million BF a year, remained remarkably constant between 1970 and 1985. The practice seems relatively insulated from wider structural changes affecting the national economy and modifications in other leisure practices.

In the Francophone community, also, gardening and do-it-yourself activities are among the most popular hobbies. Nearly half of all social groups take part (with a slightly lower proportion for gardening in Brussels). Home computers are owned by less than 5 percent of the population: the revolution taking place in other countries had not yet reached Belgium in 1983 and will not be discussed here, though it will certainly affect the country's future leisure patterns as it is already doing elsewhere.

**Participation in community life and associations**

Participation in associations and clubs is an important leisure activity in Flanders. In 1983, 43 percent of the population belonged to clubs or associations (47 percent of men and 40 percent of women). The most popular were sports clubs (19 percent), followed by cultural associations (11 percent), youth associations (9 percent), socio-cultural associations (9 percent), hobby clubs (6 percent), political and work-related groups (5 percent) and youth clubs (5 percent). Participation in clubs declined between 1980 and 1983 in Flanders, most notably in socio-cultural associations, from 34 to 18 percent, and in sports clubs from 25 to 19 percent.

## Policy implications

From an economic perspective, leisure can be treated as a commodity which responds, in part, to price fluctuations. Some leisure activities are free of charge, while others involve costs ranging from the purchase of equipment to regular expenditure on participation. Many leisure activities requiring specialised equipment are marketed by the leisure and cultural industries, which compete not only for consumers' money but also for their time. Yet leisure can also be viewed as a socially useful activity for individuals and for society. This is reflected in the legislation begun at the turn of the century establishing and recognising legal free time. The state has played a continuing role in leisure, assigning the development of leisure policies to specific institutions, and allocating budgets to finance and subsidise specific leisure activities for different population groups ranging from sports to cultural and self-development opportunities.

If the often significant differences observed in leisure between 1980 and 1983 in Flanders are related to the crisis and do not represent simple fluctuations, then overall participation in cultural and self-development activities seems on the decrease, while domestic leisure activities, particularly utilitarian hobbies (do-it-yourself), are taking on increasing importance. What does this mean? Where will it lead? Shifts are occurring among leisure activities, the implications of which are often not yet clear. As a result of the crisis more and more utilitarian leisure values are coexisting alongside traditional, internalised leisure values, and this coexistence seems likely to continue. This interaction entails contradictions between aspirations, values and activities, the availability of time and money, and the need to work more to order to satisfy leisure goals. Values of competition, as disseminated in the media and the workplace, at some point are bound to conflict with values of altruism and solidarity in human relations.

Disparities appear to be increasing between various groups in their participation in many leisure activities. The universal ownership of TV represents a recurrent monthly cost which must affect participation in other leisure activities which cost money. This competition, independent of the free time available, reinforces inequalities in access to out-of-home leisure. Inequalities in access to leisure are particularly important for the two growing, non-economically active population groups, the unemployed and the elderly, who have relatively small disposable incomes. The rich retiree basking happily in the sun or going to the opera is a social image that applies to only a small minority in Belgium. Although these two social groups are increasing numerically, they can be neglected politically, and by social science, because they fall outside the conventional work–leisure paradigm. From a traditional viewpoint, retirees and the unemployed do not work, and so have privileges in terms of free time. Yet they are not leisure classes. Rather, their situations are similar to those of pre-1968 housewives who were sometimes mis-defined as a sort of privileged leisure class since housework was not considered as work but as free time, leisurely, relaxing and fulfilling. Likewise, the imposed free time, or unoccupied time, of the unemployed and the elderly has a different relation to work than for other population groups. It has entirely different implications for identity, income and the performance of other social roles, including family roles. The family role of the father is not the same when he is unemployed. Being no longer part of the labour process, and hence having lost a social role and an important dimension in social identity, unemployed men's social interactions are impoverished. The young unemployed are confronted with the gradual disappearance of school friendship ties while the family relationship is also, it appears, modified in times of economic crisis. Concerns for social development and for equity, as well as for economic development, all indicate the need to take into account more fully the leisure needs of the unemployed, and of older citizens too, in order to offer them equal possibilities for self-development, relaxation and dignity.

In industrialised societies, where professionalisation and individualism are spreading, the marginalisation and isolation of the elderly is being exacerbated by their loss of occupational roles and identities. Their participation in leisure activities appears, from all the available data, to be lower than for other population groups. This is not, of course, to say that the elderly are totally neglected. Already by 1978 there were over 300 clubs or associations for the elderly in Brussels alone (Deliege, 1978), indicating a will and possibility to fight isolation and lack of social contacts. However, such associations reached just 20 percent of the elderly population. There is a need for research and action to make a clear distinction between the third and fourth age instead of aggregating as a group all those over 60 or 65 years. Leisure research has often paid insufficient attention to the unemployed and the elderly, thus reinforcing their socioeconomic discrimination and marginalisation. Existing leisure opportunities are often under-utilised by the unemployed, while there is a scarcity of leisure opportunities for the elderly. These problems appear to exist in all industrialised countries. They represent one of the most critical instances of the overall, negative effects of socioeconomic changes in the 1980s on leisure activity and participation, and so may serve as a focal point for further investigation and for policy action. However, this must not lead us to forget the strong and positive cultural policies of recent decades in Belgium, or the efforts that are still being made in support of the democratisation of culture and better professional education.

## References

Beckerman, W., W. Van Ginneken, R. Szal and M. Garzuel (1979) *Les Programmes de Maintien du Revenu et leur Impact sur la Pauvreté*. Geneva: BIT.

Best, F. (1980) *Exchanging Earnings for Leisure*. Washington, DC: US Department of Labor Monograph, 79.

Bouillin-Dartevelle, R. (1986) 'De l'obsession de Persister a l'angoisse de Resister: Nouvelles Stratégies du Loisir en Temps de Crise?' Paper presented at the World Congress of Sociology, New Delhi.

Cahiers de l'Institut universitaire d'études du développement (1984) *Crise et Chuchotements: Interrogations sur la Pertinence d'un Concept Dominant*. Geneva: PUF.

Commission of the European Communities (1987) *Europeans and their Holidays*. Brussels.

Deliege, P. (1978) *3e Age: Colloque 'Quelle Culture à Bruxelles? Avec quels Moyens?'*. UCL/Campus de Woluwe St Lambert: Commission Français de la Culture de l'agglomeration de Bruxelles.

Drumeaux, A. (1986) 'La Dépense Culturelle et de Loisirs aux Différents Niveaux de l'appareil Institutionnel', Institut de Sociologie de l'Université Libre de Bruxelles.

Dumazedier, J. (1974) *Sociologie Empirique du Loisir*. Paris: Seuil.

Freudenheim, M. (1987) 'Business and Health: Coping with Stress at Work', *New York Times*, 26 May.

Fukasz, G. (1982) 'Les Changements dans les Loisirs des Ouvriers Hongrois', *Loisir et Société*, 2, Prague.

Govaerts, F. (1975) 'Femmes et Idéologie de la Jeunesse dans le Discours Publicitaire', *Cahiers JEB*, 4, Ministère de l'Education Nationale et de la Culture Française, Bruxelles.

Govaerts, F. (1979) 'Modèle de Connaissance Publicitaire et Idéologie de la Consommation', *Revue de l'Institut de Sociologie*, Université Libre de Bruxelles, 3–4: 223–37.

Govaerts, F. (1986) 'Les Loisirs à Bruxelles', *ELRA Research Group Editions*, 2, Institute for Culture, Budapest.

Govaerts, F. and J. Marques-Pereira (1986) 'Isolation, Housing and Income:Towards a Policy for the Elderly in Belgium', Paper presented at the World Congress of Sociology, New Delhi.

Institut de Sociologie (1986) *Les Pratiques Culturelles dans la Communauté Française: Quelques Analyses Approfondies de l'enquête Quantitative*, 1, Université Libre de Bruxelles.

Institut de Sociologie ULB et Institut des Sciences Politiques et Sociales UCL (1985) *Les Pratiques Culturelles dans la Communauté Française, Principaux Résultats de l'Enquête Quantitative, Étude Realisée à la Demande de la Communauté Française*, Université Libre de Bruxelles.

INS: Institut National de Statistique (1975) *1971 Census*, 5: 28–30, Brussels.

INS: Institut National de Statistique (1980) *Bulletin de Statistique*, Brussels.

INS: Institut National de Statistique (1982) *1981 Census*, Brussels.

INS: Institut National de Statistique (1985a) *Annuaire Statistique de Poche*, Brussels.

INS: Institut National de Statistique (1985b) *Annuaire de Statistiques Régionales*, Brussels.

INS: Institut National de Statistique (1986a) *Aperçu Statistique de la Belgique*, Brussels.

Institut National de Statistique (1986b) *Les Comptes Nationaux de la Belgique, 1976–1985, Etudes Statistiques no. 78*, Brussels.

Institut National de Statistique (1986c) 'Affectation du Produit National, Estimations aux Prix de 1980', *Tableau 111–4. Documents non Publiés*, Brussels.

Lebaube, A. (1986) *Vivre avec la Crise, Le Monde, Dossiers et Documents*, (October), Paris.

Mabille, X. (1986) *Histoire Politique de la Belgique, Facteurs et Acteurs du Changement*. Brussels: CRISP.

Mattelart, A. and J.M. Piemme (1980) *Télévision: Enjeux sans Frontières, Industries Culturelles et Politiques de la Communication*. Presses Universitaires de Grenoble.

Ministry of the Flemish Community, Tourist Office for Flanders (1984) *Tourism (English Summary)*. Flanders.

Naeyaert, D. and U. Claeys (1984) *Vrijetijdsbesteding in Vlaanderen anno 1983*, Deelrapport 1, Sociologisch Onderzoeksinstitut, Katholieke Universiteit, Leuven.

OECD: Organisation for Economic Co-operation and Development (1986) *Politique du Tourisme et Tourisme International dans les Pays Membres de l'OCED*. Paris.

Samuel, N. with M. Romer (1984) *Le Temps Libre, un Temps Social*. Paris: Librairie des Méridiens.

Weisgerber, P. (1986) *L'Evolution du Tourisme*. Liège: Actes du Pre-Congrès Furatour.

# 6

# Brazil: A New Cycle of Modernisation

## Renato Requixa and Luiz Camargo

### Free time in Brazilian society

At the beginning of the twentieth century, when Brazilian industrialisation was still in its initial stages, the typical labourer worked 5000 hours a year (Dias, 1977: 226). Nowadays, with a working week of 48 hours and an official working year of 273 days, the typical labourer works just 2200 hours anually. White-collar workers such as office and bank employees, with working weeks of 40 hours, are today on the level that European and American workers had reached at the end of the 1970s with approximately 1800 working hours per year (Dumazedier, 1979: 32).

Not every Brazilian adult finds a regular occupation in the labour force. Even in urban areas 40 percent of the economically active population still make their livings from sporadic jobs, through self-employment, or from tasks which make up the so-called casual sector of the economy. Here much of the work is seasonal. People work hard, for long hours, but only at certain times of the year. At other times the pressure is far less intense. However, Brazilians with full-time and permanent employment work more hours, both weekly and annually, than their European or American counterparts who are now benefiting from the gradual introduction of 36-hour working weeks.

In Brazil there has been only one time-budget survey using internationally accepted parameters (De Souza, 1975). This survey was in 1973, in Rio de Janeiro and satellite towns. A representative sample of 332 persons aged 18–65 were asked to keep time-books recording their activities during each of the 1440 minutes of the day for an entire week. Their activities were classified into 72 categories which were then grouped into four main classes – professional work, domestic work, hygienic care, and free time. Despite the time which has elapsed, the results remain useful since no significant change has taken place in the number of working hours. This survey found that the typical Brazilian factory worker spent a total of 59 hours weekly working and commuting. Even for office workers the weekly average was a high 55 hours. These figures are high when compared with those recorded in surveys in industrialised European countries and North America, where the average working week including commuting is now between 40 and 45 hours. And free time? Naturally it is affected by the longer working week in Brazil and varies between 27 and 30 hours according to the same 1973 survey. In the following sections the main ways in which the Brazilian population spends its work-free time are examined.

*Free time is used basically as leisure time*
The time-budget survey included under the heading 'free time' not only recreation but also religious and political activities, and non-compulsory studies. How is free time allocated among these different activities in Brazil? Not surprisingly, as in other societies, free time is used by Brazilians almost entirely as leisure, for recreation and relaxation. In the different social classes that were surveyed, the amount of time devoted to political, religious and educational activities never exceeded 10 percent of all free time. At weekends the additional free time available was leading to a corresponding increase in the time devoted to leisure.

*Time available for leisure is significantly affected by the*
*various forms of mass media communication*
Is television the Brazilian population's only form of leisure? The influence of the TV set on viewers' lives is often extremely strong. Recent surveys show that 95 percent of the urban population watch television on weekdays and 90 percent at weekends. There is, furthermore, an army of super-enthusiasts, 26 percent of the urban population, who spend more than six hours in front of the television on Sundays. Apart from television, other popular activities include listening to AM and FM radio, reading newspapers and magazines, and listening to records, that is to say, entertainment financed by commercial enterprises which are collectively called the culture industries.

These facts suggest to many that Brazilian leisure is mostly directed towards passive consumption, or activities that lead to consumption. Almost half the time available for leisure is spent on pursuits associated with the culture industries: watching television in first place, listening to the radio in a distant second place, and last by far, listening to records and reading books, newspapers and magazines. However, it is important to note that such means of mass communication are nothing more than the reproduction of the contents of other leisure activities. The number of classical or pop music concerts on the radio and television is incomparably greater than live shows or concerts. The same is true for other artistic performances such as the theatre and dancing, and for sports events, gardening, cooking and news in general.

Obviously, passive consumption is an important part of Brazilian leisure, but it is wrong to imagine that this consumption is taking the place of practice (Camargo, 1982: 192–5). Quite the opposite is the case; for example, the presentation of a ballet on television encourages some to engage in this pursuit. Also, the great attention which television has given to volleyball over the last few years has been one of the main reasons for the increase in the practice of this sport among the general population. Also, if almost half of all leisure time is associated with the mass media, it stands to reason that more than half of this time must be devoted to other leisure activities.

*Leisure time is the training field for a varied cultural life*
Some people imagine that when it comes to sport, the Brazilian predilection is for football. A liking for football exists, and increases with age among both men and women. Among the younger age groups, however, where women's tastes seem to weigh heavily, other activities predominate, in the following order: swimming, volleyball and basketball. This is probably due to the advance in schooling and aggressive marketing by the organisations connected with these sports (Camargo, 1982: 195–209).

These generalisations are valid for sporting preferences whether one considers the numbers playing or following the sports on television and in newspaper reports, or watching events at gymnasiums and sports stadiums. Brazilians are less involved in sport than some observers might imagine. The time spent practising sports is high at school age, but drops sharply after leaving school. Only 8 percent of adults practise any sport, even casually. However, gymnastics has become increasingly popular over the last fifteen years. In Sao Paulo some 24 percent of the population over the age of 18 practise some form of gymnastics either in gymnasiums or in their homes.

With regard to hobbies the variety is much greater: repairing electrical appliances, repairing and painting homes, simple carpentry, car and motorcycle repairs, gardening, breeding pets, cooking for pleasure and similar activities are commonplace in the lives of 70 percent of the urban population. For artistic activities the figures are equally notable. It is estimated that 8 percent of the population have some form of literary activity, 17 percent practise photography and 12 percent play some type of instrument even if this is only for their families and friends. Travelling is also common. Petrol and accommodation are expensive, but this does not prevent 2.5 million people leaving Sao Paulo alone during holiday weekends. More than 70 percent of workers go away on vacations and more than 80 percent go on some trip during the year in the name of leisure. Possession of a car is certainly important. From 1973 to 1980, despite the energy crises, the number of households that owned a vehicle rose from 14 to 28 percent in urban areas, and from 2.5 to 9.5 percent in rural areas.

There has also been an increase in involvement in recreational organisations and societies. Although the number of recognised organisations in an average Brazilian city rarely exceeds 100, while in a French city like Annecy (Dumazedier, 1974) there are more than 600, one cannot speak about a precarious state of community life in Brazil but rather about a lack of any tradition of formal community life. In reality, most organisations that are formed go out of existence through lack of financial support and recognition by the community.

**Tendencies in Brazil which affect leisure**

What are the prospects for leisure in Brazil during the remainder of the twentieth century? Leisure time grows as working hours are reduced, so the first issue to be considered is the likely development of legislation affecting working hours. But leisure time also results from the streamlining of chores. And as Dumazedier (1974) has said, leisure is also a result of an aesthetic ethic whereby a society revises its values and incorporates, by means of voluntary, liberating, personal and hedonistic activities, new forms of daily life (Dumazedier, 1979: 28). The following trends will be analysed from these perspectives:

1. accelerating technological development which should lead to further reductions in working hours;
2. the development of a new work ethic which allows for the adaptation, in a more integrated form, of the utilitarian values of work and the existential values of leisure;
3. the secularisation of urban customs favouring new forms of community life and more recreation centres;
4. the deconsecration of working hours which will permit a more natural organisation of the daily demands of both work and leisure.

*Accelerating technological development*
This means an intense introduction of new scientific and technolo-

gical knowledge in the field of industrial production. The close connection between science and industry has given rise to a series of social developments with identifiable phases (Dumazedier, 1981).

In the initial stage, the adoption of the most modern scientific and technological knowledge by industry leads to increased productivity. With this comes an excess of production, which is not absorbed by the consumer. In the second phase of this process companies try to reduce costs so as to make their products cheaper in the hope of increasing consumption. Then they appeal for mass dismissals of workers and/or for production restrictions. In the following stage the unions try to avoid mass dismissals by proposing reductions in working hours. At this point there is a delicate period of negotiation. Companies accept reductions in working hours provided that there are proportionate reductions in the workers' wages. The unions do not agree to this and insist on retaining full wages. Then comes a longer period of negotiation while society at large considers the pros and cons of reductions in working hours. The end result, in general, is a reduction in working hours. This analysis is obviously over-simplified. In reality the process is much more complex and includes innumerable variations in degree and intensity. But, as a general rule, the result is a reduction in working hours without any corresponding reduction in workers' wages. As by the turn of the century there will certainly be a continuous and progressively greater implementation of modern technology in industrial production (especially in automation and cybernetics), it is not difficult to foresee a continuation of the process described here, with over-production, with unemployment followed by negotiations, the outcomes of which favour an increase of free time.

In any case, a paradoxical situation currently exists in Brazil with the burden of long working hours for some and unemployment for others. On the one hand there are labourers working eight hours a day, 48 hours a week, and on the other hand a large proportion of the would-be workforce is unemployed because of the non-existence of jobs. It is an odd situation which common sense rejects and public opinion is unable to comprehend. After all, why not reduce the number of working hours so that everybody has the chance to work? Dumazedier (1974) points out a double paradox in modern industrial society. Until recently, to obtain an increase in production, people had to work more (Dumazedier, 1979: 29). The first paradox is that today the industrial system can, thanks to science, produce more while people work less. The second paradox is that the industrial system is resistant and does not easily accept a reduction in the number of working hours.

France offers an outstanding example of the pace of the current productivity increases as a result of the implementation of scientific knowledge in industry. From 1880 to 1953 French productivity doubled. It took 73 years for this to happen. Then, in the following ten years from 1953 to 1963, French productivity doubled again (Dumazedier, 1979: 32). It is curious to note that the industrial system today can produce the same, or even an increased, quantity of goods alongside a reduction in the labour force in terms of the time spent in production. This leads to an extraordinary vision of the future which has still not been widely recognised. This is why resistance to the reduction in working hours remains an ever-present feature of the industrial system. The United States offers interesting data in this respect. From 1900 to 1920 the average working week in the United States dropped from 58.5 to 50.6 hours. There was, therefore, a decrease of eight hours in the average working week during this 20-year period. However, in spite of the extraordinary increase in productivity in that country, it took another 50 years, from 1920 to 1970, for the average working week to be reduced by another eight hours.

Taking the case of Brazil, when industrialisation started at the beginning of this century the average working year was approximately 5000 hours. Today the average is around 2200 hours. This average is greater than the annual averages of European and North American workers, which are around 1800 hours. The widely held belief that Brazilians do not work very hard is a myth. Brazilians work, and work hard. In addition to the high average working week of 48 hours, consider the circumstances in which the workers live: their salaries, housing, health, social payments, and also (bearing leisure time in mind) the great distance between their domiciles and places of work. In the case of a typical worker in Sao Paulo, travelling to and from work takes up between two and a half to three hours a day. Furthermore, the 1980 census showed that out of every two Brazilians over the age of ten years, one worked. And of the 44 million who made up the workforce in Brazil, according to the same census, approximately 13 million worked more than 48 hours per week. Finally, to complete the picture, it should be borne in mind that these 44 million represent only 36 percent of the population. This means that this 36 percent are responsible for supporting 64 percent of the people. This is a very different situation from countries like the United States where 47 percent support 53 percent of the population, while in Japan the balance is almost fifty-fifty. National and international data point towards a gradual reduction of the number of daily, weekly and annual working hours of the Brazilian worker by the end of the century.

*The new work ethic*

Scientific and technological developments are of great importance to the increase of free time in reducing the number of working hours, though this consequence is not automatic, owing to the previously mentioned resistance. Simultaneously, a new ethic relating to work and new ways of thinking is permeating Brazilian society. A new work ethic is emerging, breaking down barriers that were rooted in values received and founded in a society that is fast disappearing.

Work and leisure sociologists have written about a progressive demystification of the traditional work ethic. This ethic insists on a moral supervalorisation of work. It treats work as a guarantee of the ennoblement of human existence, and of dignity. It prescribes an austere and hard-working life of asceticism, sobriety and frugality, plus habits of parsimony and economy. This ethic is still in existence, especially among older people. However, it represents a set of values that are fast being eroded. Research into existential satisfactions *at work* and *outside work* among young people in various countries (Institute Gallup, 1979) reveals that for most young people life outside work offers more satisfaction than life at work. In Brazil 335 youngsters were interviewed in five major cities – Sao Paulo, Rio de Janeiro, Porto Alegre, Belo Horizonte and Salvador. Out of the 11 countries where the survey was carried out there were only two (India and the Philippines) where young people found more satisfaction in work than outside. In the other countries where the survey was conducted (Brazil, Japan, Switzerland, West Germany, the United States, Sweden, England, Australia and France) young people found more satisfaction outside work. The cases of India and the Philippines are explicable, perhaps, by the fact that most of the young people who took part in the survey worked for themselves and not as employees.

The idea itself that work ennobles does not seem widespread among workers any more. Nowadays it is unusual for workers to find in their jobs the necessary elements that supply meaning to life as a human being. Jobs that are monotonous and repetitive, and which lack incentive and creativity, do not provide a sufficient motivating force to arouse enthusiasm in the worker. In 1980, in a survey carried out in the city of Sao Paulo, out of total of 382 adults aged over 18, selected at random from the regular working population who were interviewed, 52 percent opted for vacations of 30 days in preference to vacations of 20 days plus 10 paid working days. Only 44 percent preferred the latter while 4 percent were undecided. It is significant that this decline in the moral valorisation of work is now occurring in practically all industrial countries, even in those with protestant, puritan or Calvinistic religious traditions where, until recently, profit, wealth and financial success were considered the greatest proof of divine grace.

In contrast to this now-declining work ethic, a new leisure ethic is spreading which treats life experience as a value in itself and not simply as a means of recuperating energy for the daily and weekly return to productive activities. The recognition of leisure as a value in itself is the source of an important social transformation. Accepting leisure with values that go beyond relaxation and rest means injecting into other spheres those values that emerge from the actual practice of leisure. Individuals become aware of the importance of leisure, above all, by practising leisure activities. It is through this dialectic that new cultural values become established. These values are introducing new ways of thinking, feeling and acting. There is, then, in Brazil, an impending cultural revolution with roots in leisure activities. This revolution is likely to transform ideas and concepts relating to work, the family, religion and politics. This great revolution of our age is independent of any political ideology. At present it is challenging standard traditional values. Our prediction is that by the end of the century this new leisure ethic will be firmly established and dominant.

*Secularisation of customs*
The secularisation of customs is a phenomenon that accompanies urbanisation. Brazil is still undergoing an intense and continuous process of urban growth. In 1940 the population of Brazil was 41 million, of whom 31 percent were urban and 69 percent rural. By 1980, with a population of 119 million, this situation was practically inverted. The urban population had risen to 68 percent and the rural population had fallen to 32 percent. Another important feature of contemporary Brazil is the increase in the number of cities. The data are highly significant. At the time of the 1980 census Brazil had 3991 cities; 2737 were considered small, that is with less than 30,000 inhabitants, 1112 were medium sized with 30–250,000 inhabitants, and 142 were big cities with more than 250,000 inhabitants. Comparing the 1940 census with the 1980 census reveals an increase of 182 percent in the number of small cities. Meanwhile, in the same period, there was an increase of 828 percent in the number of medium-sized cities and 930 percent in the number of big cities. So the country is becoming increasingly urbanised, with the population living more and more in medium-sized and big cities, but mainly in big cities. By 1980 the medium-sized and big cities, which represent only 30 percent of the total number of cities, were inhabited by 80 percent of Brazil's total urban population.

It is estimated that by the end of the century about 90 percent of the Brazilian population will be urban, concentrated in medium-sized and big cities, especially in the latter. This urban population will increasingly be subject to the social implications of the secularisation of customs. This means that the traditional influences of the family, religion and politics will undergo an appreciable reduction. The larger the city, the greater the erosion of the traditional authority of the father of the family, the political chief and the religious leader. Their authority is still strong in rural areas. The urban world, with its new values, undermines traditional forces and thus causes a reduction of time spent on family, religious and political obligations. One result is an increase in free time, which in turn becomes a force affecting urban community life, and amplifying its differences from rural life.

*The deconsecration of working hours*
During the remainder of the twentieth century the growth of free time will not depend entirely on the legal reduction of daily and weekly working hours. Up to now free time has been greatly restricted by traffic jams, and by the great distances between many people's homes and their places of work. Flexible working hours and the four-day week are likely to become increasingly common. Flexible working hours originated in Germany. Because of problems with household tasks involving young children, an employee in a West German office asked if she could begin work at 10 a.m. instead of 8 a.m. and offered to make up for the two hours at the end of the working day. Her suggestion was accepted, then widely copied. Nowadays flexible working hours have been adopted by thousands of companies all over the world. Basically, the system of flexible working hours functions as follows: while continuing to work 8 hours a day, the employee has the right to choose which 8 hours out of a longer period of 12 or even 14 hours. He or she must be at work for a certain number of hours in the morning and in the afternoon: these are the core hours. The other hours are flexible according to his or her personal interests. The system offers advantages to employers, such as reductions in the number of absences, late arrivals, overtime, and requests for time off for medical reasons. A survey into the effects in West Germany also revealed a reduction in the number of traffic accidents, a drop in accident insurance settlements, and lower fuel consumption as a result of fewer traffic jams.

The four-day week of 10 hours per working day, then a three-day weekend is another example of liberalisation. Paul Samuelson, a Nobel prize-winner in economics, has analysed the effects of this four-day week, and has concluded that free time increases by about 20 percent. This system started in the United States in a chain of shops which sold tyres. It was observed that most purchases were made on Thursdays, Fridays and Saturdays. The three days off alongside a four-day working week need not coincide with the traditional weekend, but can depend on various factors. Again, surveys reveal many advantages.

Both of these systems are important partly because they illustrate a new mentality towards working hours. In Brazil until now, working hours have been very rigid, truly sacred and untouchable. No change whatsoever was normally permitted. Work time was an integral part of the mentality that understood work as a real punishment for man. Five minutes late on arrival brought financial penalties. The deconsecration of working hours does not mean their reduction, but means, rather, important changes in attitudes towards work in general and the acceptance of new cultural values.

A result of both systems is an increase in free time, partly as a consequence of fewer traffic jams in big cities. Because of the success of these procedures they will certainly spread. Brazilian politicians and companies are becoming interested in such new procedures, which bring new existential conditions and foster new social aspirations.

In addition to the four trends analysed in the previous sections, other factors of a social and technological nature are likely to generate more free time. It seems obvious, for example, that improved public transport will considerably increase free time. The buses that run from the north to the south of the city of Sao Paulo currently take about two and a half to three hours. The subway takes 20 minutes to cover the same route. The use of electronic equipment and semi-prepared food save time in the home, especially for women. Women with paid employment have less free time than other adults since in addition to their professional work they spend more time on household chores than men. There has been an extraordinary increase in the number of women in the Brazilian workforce. In 1970 Brazil's workforce was around 30 million. By 1980 this had risen to 44 million, an increase of almost 50 percent. However, the growth of the economically active female population was even greater. In 1970 there were 4.7 million women in the Brazilian workforce. By 1980 there were 10.3 million, which means that the number of female workers had risen in ten years by more than 100 percent.

**Conclusions**

The proximity of the new millennium encourages speculation. Sombre perspectives include forecasts of ecological disaster and nuclear holocaust, and compete with hopes for a happy future for humanity. Brazil offers grounds for worry, yet, on balance, socioeconomic considerations over the medium and longer term favour optimism.

Today Brazil has 125 million inhabitants. By 1990 there will be 150 million. This population is predominantly urban with two-thirds living in cities and one-third in rural areas. Furthermore, this urban population is increasingly concentrated in medium-sized and big cities. The latter comprise the nine metropolitan regions with more than a million inhabitants in each. In addition to this, it must be stressed that the population of Brazil is predominantly young, with 36 percent under 14 years of age and 46 percent under the age of 20.

The Brazilian workforce totals about 50 million registered employees, to whom can be added a further 10 million so-called 'invisible' workers. This workforce is responsible for a gross national product of over 300 billion US dollars which represents 60 percent of the output of the whole of Latin America, and places Brazil as the eighth largest economy in the world. After some years of recession, the country has returned to the same levels of growth as in the 1970s, with an increase of 7 percent per year in the gross national product. With such a level of economic growth, it seems right to think, as government planners do, that the evils of poverty and misery which still affect 20 percent of Brazil's population will finally be resolved, together with problems of malnutrition, life in shanty towns, high infant mortality rates, and minors abandoned and condemned to live as outcasts. These are our forecasts for the year 2000, when it is hoped that Brazil will be on the same social and welfare level as countries such as Spain and Greece.

Thus, a new cycle of modernisation of Brazilian life comes into sight. Our perspective is basically optimistic. After all, the growth of the country will open the door to the tendencies discussed earlier. Modernisation should encourage Brazilian employers to take a more balanced view of their social rights and responsibilities, especially those which affect the daily lives of their workers. This same modernisation should, in turn, bring with it enlightened actions from the trade unions with regard to systems which are already in operation in more developed countries, such as the possibility of reducing work time without affecting production, and introducing flexible working hours. It is hoped that these trends will allow greater control of the harmful aspects of Brazilian industrial life, and have a positive influence on community life and the leisure of the population in general.

The social control of Brazil's culture industries has become important because all modernisation brings with it a disregard for traditional culture, for patrimonial culture, and for the environment. These trends threaten the social–cultural identity of the Brazilian population. Care must therefore be taken that economic growth does not bring with it, as in the 1970s, pollution in the countryside, in the urban green spots and in other open spaces accessible to the inhabitants of big cities. Traditional cultural activities must not be undermined ahead of any replacements. Above all, the absolute mystification of economic growth must be avoided. Economic development is not the same as development in itself. It will amount to progress only if accompanied by appropriate political, social and cultural changes. Furthermore, the idea that everything can be instantly reorganised alongside economic change must be resisted. Much that is irrecoverable could be lost on the way.

Leisure problems are certainly not exclusive to Third World nations. Economically rich countries also face problems, often of an even more serious nature. These include a frightening range of pathologies bearing on the use of free time, such as violence and the abuse of drugs. According to the professionals who study leisure, to grow without losing the special traits that distinguish Brazilian culture is the challenge for this society up to the end of the twentieth century.

## References

Camargo, L. (1982) *Genèse du Loisir dans les Pays en Voie de Développement – le Cas du Brésil.* Doctoral thesis, Sorbonne, Paris.

De Souza, A. (1975) *As 24 Horas do Carioca.* Rio de Janeiro: IUPERJ.

Dias, E. (1977) *Historia das Lutas Sociais no Brasil.* Sao Paulo: Alfa-Omega.

Dumazedier, J. (1974) *Sociologie Empirique du Loisir.* Paris: Seuil.

Dumazedier, J. (1979) *Sociologia Empirica do Lazer.* Sao Paulo: Perspectiva.

Dumazedier, J. (1981) 'Lazer e Trabalho', *Conferencia,* Sao Paulo (August).

Institute Gallup (1979) *International Research on the Youngsters' Values and Attitudes towards Work.*

# 7

# Puerto Rico: Consumerism as a Way of Life

*Nelson Melendez*

On 23 February 1987 the Secretary of the Interior of Puerto Rico announced a far-reaching income tax reform plan. Behind this reform lies the government's avowed aspiration of dramatically modifying the Puerto Rican life-style. This life-style is characterised by heavy consumer spending, large personal debt, dependence on multiple forms of credit, recurrent loans, and an almost total absence of savings. Most economic analysts are critical of the way the average Puerto Rican has grown accustomed to living by credit in order to satisfy his or her consumer appetite (*El Mundo*, 23 March 1987).

What connection, if any, does the above have to leisure? The following pages discuss a number of issues that, in aggregate, lead to a better understanding of the relationships between leisure and socioeconomic change in Puerto Rico, and indicate a very close relationship between the proposed income tax reform and leisure. It is as well to understand, however, that tax reform will tackle only a symptom, and that the essence of the relationship between leisure, the economy, social change, life-style, and quality of life in Puerto Rico remains virtually uncharted territory. Indeed, this chapter is conceivably the first expedition in search of such relationships.

Before proceeding, some basic information about Puerto Rico is necessary to provide a frame of reference. Puerto Rico is a tropical island in the Caribbean Sea with a land mass of approximately 4000 square miles. It is the fourth largest island in the Caribbean archipelago which is composed of some 7000 islands. The current resident population is 3.2 million although the total number of Puerto Ricans is close to 5 million, the balance now living outside the island. Its strategic location between North and South America has greatly influenced Puerto Rico's history and the character of its people.

The Spanish explorer Christopher Columbus landed on the island during his second voyage in the 'New World' on 19 November 1493. Subsequently Spain colonised the island and held it until the Spanish-American War of 1898 when control was lost to the United

States of America. The island has been under the political and economic influence of the USA ever since. Currently Puerto Rico is related to the USA in political terms as an associated free state; a political formula that affords a degree of internal self-rule such as the free election of a chief executive (governor), mayors and legislators. This political formula came into being on 25 July 1952 and the island has subsequently been known as the Commonwealth of Puerto Rico, or the Free Associated State of Puerto Rico. In 1953 the United Nations (UN) recognised the new political status in a resolution which stated that 'the people of Puerto Rico have been invested with attributes of political sovereignty, which clearly identify the status of self-government attained by the people as an autonomous political entity'. Currently the political status of Puerto Rico is under debate in the same forum (the UN) in the Decolonization Committee.

The form of government is a representative democracy with executive, legislative and judicial bodies balancing each other's power. General elections are held every four years and at present there are four registered parties: the Popular Democratic Party (currently in power), the New Progressive Party, the Puerto Rican Independence Party and the Puerto Rican Socialist Party. The governing party wants to preserve the status quo, the second wishes the island to become a state of the USA, and the last two seek greater independence.

In Puerto Rico, as elsewhere, it has proved impossible to keep politics and leisure in entirely separate domains. In 1980 the Puerto Rico Olympic Committee defied a government boycott of the Moscow Games. In so doing the committee was establishing that it was a private body, free from government interference as long as it operated within the law. But what was really at issue was the sovereignty of the island. The USA was boycotting the Moscow Games. Participation by Puerto Rico was an assertion of national independence, which was achieved, in international sport. Sending a Puerto Rico team to Moscow satisfied some islanders' aspirations for greater independence from the USA, while, at the same time, maintaining the client status in other spheres.

There are 78 municipalities or cities in Puerto Rico with populations ranging from 452,224 in the capital, San Juan, to 1298 in the city of Culebra. However, approximately half of the island's total population is concentrated in the metropolitan area of San Juan, which encompasses six municipalities. The island's economy is not dominated by a single economic sector; several share the load. The major sectors are manufacturing, trade, finance, public administration, and services. Tourism, which is sometimes mistakenly treated as a major force in the economy, is responsible for only approximately 5 percent of the gross national product (GNP), while manufacturing accounts for nearly half.

Ethnically Puerto Ricans are a mix of three main cultural groups: Mesoamerican Indians, Europeans (mostly Spanish), and African blacks. To this a further ingredient of North Americans (mostly white) can be added as a result of US influence over the island.

## Selected socioeconomic trends

### Population

A significant phenomenon in Puerto Rican demographics, and consequently in any socioeconomic analysis, is migration. At the beginning of the twentieth century Puerto Ricans began a migratory movement to the United States mainland (including Hawaii), where some 2.5 million Puerto Ricans must now be living. A total of 157,000 left the island during the period 1980–85 alone. The most frequent motivation to migrate has traditionally been job-seeking.

As in most partly developed countries, population growth in Puerto Rico has been slowing down. The total population, in terms of numbers, is stabilising and is also growing older, although less so than in most fully developed countries (see Table 7.1). Following international trends, the divorce rate has almost doubled since 1970, and currently one out of every two marriages ends in divorce.

Table 7.1   *Population by gender and age groups (000s)*

|  | 1970 | 1980 | % change |
|---|---|---|---|
| Total population | 2721.7 | 3196.5 | +17 |
| Females | 1388.1 | 1630.2 | +17 |
| Males | 1333.6 | 1556.3 | +16 |
| Persons in age groups |  |  |  |
| 0–19 | 1329.2 | 1368.9 | +3 |
| 20–39 | 666.5 | 877.8 | +31 |
| 40–59 | 456.2 | 581.7 | +27 |
| 60–+ | 296.8 | 368.1 | +24 |
| Median age (years) | 20.7 | 24.0 | +16 |
| Population density (per sq. mile) | 795.1 | 933.8 | +17 |
| Life expectancy (years) | 72.0 | 74.0 | +3 |
| Population growth | 20.4 | 16.7 | −18 |
| Fertility rate | 27.1 | 23.2 | −14 |
| Mortality rate | 6.7 | 6.5 | −3 |

*Source:* United States Bureau of the Census (1984)

*Education*
Education is mandatory in Puerto Rico until the eighth grade, and the system is bilingual (Spanish and English). The island's literacy rate is comparable to standards in most industrial nations. Since 1970 there has been a significant growth in the numbers attending and graduating from universities (see Table 7.2). This has been the result of substantial financial assistance to prospective students through a United States government programme known as the Basic Education Opportunity Grant (BEOG). Government spending on education in Puerto Rico has risen considerably. There has also been a rapid growth in what many are now calling 'the educational industry': a large number of private post-secondary institutions offering technical and professional programmes. Private expenditure on education has more than tripled in the past ten years (from $34 million to $128 million), while in the public sector the increase has been considerable but not quite as strong (from $255 million to $646 million).

Table 7.2   *Enrolment in schools and universities, literacy and desertion rates*

|  | 1970 | 1980 | % change |
| --- | --- | --- | --- |
| Persons enrolled in school | 821,046 | 971,592 | +18 |
| Persons attending universities | 63,329 | 134,677 | +113 |
| Number of high-school graduates | 179,108 | 332,770 | +86 |
| Number of university graduates | 72,367 | 147,920 | +104 |
| Literacy rate (%) | 89.3 | 91.8 | +3 |
| School desertion (%) | 5.6 | 3.7 | -34 |

*Source:* Universidad Interamericana de Puerto Rico (1980: 47)

*The economy*
Following international trends, unemployment has risen dramatically in Puerto Rico, by 65 percent since 1970. By 1986 the unemployment rate had reached 23.9 percent. Some analysts say that the real figure is close to 40 percent if one takes account of those who are no longer actively seeking jobs. The largest gains in employment have been in professional and managerial occupations (30 percent). Unemployment rates are twice as high among males as among females. The latter are quickly gaining ground in economic participation particularly in technical, sales, clerical, professional and managerial jobs (see Tables 7.3 and 7.4). What is particularly noteworthy, however, is the recent growth of public administration as a source of employment. In 1970 this ranked fourth among all sectors of the economy in terms of jobs, and employed 111,000. By

1980 employment in this sector had increased by 66 percent to 184,000 jobs. Public administration has become Puerto Rico's number one growth sector in terms of employment. The growth of government bureaucracy, and its influence on the job market, has been severely criticised. The political clout wielded by any administration that controls close to one in every three jobs must surely be cause for alarm in a democratic system.

Another point of interest is the dramatic rise in unemployment among persons with high educational levels (more than 13 years at school). Although job opportunities for this group have traditionally been better than for the rest of the population, it is in this very group that the recent increase in unemployment has been greatest (see Table 7.5). This perhaps suggests either a drying up of professional-type jobs, or an incorrect orientation of higher education on the island, which is no longer preparing people for the types of jobs available.

Table 7.3   *Labour force and employed persons (000s)*
*(over 16 years of age)*

|  | 1970 | 1980 | % change |
| --- | --- | --- | --- |
| Labour force | 765.0 | 996.0 | +30 |
| Employed persons | 634.9 | 733.9 | +16 |
| Employed males | 438.9 | 465.3 | +6 |
| Employed females | 195.9 | 268.5 | +37 |
| Ratio of employed persons to all persons (%) | 38 | 35 | −9 |

*Source:* Universidad Interamericana de Puerto Rico (1980: 55)

Table 7.4   *Employed persons by occupation (% of employed persons)*

|  | 1970 | 1980 | % change |
| --- | --- | --- | --- |
| Professional and managers | 15.5 | 20.3 | +30 |
| Technical, sales and clerical | 23.2 | 27.2 | +17 |
| Services | 12.6 | 14.6 | +16 |
| Agriculture | 8.0 | 3.5 | −56 |
| Labourers and operatives | 25.3 | 22.0 | −13 |
| Entertainment and recreation services (total) | 0.01 (5,700) | 0.01 (5,504) | − |

*Source:* United States Bureau of the Census (1984)

Puerto Rico's recent economic history has been remarkable to say the least: a sort of rags to riches story, from being the poor relation of the Caribbean to enjoying the highest living standards of any Latin American country, in less than 40 years. A massive

Table 7.5   *Unemployment: total, by age group and by years of school completed (% of labour force)*

|  | 1970 | 1980 | % change |
|---|---|---|---|
| Unemployed, total | 10.3 | 17.0 | +65 |
| Unemployed males | 11.0 | 19.4 | +76 |
| Unemployed females | 9.0 | 12.2 | +35 |
| 16–19 years | 27.7 | 45.3 | +63 |
| 20–24 years | 17.7 | 30.5 | +72 |
| 25–34 years | 8.9 | 16.1 | +81 |
| 35–44 years | 6.8 | 11.0 | +62 |
| 45–54 years | 6.2 | 10.6 | +71 |
| 55–64 years | 6.6 | 11.6 | +76 |
| 0 years completed | 11.6 | 19.2 | +65 |
| 8 years completed | 13.3 | 23.4 | +76 |
| 12 years completed | 9.7 | 15.9 | +64 |
| 13 years completed | 2.8 | 7.8 | +178 |

*Source:* Universidad Interamericana de Puerto Rico (1980: 56)

industrialisation programme called 'Operation Bootstrap' (*Manos a la obra*) was largely responsible for this turn-around. This programme transformed the Puerto Rican economy from one based on the uncertainty of a single crop (sugar) to a broad-based manufacturing economy. Per capita income has grown from US $121 a year in 1940 to $4000 a year in 1986, and in the process a middle class of considerable proportions has been created. At present, however, 62 percent of all families are still living below the poverty level (established at $7500 per annum for a family of four).

Even when one considers only the period 1970 to 1980, economic growth has been striking, though at quite a cost. The island now has a very serious debt problem amounting to 12.6 billion dollars in combined public and private debt in 1984 (see Table 7.6). By 1986 private debt had risen dramatically to more than 6 billion dollars (almost $2600 per person). It is now equivalent to 45 percent of disposable annual income, which is a phenomenal rise from 11.9 percent in 1960. Ironically, the macro-financial scene is quite strong, as bank assets have risen by almost 300 percent during this same period (see Table 7.7). This situation serves to fuel further borrowing, as banks are eager to lend money and have reduced interest on loans to rates once unheard of. Thus consumer expenditure has risen dramatically, by almost 200 percent, thereby pushing the island further along the international trend towards consumerism as a way of life. We will return to this theme later on.

The annual growth rate of the Puerto Rican economy in 1986 was just over 2 percent. Although not spectacular, this growth rate

Table 7.6   *Debt: public and consumer (US $ millions)*

|  | 1974 | 1984 | % change |
|---|---|---|---|
| Public debt | 3725.8 | 8690.9 | +133 |
| Consumer debt | 1414.0 | 3928.6 | +178 |
| Consumer debt to personal income ratio (%) | 21 | 38 | +81 |

*Source:* Junta de Planificacion de Puerto Rico (1984: 32)

Table 7.7   *GNP, personal income and expenditure
(US $ millions)*

|  | 1970 | 1980 | % change |
|---|---|---|---|
| Gross national product | 4688 | 11,105 | +137 |
| Disposable personal income | 3565 | 10,494 | +194 |
| Personal consumer expenditure | 3746 | 11,118 | +197 |
| Ratio of personal income to expenditures (%) | −5 | −6 | −1 |
| Personal income per capita | 1353 | 2860 | +111 |
| Average family income (US$) | 5674 | 12,928 | +128 |
| Private savings accounts | 94 | 423 | +350 |
| Assets in banks | 3322 | 12,223 | +268 |

*Source:* Puerto Rico Planning Board (1980: 3)

might be considered solid. However, this growth, like the entire
Puerto Rican economy, is terribly dependent on the USA because
of the 'colonial' nature of the political relationship. In fact the
comment is frequently made that the Puerto Rican economy can be
best described as artificial, as it depends so heavily on the transfer of
funds from the USA. In the 1987 fiscal year such transfers totalled
US $6 billion, which was more than the gross national products of
many Latin American countries including Paraguay and Panama,
and these countries are considerably larger than Puerto Rico.
Conversely, economic activity in Puerto Rico creates significant
benefits for the US economy. For example, in 1985 just one sector
in the Puerto Rican economy generated over 200,000 jobs and more
than US $100 million profit for US businesses.

The fund transfers from the USA are close to half of Puerto
Rico's GNP and are used to subsidise large programmes of
government spending on welfare, public services and jobs. The
public sector is now the source of approximately one-third of all
jobs. The artificiality of the economy is seen as responsible, in the
eyes of many, for a breakdown of the work ethic in Puerto Rico. It
is argued that many people see no point in working when they can
achieve close to the same living standard on welfare benefits. The
minimum wage on the island is US $3.35 per hour and the standard

working week is 37.5 hours. More than half of Puerto Rican workers earn this minimum wage, which amounts to a little over US $500 per month before deductions. The net income might, after deductions, be close to US $400. With that kind of income one can hardly cover the basic necessities given the cost of living in Puerto Rico (which is higher than in the USA). This is without considering the typical expenses involved in going to work such as transportation, clothing, materials, and food away from home.

## Work ethic versus consumer ethic

It is doubtful whether a work ethic has ever existed in Puerto Rico. Such an ethic is difficult to foster in colonial situations where the indigenous people do not control or own the means of production, receive few of the benefits, and are considered by the governing power as tools in the production process. This attitude is likely to be reciprocated by the workers. Most workers in Puerto Rico seem to have an instrumental view of work. In other words, work is not seen as good in itself; it is considered good only in so far as it produces benefits extraneous to the content of work, like an income. When that income is no greater than one can receive in benefits or welfare assistance from the government, there seems to be little purpose in working. Many citizens in Puerto Rico do not work. Sometimes this is because they cannot find jobs; in other cases it is because they choose not to work except in well-paid jobs. As many as 53 percent of Puerto Rican families do not have any members working.

Members of these families have considerable unoccupied time on their hands, but they are not the only ones with disposable time. The average worker puts in only 1600 to 1700 working hours a year (19 percent of total time), which places the island at the 'forefront' of the advanced industrial nations in terms of the total amount of work-free time per year. The workers seem quite content with this, whereas business leaders and managers are not. The latter are often extremely critical, particularly of official paid holidays. Puerto Rico has 19 of these, which probably makes the country the world leader. Managers say that the island loses its international competitive edge because of the large number of holidays, which also turns away investors who are looking for long production cycles. Managers say that 212 work days a year are simply not enough.

What is sometimes overlooked is that holidays or non-work days often turn into shopping days, which are a boon to the economy. During 1986 retail trade and services amounted to US $4.1 billion, or 31 percent of the net income that the economy generated. In economic terms each citizen can be viewed as a producer and also as a consumer. The amount of free time in Puerto Rico has a direct bearing on the amount of working hours and the economic production derived from these, but just as importantly it affects consumer markets because of the growing demand for leisure goods and services to be used during free time. It seems that while working hours have decreased (or totally disappeared for some), simultaneously people have become more affluent thanks in great measure to easy credit.

Consumer expenditure related to leisure has increased spectacularly in nearly every developed country and in many developing ones. In Canada and the USA respectively consumer expenditure on leisure surpassed $67 and 300 billion a year in 1985. The situation in Puerto Rico is not very different. Table 7.8 shows the rank that expenditure on recreation occupies among all consumer expenditure in Puerto Rico. The amount spent on recreation is not only considerable and obviously highly important from the viewpoint of the consumer, but also in macroeconomic terms. It should be borne in mind that this leisure expenditure is computed only on the basis of gate receipts at recreational spectacles such as the cinema, shows, fairs, sports events, concerts and suchlike, and does not include items such as travel to these, or leisure.

Table 7.8  *Personal consumption expenditure, 1984*

| Type | Amount (US $ millions) |
| --- | --- |
| Food | 3130 |
| Transportation | 2029 |
| Housing | 1688 |
| Household operations | 1571 |
| Clothing and accessories | 1225 |
| Recreation | 1047 |
| Medical care | 1023 |
| Foreign travel | 579 |
| Alcoholic beverages | 566 |
| Personal care | 436 |
| Business services | 426 |
| Education | 304 |
| Tobacco products | 274 |
| Miscellaneous purchases | 141 |
| Religious and non-profit organisations | 86 |
| Total | US$13,836 |

*Source:* Junta de Planificacion de Puerto Rico (1984: 10)

It should be noted that expenditure *strictly* on recreation is greater than on medical care and education. However, the total amount of consumer expenditure related to leisure will be much greater than Table 7.8 suggests if one assumes the following: (1) that 100 percent of expenses on alcoholic beverages and religious institutions take place within the context of leisure; (2) that 50 percent of expenditure on foreign travel and tobacco products can be directly related to leisure; and (3) that 14 percent of expenditure on clothing and accessories, transportation, housing, food, household operations, personal care, and miscellaneous expenses are related to leisure activities or experiences. When these assumptions are made, a figure of US $3.5 billion is obtained, which represents 25 percent of all consumer spending. In other words, 25 cents of every dollar spent by Puerto Ricans is related to leisure. It can be argued that this estimate is rather conservative and that the real figure could be even higher.

Interestingly, the leisure industry in Puerto Rico, which is both well established and large, has traditionally but mistakenly been connected to, or perhaps confused with, tourism. Tourist expenditure on the island is really not as significant a contribution to the economy as one might think. For the year 1984 such expenditure represented only 5 percent of GNP. The detailed economic impact of leisure on the island is still largely unknown, and what is striking is not so much the lack of knowledge but the lack of interest shown in leisure as an increasingly important socioeconomic phenomenon. For a country of only 3.2 million people, a lot of money circulates in Puerto Rico; a GNP of over $14 billion dollars, and a similar level of consumer expenditure are considerable, and these figures do not take into account a subterranean economy which could be huge. Leisure is related to a substantial part of this economy.

## Consumption as a way of life

It seems that in Puerto Rico, as in many other countries, consumption must be regarded as the predominant aspect of the economic role of leisure. According to the Commerce Department, consumer expenditure during 1984–5 amounted to 103.5 percent of the GNP and by 1985–6 this had increased to 104.2 percent. In other words, the consumer is spending more than the total production of goods and services, in monetary terms. The sale of retail goods and services has been reaching record figures. In 1984 retail sales reached $5667 million, by 1986 they had increased to $7026 million, and forecasts for 1987 pointed to breaking the eight million mark.

The top five types of establishment in terms of increased sales volume for 1986 were: lumber, hardware stores and mobile homes (36.1 percent), shoe stores (28.1 percent), new and used motor vehicles (22.9 percent), drug stores (22.7 percent), and car parts and accessories stores (22.6 percent). Other notable increases were recorded in furniture (7.2 percent), men's clothing (9.9 percent), jewellery (9.6 percent) and restaurants (17.6 percent). In 1986 the trade and service sectors generated 30.6 percent of the economy's net income, and 39.4 percent of the total number of jobs. A total of 36,417 retail establishments operated in the island during the year and an increase of 1.4 percent was forecast for 1987.

The Puerto Rican consumer now has more money available than ever, because significant reductions in interest rates allow him or her to take out more loans at lower payments, and also because low oil prices have kept petrol and electricity costs down (these have traditionally been big expenses, see Table 7.8). Another important factor has been the stability in the consumer price index in recent years. The index actually decreased by 0.2 percent in 1984–5 and this stimulated people to buy more. The problem, however, is that consumers are spending much more money than they earn, thus creating negative consequences for family economies and also for the country. Simply put, the consumer cannot keep spending indefinitely. An important indicator is the proportion of personal loans to all loans (including mortgages and commercial). In 1975, 18.3 percent of all loans were personal loans, and by 1986 this proportion had more than doubled to 37.9 percent. In 1984 the consumer debt amounted to 32 percent of disposable personal income and by 1986 it had increased to 45 percent. Also, during this year the number of bankruptcies rose by almost 50 percent, from 1544 to 2285. What is particularly alarming is the explosion in the number of personal bankruptcies, which represented 82.3 percent of the total during 1986. Certainly this is not a healthy picture. If one takes stock of the increases in spending, borrowing, and the types of expenditure (most of the increases in sales mentioned earlier can be considered discretionary spending) then it can be argued quite easily that a high level of consumption is an integral part of the life-styles of most Puerto Ricans.

How a consumer ethos developed in Puerto Rico is a question that cannot be answered fully here. Suffice it to say that consumption is a feature of the culture; a culture in transformation, still undergoing significant and thorough changes that began after the Second World War. Certainly the influence of the USA on Puerto Rico, as on so many other countries, played a major role in the emergence of a consumer culture. But to discover how consumption became a cultural ideal requires looking closely at the powerful institutions and individuals who conceived, formulated and then disseminated the consumer ethic. The origins of a consumer culture in the USA can be traced to the activities of urban elites during the last two decades of the nineteenth century. Three developments were of significance in this context: the maturation of the national market-place, including the establishment of national advertising; the emergence of a new stratum of professionals and managers rooted in a web of complex new organisations (corporations, government, universities, professional associations, media and foundations, among others); and the rise of a new gospel of therapeutic release preached by a host of writers, publishers, ministers, social scientists, doctors and advertisers (Fox and Lears, 1983).

Consumer culture is more than a leisure ethic; it is a set of values, a standard of living and also a power structure. Life for most middle- and working-class Puerto Ricans during the past 20 or 30 years has been an endless pursuit of the 'good life' (the pursuit of happiness is stated as the underlying precept in the island's constitution), and a constant reminder of their powerlessness as well. Consumers are not only buyers of goods, but also recipients of professional advice, marketing strategies, government programmes, electoral choices, and advertisers' images of happiness. Although the dominant institutions purport to be offering the consumer a fulfilling participation in the life of the community, in practice they present the empty prospect of taking part in the market-place of personal exchange. Individuals have been invited to seek commodities as keys to personal welfare and, in some cases, to conceive of their own selves as commodities.

The choices required in the use of leisure are in the same category as those involved in general consumer behaviour. Depth research, using psychoanalytical techniques, has discovered that the prime motivation in consumer behaviour is the pursuit of an acceptable identity. The identity sought must not only be acceptable personally, that is by the individual confronting himself, but socially as well. Fulfilment in itself is conceived in terms of the identity that a given pattern of behaviour indicates. Equally, the persuasion process, which is an integral part of the marketing function in modern business, relies for its effects on the identities that are considered desirable by sufficient numbers of consumers. 'I draw attention to the persistent need to search for an acceptable identity as the leitmotiv of behaviour, and to the pattern of choices that result from it, as key determinants in studying the sociology of leisure' (Glasser, 1970).

The pursuit of an acceptable identity, it seems, motivates choices in the construction of the life patterns that people follow. Naturally, identity can be reflected in a variety of the roles that any person plays, including leisure roles. The marketing component of the modern business enterprise has been extremely successful in creating identities for consumers to adopt, and this process is intimately linked to leisure since most identities can only be assumed or enacted within the context of leisure. Veblen was the first modern writer to discuss the emulative process in the new industrial and urban society where the working and emerging middle classes began to pattern their lives on those of the 'leisure class'. Today the massive commercial exploitation of the emulative process spreads over a wide spectrum of activities and contexts, one of the most important being leisure. Consumers are led to believe that the goal of leisure is the 'good life' and that the way to reach it is through consumption. A radio advertisement for a local bank has a vacationing couple saying, 'Now we are determined to be happy. We are going shopping with our new credit card.'

There is little doubt about the pivotal role played by advertising in the creation and maintenance of consumer appetites. Advertising in Puerto Rico is very big business. According to a report in *The Economist* (9 March 1985), the island spends more on advertising than any other country in the world as a proportion of its GNP. In 1982 2.3 percent of Puerto Rico's GNP was spent on advertising, which was close to US $300 million. The countries that follow are Australia and the USA. The sum mentioned is spent on TV, radio, press, posters, direct mail and on-the-spot publicity. Advertising industry spokesmen have justified such levels of expenditure by declaring that product competition is intense because there are few restrictions on the import of products, and also that US industries use the island as a testing ground for products that they intend to market elsewhere in Latin America. Quite naively one spokesman has stated that if so much money is spent on advertising it must be because there is a lot of consumer activity on the island (*Nuevo Dia*, 29 March 1985). There are at present 135 advertising agencies on the island, which must also be some kind of a record figure if one bears in mind that the population is only 3.2 million.

The advertising industry could not be sustained without a technologically advanced and well-established media infrastructure. Puerto Rico has it. In 1986 there were six island-wide newspapers and dozens of regional and local ones. There were 67 AM and 44 FM radio stations, and 29 duly licensed and fully operational TV stations (10 locally owned, the rest foreign). Few countries in the world have such massive media establishments. Of all the forms of media, TV has the greatest impact in capturing and maintaining the interest of Puerto Ricans (*San Juan Star*, 7 August 1986).

Television became technically feasible in the late 1930s and early 1940s, but in Puerto Rico the first television broadcast took place only in May 1954. The first TV commercial was a Coca Cola ad. By 1970 Puerto Rico was the Latin American country with the highest per capita number of TV sets. By 1985 there was at least one TV set in 97 percent of Puerto Rican households, and average viewing hours per day amounted to 5.2. The latter add up to approximately 1900 hours a year (22 percent of the total) which is greater than the average number of working hours for the Puerto Rican worker, and more hours than a youth spends in school! Further, the average TV viewer is exposed to approximately 7600 commercials a year! An additional finding from media research in Puerto Rico is the correlation between low income and low educational levels, and high levels of TV viewing time. The better educated and higher income groups seem to have more alternative leisure pursuits. Television viewing is the most popular leisure activity in Puerto Rico in terms of total time spent.

In February 1986, the Centre for the Study of Free Time (CETIL) undertook a study aimed at discovering whether the messages transmitted by television commercials made reference to leisure behaviour, thus inducing viewers to engage in consumption through leisure activities (Melendez and Betancourt, 1986). This study involved recording 20 hours during selected days and hours, of TV transmission offered by each of the two largest broadcasters in Puerto Rico: WKAQ-TV and WAPA-TV (Stanford Klapper, 1985). This research captured a total of 1005 commercials which were later edited to eliminate repeats. Thus 317 different commercials were identified and analysed. Content analysis was employed and, in keeping with the study's purpose, 13 categories of commercials were established. The most pertinent for our purpose were the context of the commercial (type of activity developed therein and the setting) and the content of the commercial (the message). The findings for the first category revealed that 33 different types of activity were portrayed in the commercials. These were classified into two broad divisions: non-leisure activities (54.8 percent) and leisure activities (45.2 percent). The latter category was further divided into participatory leisure activities and spectator leisure activities, with frequency distributions of 41.2 percent and 4 percent respectively. The second category of analysis (content of the commercial message) sought to explore the inducement generated by the messages. Two broad classes of message were constructed: where the commercial message induced the viewer to engage in a leisure behaviour, and where the message induced the viewer to engage in non-leisure behaviour. The results showed that close to one in three messages (31.9 percent) induced the viewers to engage in leisure behaviour.

The findings of this study confirm that there is a strong link between consumption and leisure, and that the television commercial is an important part of this link. It is noteworthy that nearly half of the commercials in the sample had a leisure context. This clearly serves to build in the viewer's mind a bridge between engagement in leisure activities and the consumption of goods and services. Furthermore, the suggestion is made that such consumption is either a requisite or an integral element of the leisure behaviour to be engaged in, thus creating and fortifying the link between the two. The viewer soon realises that satisfaction, as well as the attainment of the idealised identity discussed earlier, can and should be through the purchase of some item or service that is not only portrayed as a fundamental part of the leisure experience but something that, as an activity in time, takes place during leisure, thus consuming free time that could otherwise be devoted to some other activity. Here then is another dimension of the link between leisure and consumption; not only is the content of leisure influenced or defined by consumption, but also the time available for engagement in leisure behaviour is affected by the actual practice of consumption, be it shopping or using some good or service.

It would be interesting to study the influence of a wide variety of TV programmes on the relationships between leisure and consumption, particularly the growing breed of extremely popular contest shows and 'shop by TV' shows. If one reflects on the popularity of the latter, then the trend towards the rapidly growing influence of television on consumer behaviour that is perceived as a leisure pursuit and also happens in free time, is further confirmed.

Another aspect of the link between socioeconomic change and leisure in Puerto Rico is the growing importance of shopping centres and pedestrian shopping districts. The importance of these urban spaces is reflected not only in their increasing number, size, visitation, variety and profitability, but also in the way they have become attractive leisure destinations. This is yet another testimony to the notion that consumerism is at the centre of leisure behaviour on the island. Two recent studies provide evidence in support. One focused on covered shopping centres (or malls as they are often called) and the other on pedestrian shopping districts. It should be noted that both studies were comparable in research interest and methodology to studies by Dutch and German geographers in the 1970s and 1980s. Thus a valuable cross-cultural perspective has been created, providing evidence to suggest an international trend in the consumer dimension of leisure in the 1970s and 1980s.

The Puerto Rican study of shopping malls was undertaken during the latter part of 1986. The principal purpose was to discover what motivated people to visit these centres (Melendez, 1986). A shopping centre is defined by the Department of Commerce as a series of independent commercial units, physically separated but within the same building, and integrated with the purpose of offering a complementary set of goods and services. The first shopping centre in Puerto Rico was built in 1949, but it was not until the 1960s that construction of these facilities really took off. Incidentally, in 1960 the first covered centre was built, and through later expansion it has become the largest covered shopping centre in Latin America, with 110 acres of rentable space (Plaza Las Americas). By 1980 there were 301 shopping centres on the island and since then 20 more have been built or are nearing completion. The total rentable space in the island's shopping centres is now well over 12 million square feet.

The study conducted by CETIL covered the three largest and most frequently visited malls on the island. As previously mentioned, the principal objective was to discover why people visit these places, and visitation rates were heavy; the aggregate number of visitors to the three centres was 605,000 per week. The data for the study were collected by interviews. A total of 1048 visitors were interviewed by a team of 18 interviewers during three different days of the third week in October 1986. This study yielded interesting and revealing findings, many of which dispelled widely held notions, such as that more women than men visit malls, and that the predominant occupational category among the visitors is housewife. The findings indicated that just as many men as women were visiting the malls, and that the most frequently mentioned occupational category of visitors was professional (27.8 percent). Other pertinent findings include the following: the greatest proportion of visitors (24.7 percent) were in the 18–23 age group, indicating the attractiveness of the malls to youth; the majority of visitors (66.8 percent) were accompanied by at least one person thus suggesting that visits are gregarious and often family activities since in two out of three cases the companions were relatives. The findings most relevant to the present discussion are those indicating the proportion of visitors who were not in the malls to shop, but in response to a self-declared interest in leisure; these amounted to almost one in every three visitors (31.9 percent). Among the shoppers, less than half were seeking items of necessity (42.4 percent). Other important findings included the frequency and length of visits; 67.2 percent of the sample visited the malls at least once a week, and 61.4 percent stayed more than one hour on each occasion.

The above findings certainly lend credence to the earlier contention, that socioeconomic change in Puerto Rico in the last decade or so has created a strong link between consumption and leisure, and has strengthened a consumer ethos that seems at times to be the same as a leisure ethos. This point is further endorsed by comparing the number of people who visited the malls with a leisure motivation (31.9 percent), and the total number of people visiting the three largest urban parks on the island. After computing weekly visitation rates for these parks in 1986 it was found that there were over three times as many visitors to the malls as to the parks (192,995 and 59,576 respectively). Another surprising fact was that the total rentable area of the malls was slightly larger than the total surface area of the parks.

The other study of shopping districts was undertaken by Professor Piovanetti of the Social Sciences Faculty at the University of Puerto Rico. The principal purpose of this study was to compare the attractiveness of two pedestrian shopping districts in the metropolitan area of San Juan. A finding, secondary to the study but crucial to this discussion, was that 45 percent of the respondents considered themselves visitors rather than shoppers when they went to the pedestrian shopping districts. This finding again confirms the close relationship between leisure and consumption in present-day Puerto Rico.

Geographers have sought to classify the different physical elements that compose the total system of resources serving the leisure functions of the city. Traditionally the shopping areas, whether malls or pedestrian districts, have been identified as secondary elements in these leisure functions (Jansen-Verbeke, 1985). In Puerto Rico it seems, and the comment may apply also in other countries, that these shopping areas constitute a primary element in the leisure resources of the city, sharing the same role as parks, sports and arts facilities, among others.

Needless to say, Puerto Rican leisure is not wholly consumerism. Puerto Ricans traditionally regard themselves as sports-loving people. Nowadays this 'love' means 'following' more often than actually playing. A recent CETIL study has shown that sport accounts for 19.4 percent of all space in the Puerto Rican press. This research also found that 73.2 percent of the urban population was following sport through the media – daily in the case of 41.3 percent of the entire sample. Still, 35.5 percent were playing sport at the time of the survey, and just under half of these participants were playing at least once a week.

In conclusion, there seems ample justification for stating that in Puerto Rico the socioeconomic changes of the last five or six years have had a significant impact on leisure. Such impact is related to what people perceive to be desirable leisure pursuits. The view has gained ground that a higher quality of leisure experience is achieved by acquiring and consuming more goods and services. At the same time, a general all-encompassing consumer attitude or ethic has been spreading. So perhaps the phenomenon is two way; people's consumer appetites are manifested in their leisure pursuits, but these also serve to consolidate the consumer view of the world.

The above is not an entirely grim scenario, although it is far from healthy economically or psychologically. A number of benefits have accrued from socioeconomic changes in the 1980s, most notably an unprecedented improvement in the quantity and quality of leisure services on the island, both public and private. For the first time in its history, Puerto Rico has university-level programmes designed to educate the professionals needed to handle leisure service provisions. Public and private agency budgets are growing, and diverse facilities are starting to appear.

Will the tax reform plan succeed in modifying the consumer behaviour of Puerto Ricans? Perhaps not. What could pay good dividends, however, might be a closer look, from a multi-disciplinary perspective, building on the analysis in this chapter, into the relationships between the economy, social change, life-style, quality of life, and leisure.

## References

Fox, R.W. and T.J. Jackson Lears (1983) *The Culture of Consumption*. New York: Pantheon Books.

Glasser, R. (1970) *Leisure: Penalty or Prize*. London: Macmillan.

Jansen-Verbeke, M. (1985) 'The Inner City as a Leisure Project', *World Leisure and Recreation*, 27(2).

Melendez, N. (1986) *Los Centros Comerciales y el Tiempo Libre: Nuevos Usos de los Espacios Urbanos*. Bayamon: CETIL.

Melendez, N. and A. Betancourt (1986) *Los Comerciales de Television y su Influencia Sobre las Conductas de Tiempo Libre*. Bayamon: CETIL.

Puerto Rico Planning Board (1980) *Estadisticas Socioeconomicas*. San Juan.

Stanford Klapper Associates Inc. (1985) *Mediafax Television Audience Measurements, Puerto Rico, October 30–November 19, 1985*. New York.

United States Bureau of the Census (1984) *1980 Census of Population and Housing, Commonwealth of Puerto Rico*. Washington, DC.

# 8

# Japan: Homo Ludens Japonicus

## *Sampei Koseki*

*Born to play,*
*Born to enjoy,*
*Merry infants'*
*Cheerful voices*
*Sound to hearts*

*From a book of popular songs, edited in the twelfth century*

### A cynical prologue

Japan – an enigma, a curious Wonderland, a Lilliput that actually exists in the northwest Pacific Ocean. This land is made up of small islands, but has become a country of great economic strength whose output now amounts to 10 percent of the entire world's. Following the example of Europe, more than 120 million diligent Japanese have made a success of industrialisation, and in less than 100 years.

The culture of Japan is a unique blend of East and West, a reborn Far Eastern Roman Empire at the end of the twentieth century. In this culture a naive animism coexists with sophisticated high-level technology, by means of which numerous 'worker bees' gain large sums of money and enjoy their leisure. Their surprising energy is consumed in hard work, and in the pursuit of pleasure. The Japanese are more than economic animals; they are also *homo ludens*, and herein lies the Japanese paradox. This Wonderland, in the eyes of T.S. Eliot, would appear a waste land. The sales force sells products Made in Japan, gets money, exploits the natural resources, and despoils the globe. They lay waste their own green space of mind and spirit. A superficial hedonism seems to be making them into hollow men whose hearts are dry and dying. 'Tokyo Desert' is the title of a song well known among the inhabitants of the Japanese capital.

### The prosperous 'Yellow Yankee's' international status

There is no doubt that Japan has enjoyed prosperity even in the midst of the economic crises of the 1980s, which makes it an exception among the developed countries. Its GNP ($1,344,700

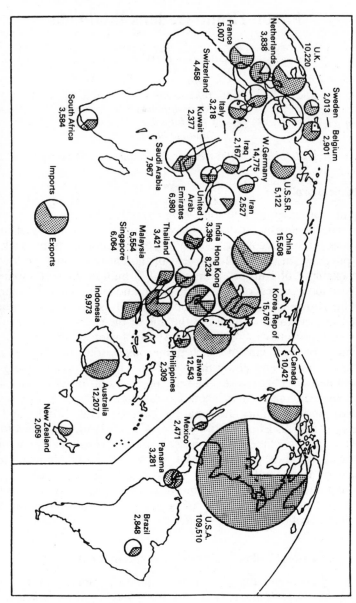

Figure 8.1   *Japan's foreign trade, by countries (1986) (US$millions)*

*Source:* Nippon (1987) *A Chartered Survey of Japan 1987—88.* Tokyo: Kokuseisha Corporation

million in 1985) is second in the world, one-third of that of the United States and more than double that of West Germany. The surplus in balance of trade, which has increased steadily since 1964, amounted to $92,799 million in 1986. Japan's main suppliers of imports are Asia (42.7 percent), North America (26.7 percent), and Europe (14.4 percent), while its main export markets are North America (41.2 percent), Asia (23.9 percent) and Europe (18.8 percent). Trade with Latin America, Africa and the USSR is infrequent (see Figure 8.1).

Supported by the increasing value of the yen, Japanese business people and tourists travel all over the world, and make approximately 5 million trips a year nowadays (see Figure 8.2). Their destinations are mainly Asia, the United States, and West Europe, an order of preference which corresponds to the national origins of foreigners visiting or living in Japan. As the Japanese are more oriented to Western people than to their Asian neighbours, these neighbours experience frustration in their relationships with the Japanese and resent the discrimination shown against them. As a result, the arrogant 'Yellow Yankee' is sometimes condemned by his neighbours, especially in those countries which have been dominated or occupied by aggressive Japanese.

Figure 8.2   *Travel abroad and foreign visitors*

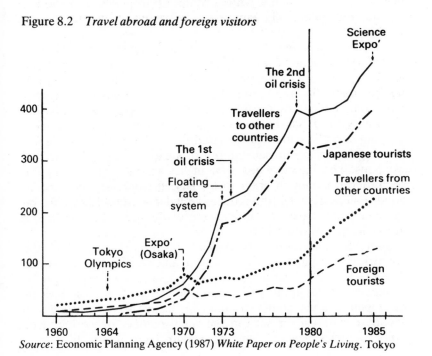

*Source*: Economic Planning Agency (1987) *White Paper on People's Living*. Tokyo

The prosperity of Japan should not be exaggerated, as it conceals many difficulties resulting from the country's inherent weaknesses. Japan at first glance seems similar to Great Britain, but Japan is seriously disadvantaged. Its habitable area is only one half that of Britain, and the population density in that area is more than four times that of Britain. The territory devoted to agriculture, which decreased notably after industrialisation, is 14.6 percent of the total, and only 2.4 percent (920,000 hectares) was given to housing space in 1984. This 'empire', furthermore, has neither slaves nor natural resources other than water, wood, rice and sea food. Japanese per capita income is less than that of Switzerland, Norway or Canada. In a recent OECD report the average Japanese house was described as a 'rabbit hutch', an evaluation with which many Japanese would agree. Residents of the larger cities suffer from unbelievably crowded trains, buses and roads as they commute to school and to work. Living costs are quite high; housing and food are abnormally expensive by European standards. Trade, then, is the only peaceful solution to Japan's dilemma, the only means for it to survive. Fortunately a 'rabbit' has long ears, which are useful for catching all kinds of information. The Japanese have listened, studied, worked hard, made sales and made money. And then 'Japan bashing' began, especially in the United States. Europeans, too, became anxious and jealous. The Japanese were paying a high price for their wealth.

To have amicable relations with all countries is absolutely necessary for Japan. The gap between ideal and reality, however, is great. Japan receives the 'protection' of the United States' military nuclear umbrella, and both her diplomatic relations and life-styles have come under strong American influence. As a result, it has not been easy for Japan to develop friendly relationships with neigh-bouring socialist countries. In addition, the United States is now pressing Japan to purchase more of its exports, including military weapons. The Japanese government has appealed to its people to spend more money in order to increase the domestic demand for goods and thereby help to reduce the balance of trade surplus, but these appeals have had little success, though the tariff wall is gradually being lowered.

Some foreign journalists criticise Japan's 'invasion' of other countries – the purchase by large companies or wealthy individuals of overseas firms, land, hotels, casinos, and even castles. Branches of Japanese firms in other countries often create friction by insisting on Japanese-style administration. In Japan itself, insistence on Japanese style can be seen in the small number of workers from other countries. Severe immigration control is maintained.

Although Japan has replaced the United States as the leader among the Development Assistance Committee (DAC) countries, its provision of $11,240 million in 1985 represented only 0.84 percent of its GNP, lower than that of the Netherlands (2.14 percent), France (1.74 percent) and West Germany (0.92 percent). In addition, the attitude of the average Japanese to non-Japanese, as well as the government's diplomatic policies, are as yet so poorly developed as to make cultural conflicts and mutual misunderstanding inevitable. In spite of its growing reputation Japan is often accused of exhibiting both a servile obedience to the United States and a new colonialism. Already overripe in economic development, Japan is still immature in playing an international role.

**From business to amenities – changes in life-style**

Although the 1980s crisis is worldwide, the Japanese life-style has not been greatly affected. A more important turning point was rather in the 1970s, with the appearance of environmental pollution, the youth culture, feminism and the oil shock. Increased attention from other countries imposed on Japan the necessity for self-reflection. The inhabitants of rabbit hutches are inherently nervous because of their long ears. Some were awakened from their ignorance and complacency, and began to sound a warning bell to their fellow countrymen. Beginning in the 1970s, a certain bewilderment set in. However, in spite of advice or condemnation from the International Labour Office, it has been difficult for the Japanese to change their habits. They seem to enjoy working. It was not until the 1980s that the average Japanese became conscious of the necessity and the pleasure of taking a break.

Naturally there are some contradictions in Japan in the 1980s. Lacking long vacations, people seek eagerly for short-term distractions and pastimes. Increasingly they are working and saving money in order to consume and enjoy life. While the sudden economic growth has produced an undesirable surplus of traffic accidents, public nuisances, status seekers and juvenile delinquency, it has also brought the leisure to give attention to more than work. Today the slogan is amenities or comforts. Some frustrations that have arisen are the result of having reached a relatively high standard of living. The nation as a whole seems to have become more mature. A slowing down of economic growth is functioning as a tranquilliser. Graduating from a youthful vivacity, the Japanese have begun to gaze at the landscape of the ending century widening their perspective with cooling eyes. This change is providing a new opportunity for discovering the self.

Although national diplomacy has remained unchanged, strong waves of Americanisation have ceased to flood Japan. The Japanese appear to feel that almost everything they can learn from America has already been learnt. Yankee imperialism has lost its prestige. Mindful of their longer tradition, the Japanese have recovered their pride. Their former inferiority complex with regard to Western civilisation has been notably mitigated, while nostalgia for national folklore and local traditions has increased. The word 'ethnic' has become fashionable among young people.

In spite of, or perhaps because of, their political apathy, the young people have contributed greatly to the cultural changes of the past 20 years. These children of the affluent society prefer enjoying life to working hard. Loyalty not to a business company but to their own interests is their motivating force. Thanks to the strong yen, students in Japan can gain enough money through part-time jobs to make trips overseas. They have neither the passion to reform society nor the threat of unemployment, a situation quite different from that of their contemporaries in Europe and Third World countries. The desire of the young for self-realisation and individualism or privatism has made an undeniable impact on the life-styles of adults as well. The traditional Japanese sense of belonging has been weakened. There is a marked increase in the number of young employees who escape from after-five socialising, formerly regarded as a virtually compulsory aspect of Japanese company life. The younger people are eager to pursue their private interests or to return home immediately after work. They are co-operative on the job but not so weak as to give up their individual rights.

This budding individualism can also be seen among housewives. More than half are now employed outside the home at their own wish, though there are few occupations where there is equality for the sexes. Full-time housewives pursue their own hobbies and interests. If they are financially well off, they can enjoy visiting friends and neighbours, shopping, playing tennis or attending various kinds of classes, while their workaholic husbands endure hard stress at their jobs. The rapid extension of the lifespan among women is an important social phenomenon; the longevity of Japanese women is now the highest in the world.

The young people, called 'the new breed' by adults, and the women, may be the two prime movers of changes in the Japanese life-style. Their avant garde has introduced various new patterns of behaviour which have been given special attention in the media. The most radical attempts at changes in life-style have sprung from social groups which are economically marginal, and therefore free from the rigid confinement experienced by the worker bees. Above all, new directions are seen in fashion, play and culture, aspects of life which are little influenced by adult men.

Sexual liberation has advanced a great deal. The change is more apparent among women than men and includes an increase in the number of women who take the initiative in love relationships. Extra-marital relations are increasing, though an alleged general decrease in sexual desire is often given attention in the mass media. Formal taboos regarding sex are still strong in the tightly organised Japanese society. The flourishing 'sex industries' have suffered from the AIDS panic, but the popularity of such establishments owes much to the frustrations produced by an intolerant moral formalism coexisting with hypocrisy. The situation has its analogy in the Victorian age in Britain. Mass media and sex industries are two types of narcotic resorted to by those suffering from feelings of alienation in affluent Japan. A sense of humour, however, is especially prized by young people. Severe competition in university entrance examinations and the requisite hard study call for various forms of relaxation. Although adults are more sober minded than young people, they too suffer the frustrations of stress and ennui. As a result comedians have acquired a wide popularity on television and radio broadcasts. Reflecting this relatively peaceful age, their laughter lacks bitterness: frivolity and cheerfulness are preferred. There are few satirical elements such as are seen in the comedies of Aristophanes, Swift, Molière or Gogol. Anything serious or profound is brushed aside. Instead a light touch and a soft cynicism are most welcome.

The lack of a sense of crisis has led to a widespread political apathy. Although there are occasional bombings by extreme radicals irritated by what they consider a false peace, radical sympathisers are rare. The majority of Japanese are generally satisfied with the policies of the Liberal Democratic Party which has held power for more than 35 years. The leftist parties at times even seem out of date. Their propaganda and terminology no longer have any strong appeal, and there has been a notable decrease in intellectual sympathisers, including Marxists in universities.

In Japan there is a general spirit of tolerance but little love of polemics. This climate is due in part to the absence of grave domestic problems and in part to the decline of the spirit of criticism. It is difficult to find any passion for social reform, though there are appeals from a minority for deeper understanding of the struggles of Third World countries. On the other hand, there has been a deepening of interest in religion in a wide sense, particularly in mysticism, among serious-minded people. The ennui of a peaceful life, bringing on a sense of spiritual hollowness, has caused various religious or quasi-religious sects to flourish. The majority of these movements are not visible on the surface of society. But the attraction, no matter how slight, of irrationalism, occultism, transpsychology, divination, fanatacism and the extra-scientific cannot be denied. At the same time the merits of Buddhism, the dominant religion of Japan, are being rediscovered. This renewal of interest can be regarded as a reaction to superficial westernisation and a questioning of the value of civilisation itself. Many elderly people, whose numbers are increasing yearly, are surviving only because of the development of medicine. Their most pressing problem is how to die painlessly; some pray earnestly for the coming of death. There are temples given over to the care of such elderly people who fear the approach of senility and do not wish to become a burden to their children.

Certainly some people, feeling unfulfilled with mere material satisfaction, are losing interest in this world and are looking for a means of escape from this life. This tendency may be one of the by-products of an affluent society which has no foundation in spiritual idealism. Thus a hedonistic pursuit of pleasure exists side by side with an anomie accompanied by a hollowness or emptiness of spirit. It may be possible to find in such a situation the sneaking shadow of a mild decadence hidden under the bright and cheerful ideology of affluent happiness.

### Free time of the hard-working bees – its quantitative aspects

Unfortunately it is undeniable that the free time of the average worker in Japan is markedly less than that enjoyed by West Europeans. For instance, the yearly average for 1985, 1858 hours, was 854 hours less than the 2712 hours of workers in France. This problem is one of the most crucial in Japanese everyday life. The scarcity of time for mental composure is a decided weakness in this otherwise wealthy country. The nation as a whole is poor in leisure, quantitatively at least. The following observation appeared in a recent Japanese newspaper editorial:

> The growth of our economy is remarkable. It is shown in such varied phenomena as economic conflicts with other countries and the strong yen. Nevertheless, living in Japan one is hardly aware of the country's prosperity. Is this as it should be? Why can't we turn the results of increased productivity to improving the quality of life? This is a good chance to extend the five-day working week. . . . One reason why this system has not become well-established is the rapid ageing of the

population and the shift of concern to an extension of the retirement age
for employees. . . . We must hurry to reform such a situation.
Fortunately the appeal for increasing domestic consumption brings a
favourable wind to blow on the five-day working week system. (*Asahi
Newspaper*, 6 November 1987).

In actual practice this system has so far been adopted mainly by
large companies only. It is as yet limited to just 6 percent of all
companies and 28 percent of employees nationwide, though 50
percent of all companies and 78 percent of all employees now have
two holidays a week one or more times per month. The scarcity of
holidays and free time is the greatest price paid by the hard-working
Japanese for their material prosperity. Even the love of work has its
limits. The majority of workers wish to have more free time.

Perhaps the Japanese are more eager to try a greater variety of
diversions than people of other countries; the Japanese are full of
curiosity and have an excellent tradition of leisure pursuits and
amusements. From the high-growth period of the 1960s until 1975,
overall work time decreased steadily, and the new word 'leisure'
became fashionable. Except for the year 1975, *regular* work time
has continued to decrease. The descending line of *total* work time,
however, has changed to a horizontal one. The key is in the
*overtime* work that began with a slight increase but has now reached
one-third of total work time. Behind this phenomenon are several
contradictory factors.

The macroeconomy by nature does not bring the same influence
to every sector. Among large companies the five-day working week
has recently become more widespread. Reasons for this include
employees' requests, government policy in response to foreign
pressure, and reduced production or reduced incentives for production. All such factors reflect the reality of the 1980s. On the other
hand, there are many workers who from economic necessity cannot
shorten their work time, and others who wish to work more for
pleasure or profit. Generally speaking, the function and the
meaning of the shortening of work time are determined by two main
factors: the type of industry and whether it is growing or declining,
and the productivity of the particular enterprise.

The main difference in work time between Japan and Europe is in
the absence in Japan of a summer vacation. Holidays with pay are
rare, especially in the service industries. An employee has the legal
right to 6 to 20 days paid leave a year, but this right is not always
exercised because its realisation depends on the atmosphere in a
company and the attitudes of the workers themselves. Superiors or
colleagues may disapprove implicitly, but without saying so frankly.
Further, there is a type of worker who finds the office more

124    *Leisure and Life-style*

comfortable than home. He may not be able to relax at home either because of some unfavourable condition there, or because of his own personality. Such a situation may be difficult for members of other societies to understand, but many Japanese will point out that it is only by working long hours that they can obtain decent livelihoods, and that they have no particular dislike of the work itself. These apologies have a factual basis. Even with so much hard work, the standard of living in Japan is lower than that of Western Europe. 'Workaholism' is a kind of chronic disease of the Japanese in spite of their increased desire for the pursuit of pleasure. Even now wages are relatively low, and overtime work is taken as a matter of course. The need for it is generally recognised.

In regard to the budgeting of time for various daily activities, the surveys made by the government television station, NHK, are informative. This survey is conducted every five years to determine people's contact with the mass media. According to the 1985 survey (see Table 8.1) the average free time of an employee on a working day was 20 minutes shorter than in 1980; work time had been extended to an average of 8 hours 1 minute. Even on Sundays the

Table 8.1   *How people spend their time in Japan*
*(weekdays, nationwide average)*

|  | All people (10 years old and over) | | Males (20 years old and over) | | Housewives | |
|---|---|---|---|---|---|---|
|  | 1980 hrs/min | 1985 hrs/min | 1980 hrs/min | 1985 hrs/min | 1980 hrs/min | 1985 hrs/min |
| Sleeping | 7.52 | 7.43 | 8.02 | 7.50 | 7.33 | 7.24 |
| Eating | 1.33 | 1.33 | 1.33 | 1.33 | 1.44 | 1.42 |
| Personal chores | 1.02 | 1.04 | 0.59 | 0.59 | 1.00 | 1.00 |
| Work | 4.31 | 4.30 | 7.19 | 7.40 | 1.06 | 1.02 |
| Study | 1.27 | 1.40 | 0.06 | 0.08 | 0.01 | 0.01 |
| Housekeeping | 2.33 | 2.29 | 0.29 | 0.26 | 7.36 | 7.29 |
| Socialising | 0.36 | 0.40 | 0.38 | 0.38 | 0.51 | 1.00 |
| Resting | 0.39 | 0.37 | 0.42 | 0.41 | 0.41 | 0.42 |
| Leisure | 0.37 | 0.50 | 0.35 | 0.45 | 0.39 | 0.57 |
| Travel, including commuting | 0.54 | 0.54 | 1.06 | 1.03 | 0.23 | 0.27 |
| Newspapers, magazines, books | 0.36 | 0.35 | 0.48 | 0.48 | 0.37 | 0.37 |
| Radio | 0.39 | 0.32 | 0.45 | 0.40 | 0.45 | 0.38 |
| Television | 3.17 | 2.59 | 2.57 | 2.41 | 4.44 | 4.25 |
| Total | 26.16 | 26.06 | 25.59 | 25.52 | 27.40 | 27.24 |

Times for different activities overlap.
*Source:* Nippon Hoso Kyo Ka Broadcasting Corporation, Public Opinion Research Institute (1986) *How People Spend Their Time (Survey)*. Tokyo

employees' free time (6 hours 26 minutes in 1985) was shorter by about a half an hour compared with ten years before. More than two-thirds of the free time on weekdays was allocated to watching television (see Table 8.2). This table includes activities that may be done simultaneously, bringing the total figure to more than 24 hours.

Table 8.2   *Time distribution of employees (average)*

|  | Weekday | | | Sunday | | |
|---|---|---|---|---|---|---|
|  | 1975 hrs/min | 1980 hrs/min | 1985 hrs/min | 1975 hrs/min | 1980 hrs/min | 1985 hrs/min |
| Sleeping | 7.48 | 7.43 | 7.31 | 8.54 | 8.50 | 8.39 |
| Eating | 1.27 | 1.29 | 1.30 | 1.34 | 1.37 | 1.37 |
| Personal chores | 1.09 | 1.07 | 1.08 | 1.01 | 1.03 | 1.03 |
| Work | 7.32 | 7.41 | 8.01 | 2.12 | 2.12 | 2.24 |
| Housekeeping | 1.09 | 1.15 | 1.16 | 2.18 | 2.25 | 2.24 |
| Travel, including commuting | 1.07 | 1.12 | 1.10 | 0.43 | 0.53 | 0.59 |
| Newspapers, magazines, books | 0.38 | 0.39 | 0.39 | 0.42 | 0.47 | 0.40 |
| Radio | 0.30 | 0.37 | 0.29 | 0.32 | 0.29 | 0.20 |
| Television | 2.43 | 2.37 | 2.20 | 4.15 | 4.03 | 3.40 |
| Resting | 0.40 | 0.37 | 0.34 | 0.42 | 0.40 | 0.40 |
| Socialising | 0.32 | 0.32 | 0.36 | 1.13 | 1.18 | 1.18 |
| Leisure | 0.30 | 0.28 | 0.35 | 1.50 | 1.37 | 2.01 |
| Out of home | 10.34 | 10.50 | 11.11 | 6.50 | 6.49 | 7.32 |
| Free time in a strict sense | 3.36 | 3.18 | 3.09 | 6.56 | 6.26 | 6.26 |

*Source:* As Table 8.1

It is obvious that Japanese employees are suffering not only from a scarcity, but also from a steady decrease in free time. Probably because of fatigue the average employee devotes most leisure time to watching television, though this category has also decreased in the last 10 years. Time spent in commuting and housekeeping has increased slightly. In the larger cities commuting may require a considerable amount of time, in some cases as much as four hours per day. Increased housekeeping time is probably caused by two factors: the increase in the number of married female workers, and the increase in husbands participating in housekeeping.

Among full-time housewives free time is conspicuously increasing. The 'TV culture' is undoubtedly supported by these women, though even among this group time spent watching television has decreased by about 30 minutes on weekdays in the past ten years (see Table 8.3). In spite of sexual discrimination, full-time housewives are at an advantage with regard to free time. Their time for hobbies and recreation, even on weekdays, has increased by about 30 minutes during the past ten years. 'Out-of-home' time has increased as well, which suggests that more housewives are working

Table 8.3    *Time distribution of housewives (average)*

| | Weekday | | | Sunday | | |
|---|---|---|---|---|---|---|
| | 1975 hrs/min | 1980 hrs/min | 1985 hrs/min | 1975 hrs/min | 1980 hrs/min | 1985 hrs/min |
| Sleeping | 7.30 | 7.30 | 7.24 | 8.23 | 8.27 | 8.13 |
| Eating | 1.45 | 1.44 | 1.42 | 1.50 | 1.49 | 1.51 |
| Personal chores | 1.13 | 1.00 | 1.00 | 1.03 | 0.59 | 1.01 |
| Work | 1.10 | 1.06 | 1.02 | 0.44 | 0.34 | 0.37 |
| Housekeeping | 7.46 | 7.36 | 7.29 | 6.40 | 6.23 | 6.08 |
| Travel, including commuting | 0.12 | 0.23 | 0.27 | 0.20 | 0.31 | 0.38 |
| Newspapers, magazines, books | 0.27 | 0.37 | 0.37 | 0.22 | 0.30 | 0.29 |
| Radio | 0.33 | 0.45 | 0.38 | 0.18 | 0.22 | 0.19 |
| Television | 4.57 | 4.44 | 4.25 | 4.38 | 4.25 | 3.51 |
| Resting | 0.40 | 0.41 | 0.42 | 0.39 | 0.40 | 0.44 |
| Socialising | 0.50 | 0.51 | 1.00 | 1.11 | 1.11 | 1.17 |
| Leisure | 0.29 | 0.39 | 0.57 | 0.43 | 0.50 | 1.20 |
| Out of home | 3.07 | 3.11 | 3.40 | 3.41 | 3.44 | 4.32 |
| Free time in a strict sense | 4.02 | 4.14 | 4.33 | 4.40 | 4.50 | 5.04 |

*Source:* As Table 8.1

at part-time jobs. Much of their time spent at and away from home is devoted to various pleasures, such as cooking (as a hobby), shopping, sports (tennis, volleyball and bowling are popular), aerobic exercises, swimming, learning handicrafts and attending classes in various cultural subjects. Both employees and women at home wish to become more active, a tendency shown in the decrease in time given to television and the corresponding increase in time spent outside the home or enjoying other activities.

### Diversity and saturation of leisure activities

The concept of free time is of necessity ambiguous. Usually the term seems to mean the time free from work and other activities performed for the purpose of earning a living, while the ideal of freedom is the liberty to strive for an active self-realisation through pleasurable activities. At first glance the Japanese use of free time seems to be neither joyful nor active. A recent survey of free-time behaviour in Tokyo revealed eight preferred categories of activity (see Table 8.4). Probably most Japanese employees are tired after work. They do not appear to have much surplus energy. These hypotheses can be verified by the results of other surveys. The dominant free-time activities seem mere distractions, diversions or pastimes rather than amusing or creative recreation, as they are not

Table 8.4   *Behaviour in free time, 1987 (weekdays, Tokyo)*

| Behaviour | % |
|---|---|
| Watching TV | 56.2 |
| Resting (doing nothing) | 40.3 |
| Shopping, eating, drinking | 35.9 |
| Sports, gymnastics, taking a walk | 31.8 |
| Time spent with family | 27.0 |
| Gardening, house repairs, cooking (as hobby), sewing, knitting | 24.5 |
| Socialising with friends | 23.1 |
| Reading, studies, learning | 21.0 |

Double answers permitted.
*Source:* Leisure Development Centre (1987) *White Paper on Leisure.* Tokyo

very active, tending to function more to kill time or reduce tension. But perhaps in this regard it is better not to pass too hasty a judgement on Japanese workers, as a similar situation may exist in other countries. Respondents to the survey recognised several disturbant factors, which are listed in Table 8.5.

Table 8.5   *Disturbant factors for free-time activities (1987)*

| Disturbant factors | Sports | Travel | Culture |
|---|---|---|---|
| Too busy on weekdays | 30.1 | 10.9 | 25.8 |
| Too expensive | 17.8 | 41.2 | 21.9 |
| Time limitation of facilities | 18.4 | 0.8 | 9.1 |
| Facilities too distant | 17.7 | 1.2 | 9.0 |
| No vacations | 6.4 | 30.5 | 2.6 |
| Not enough holidays | 14.3 | 18.6 | 9.9 |

*Source:* As Table 8.4

As free time on weekdays is limited, employed people tend to take full advantage of their rare holidays. Their eagerness may in part be a reaction to the scarcity of leisure in daily life. Active enjoyment of holidays seems above all to serve as a temporary escape from the cramped and stressful circumstances of everyday living. The people eagerly seek a variety of non-routine experiences. Husbands are coaxed into taking their wives and children somewhere for amusement. So one cannot conclude that Japanese only work hard. A nationwide survey shows the 20 most popular leisure activities (see Table 8.6). In this survey, enjoying mass media and shopping were omitted intentionally as they were regarded as common to everyone.

Table 8.6    *The 20 most popular leisure activities*

| Leisure Activity | Participants (annual, 000s) | | |
|---|---|---|---|
| | 1984 | 1985 | 1986 |
| Dining (out) | 5470 | 5920 | 6110 |
| Driving | 4910 | 5560 | 5690 |
| Travel (domestic) | 4530 | 5100 | 5270 |
| Drinking (out) | 4030 | 4350 | 4080 |
| Going to the zoo, botanical gardens, aquariums, museums | 3390 | 3900 | 4030 |
| Card games | 3710 | 3820 | 3940 |
| Gymnastics (without apparatus) | 3580 | 3600 | 3780 |
| Picnics, hiking, field walks | 3050 | 3710 | 3700 |
| Sea bathing | 3790 | 3840 | 3700 |
| Amusement parks | 3320 | 3640 | 3630 |
| Cinema | 3040 | 3320 | 3480 |
| Gardening, horticulture | 3200 | 3390 | 3460 |
| Public lottery | – | 2900 | 3300 |
| Listening to music (disc, tape, FM radio) | 2600 | 3160 | 3140 |
| Bowling | 2760 | 2640 | 2890 |
| *Pachink* (Japanese pinball) | 2750 | 2840 | 2860 |
| TV games, electronic games (at home) | – | – | 2790 |
| Homecoming, travel, family reunions | 2520 | 2570 | 2700 |
| Jogging, marathon running | 2730 | 2590 | 2690 |
| Special events, expositions | – | 2630 | 2610 |

*Source:* As Table 8.4

Certain trends can be observed:

1. Drinking out is decreasing slightly, probably because young employees and their wives do not like the traditional Japanese company compulsory socialising and drinking after work.
2. The public lottery is rapidly gaining in popularity, reflecting the current 'money-game fever' and ennui.
3. TV games and electronic games played at home are increasingly enjoyed by young people.

The special characteristics of Japanese uses of leisure time are more concretely revealed in another enquiry, which shows the frequency of participation in each category of activity. Most categories are similar to those in other countries, but some are specifically Japanese. The statistics reveal how assiduously and how diversely people are enjoying their leisure time. The 20 most popular categories are listed in Table 8.7.

Table 8.7   *Frequency of participation in each activity*

| Category | % participating | | |
| --- | --- | --- | --- |
| | 1984 | 1985 | 1986 |
| Listening to music (disc, tape, FM radio) | 71.1 | 65.5 | 67.5 |
| Gymnastics (without apparatus) | 55.3 | 59.0 | 54.3 |
| Gate-ball (croquet) | – | 41.4 | 48.7 |
| Performing occidental music | 47.9 | 35.6 | 44.2 |
| Calisthenics (beauty gymnastics) | 49.9 | 47.3 | 42.4 |
| Martial arts (judo, karate, kendo, etc.) | 46.3 | 46.3 | 41.6 |
| Gardening, horticulture | 41.9 | 35.5 | 40.4 |
| Physical training (with apparatus) | 43.5 | 45.7 | 37.2 |
| Performing Japanese music | 36.6 | 35.5 | 35.0 |
| Jogging, marathon running | 38.4 | 36.2 | 34.9 |
| Rugby | – | 31.6 | 34.8 |
| Tea ceremonies | 29.0 | 29.9 | 33.3 |
| Learning, study (not occupational) | 36.0 | 35.5 | 33.3 |
| *Shodo* (calligraphy) | 38.4 | 34.5 | 33.2 |
| Flower arrangement | 31.3 | 29.9 | 33.2 |
| Aerobics, jazz-dance (rhythmic exercise) | 39.6 | 30.8 | 32.6 |
| Knitting, sewing, handicrafts | 35.6 | 28.9 | 32.1 |
| TV games, electronic games (at home) | – | 30.2 | 30.1 |
| Traditional dance | 47.9 | 46.9 | 29.3 |
| Dressmaking (occidental) | 28.6 | – | 27.7 |

*Source:* As Table 8.4

From Table 8.7 we can see the following tendencies:

Categories decreasing in popularity are: calisthenics, performing Japanese music, jogging and marathon running, learning and studying (not occupational) and *shodo* (oriental calligraphy). These activities were fashionable several years ago but have less appeal now.

Categories increasing in popularity are: gateball or croquet (which reflects the interests of an ageing population), rugby (which reflects a growing interest in more masculine sports), and the tea ceremony, which reflects a reaction among young women to over-westernisation.

Many Japanese are not satisfied with the way they spend their free time. Those who only watch television or rest hope to have a chance to travel abroad, to relax at a holiday resort, or to visit family members far away. The Leisure Development Centre has devised an Index of Growth Possibility (IGP) which relates rates of current participation in particular activities to the desire for future participation. The top five items of desired activity in the IGP are shown in Table 8.8. The level of desire is rising. People wish to be more active and creative. It is interesting, too, that women hope not only to participate in 'Western' activities, but also to study and to enjoy traditional Japanese arts. Concerning cultural activities, also, a discrepancy between reality and desire can be seen. A recent government survey (9 November 1987) gave the following results:

1. 81.7 percent answered, 'I neither enjoyed nor created anything of a cultural nature during the past year.'
2. Only 26.6 percent went to concerts, though 68.3 percent enjoyed music on the radio or television.
3. Just 23 percent visited museums, and 23 percent went to cinemas.
4. Just over 50 percent read literary works.

Nevertheless, 88.2 percent of the respondents wished to appreciate the arts or to participate in creative activities. More than 90 percent felt that their nation had an excellent culture, and 60 percent rated the level of this culture as among the highest in the world.

Table 8.8   *Index of growth possibility (IGP) of leisure activity (1987)*

| (a) Male Desired activity | IGP | (b) Female Desired activity | IGP |
| --- | --- | --- | --- |
| Travel abroad | 1062 | Travel abroad | 1023 |
| Marine sports | 320 | Golf | 531 |
| Making videos/films | 231 | Ceramic art | 358 |
| Gateball | 213 | Tea ceremonies | 228 |
| Amusement in theatre | 196 | Occidental dances | 225 |

*Source:* As Table 8.4

Japan not only has its own long tradition of arts but also shows a growing interest in Western fine arts. Japanese parvenus and dilettantes provide a lucrative market for the international art business. In 1987 a Japanese insurance company bought Van Gogh's 'Sunflowers' at an auction in London, paying 5300 million yen. This purchase may perhaps reflect the 'money-game fever' among institutional investors, and it represents only the tip of an iceberg. By the end of August 1987 purchases of Western paintings had amounted to 73,400 million yen for that year. This figure does not include prices paid for art works that came into the country though illicit traffic, like the smuggled art objects stolen in Europe. Japan is a mecca for European smugglers and art thieves. Recently a Japanese man was arrested after confessing that he had sold several of Corot's works, stolen in France. He is suspected of having some connection with the French thieves who stole Monet's 'Sunrise'. Not all buyers have the ability to appreciate their acquisitions as works of art. There are few true connoisseurs of Western art in Japan; the *nouveaux riches* and companies with surpluses regard purchases of art objects as investments.

Concerning the Japanese love of tourism, a recent official survey put the 1986 annual expenditure for domestic travel at 3.62 million yen. Yet the average Japanese household makes a trip involving at least one night away from home only 0.9 times a year, with an expenditure of 153,900 yen per household (see Table 8.9). Overnight trips averaging 5.05 days were made by 65.7 percent of the nation in 1986. The proportion of the population that had travelled abroad had reached only 15.8 percent by 1987. In 1986 just 3.6 percent of the Japanese enjoyed overseas trips unrelated to business. This figure is double that of ten years ago, and 30 times that of 20 years ago. The increase is especially marked among people over 60 years of age (10 percent of all overseas tourists), and women (35 percent). Women in their twenties, including university students, accounted for half of the latter. The Japanese by nature are full of curiosity, by which they have learnt much from foreign cultures throughout their history. In recent years this attitude has become more active. The increasing cross-cultural experiences will surely create something new in the future. But it cannot be denied that the cramped living space and tedious calm of present-day Japan cause people to desire some kind of temporary escape from the routine of everyday life.

Table 8.9  *Annual spending on leisure activities by the average family (all households) (yen)*

|  | 1965 | 1975 | 1980 | 1984 | 1985 | 1986 |
|---|---|---|---|---|---|---|
| Eating out | 14,571 | 64,620 | 105,463 | 124,471 | 127,441 | 134,279 |
| Recreational durable goods[1] | 7133 | 25,109 | 26,610 | 31,743 | 27,047 | 34,108 |
| Reading and recreation | 23,895 | 91,262 | 132,390 | 152,511 | 155,831 | 156,539 |
| Sports | 1684 | 7752 | 16,498 | 22,967 | 24,721 | 24,731 |
| Tours | 10,592 | 46,205 | 71,350 | 91,976 | 96,021 | 98,959 |
| Others | 42,048 | 174,382 | 259,477 | 293,590 | 301,391 | 332,618 |
| Total | 99,923 | 409,330 | 611,788 | 717,258 | 732,452 | 781,134 |
| Ratio to living expenditure (%) | 17.2 | 21.6 | 22.1 | 22.4 | 22.3 | 23.6 |

[1] Radios, TV sets, cameras, pianos and other musical instruments.
*Sources:* Statistics Bureau, Management and Co-ordination Agency (1987) *Annual Report on Family Income and Expenditure*. Tokyo. Office of the Prime Minister (1987) *White Paper on Tourism*. Tokyo

The leisure market is continuously expanding, even under stagflation; an overall expenditure of 49.474 million yen in 1984 rose to 54.395 million yen in 1986. The larger markets, and the percentage of expenditure in each for 1987, were as follows:

1. Eating and drinking out, 26 percent;
2. Games, 20 percent;
3. Sightseeing and tourism, 13.1 percent;
4. Audio-visual equipment, 12.1 percent;
5. Gambling, 10.5 percent.

The increases from 1986 to 1987 were especially high in admission fees for sports (10 percent), audio-visual equipment (8.7 percent), gambling (8.2 percent), and membership and lessons in sports centres (7.2 percent). But the rate of growth of the leisure market as a whole has declined a little. A popular yearbook published in English comments on this tendency:

(i)   Leisure-time activities have been so diversified that the appearance of tremendously popular new leisure activities can hardly be expected.

(ii)  As a result of, among other things, improvement of raw materials and introduction of new materials, the life-cycle of leisure commodities is shortened, and bestselling articles are replaced by new ones at shorter intervals.

(iii) Consumers are increasingly laying stress on their health and community life, and they are finding more opportunities for leisure activities at lower costs.

(iv)  High-technology leisure activities, such as those using personal computers, are rising, but they are still minor ones in the leisure market. (Nippon, *A Charted Survey of Japan 1987/88,* The Kokuseisha Corporation, Tokyo, 1987: 314).

### Behind the light – the main tendencies in the domestic economy

Japan, along with other industrialised nations, is suffering from the global recession of the 1980s. This dextrous country, however, maintained a relatively constant economic growth from 1980 to 1985. The average growth rate for these five years was 3.9 percent. Owing to government initiatives to modify the industrial structure, and to the serious efforts of business companies to save energy, Japan's defensive reaction to the first oil shock was somewhat subtle. Immediately thereafter the government took steps to strengthen friendly relations with oil-producing countries, especially those of the Islamic world, by displaying an ambiguous attitude towards the Palestinian problem.

Ironically, Japan's economic growth itself has caused problems. The strong yen has become one of the factors hindering the growth of exports as the prices of Japanese products are no longer cheap. As a result the quantity of commodities exported has actually decreased. The rate of economic growth has dropped continuously since the 5.1 percent high for 1984. The figure of 2.6 percent for

1986 is the lowest so far for the 1980s, although the rate increased in the first three months of 1987 (see Figure 8.3).

Figure 8.3   *Japan's economic growth rate (real)*

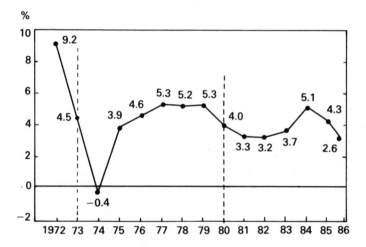

*Source*: Economic Planning Agency (1987) *White Paper on the National Economy*. Tokyo

By contrast the NIC (new industrial countries), in particular the 'Four Little Dragons' – South Korea, Hong Kong, Taiwan and Singapore – are accelerating their production, and their rates of growth have surpassed that of Japan. Now Japan must compete with these countries in foreign markets. Not only in the United States, but in Japan as well, these countries have made big headway.

A further negative aspect of growth is found in the rate of unemployment, which has shown a steady increase since 1986 and reached 3.2 percent in May 1987. The threat is especially severe for employees in small companies, and elderly employees in the older industries. Many companies are endeavouring to diversify, even to the extent of expanding their activities to include areas outside their previous experience. The unemployment figures shown for Japan in Figure 8.4, however, include individuals who were temporarily out of work, and those who were seeking to change their jobs in order to obtain more favourable conditions. Japanese youth are more fortunate by far than young people in Europe. There is little danger at present that university graduates will be unable to find any jobs at all unless they persistently set their sights too high and hold out for the most highly ranked companies or positions. The rapid development of high technology is increasing the demand for youth labour. On the other hand, a new potential demand for jobs has appeared among housewives for their own self-development, in order to have an independent income, or to supplement their husbands' income.

Figure 8.4   *Comparison of the rate of unemployment*

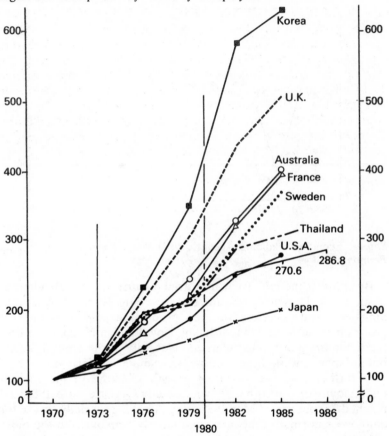

*Note*: The definition of 'unemployment' depends on the nation. The Japanese definition is rather restricted.
*Source*: As Figure 8.2

Generally speaking, few men or women in present-day Japan are truly in danger of hunger or extreme privation with no family to help them, although there can be found, especially in the larger cities, old and solitary casual labourers who live miserably. The sudden rise of land prices in the larger cities has been tremendous. The national average rate of increase in 1987 was 9.7 percent, following a decline from the 8.7 percent of 1980. In Tokyo there was an unbelievably sharp rise of 85.7 percent in 1987. With its luxury apartments selling for billions of yen existing side by side with its largest flophouse quarter (*doya-gai*) sheltering 30,000 day labourers, Tokyo wears a Janus-like aspect.

Among the highly industrialised countries Japan is an exception in the relative stability of its consumer prices (see Figure 8.5) as well as the comparatively low rate of unemployment. The rate of increase in unemployment in 1986 (0.6 percent) was lower than in 1985 (2 percent) and 1984 (2.3 percent). This was due mainly to the decrease in payments for imports, including crude oil and petroleum products. Although the quantity of imports is increasing, the strong yen has lowered the amount of money paid. However, price changes are not the same for every item of household expenditure. Rates of increase have been especially high in education (3.6 percent), housing (2.5 percent), clothing and footwear (2.2 per-

Figure 8.5   *Comparison of consumer price index (1970=100)*

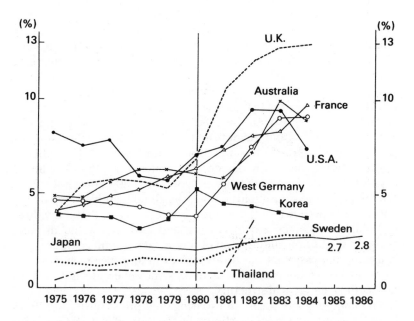

*Note*: 1986 figure added by the author.
*Source*: As Figure 8.2

cent), medical care (1.9 percent) and reading and recreation (1.5 percent). These trends have not changed for several years. Such price rises especially affect the less affluent strata. Among the Japanese, per capita calorie consumption, the proportion of animal protein in the diet, and housing space compare unfavourably with Europeans'.

### The middle class and the parvenus – levels of consumption

It is very difficult to analyse the vertical structure of Japanese society. Neither Marxist class theory nor any other stratification theories are adequate for analysing the actual state of income distribution in detail. Aspects of income and consumption vary according to occupation. Furthermore, annual income, as measured in Japan, is not always an accurate indicator of prosperity, as the former includes the sale of real estate. If in a particular year a private individual sells some real estate, this occasional income is limited to that year and does not indicate a consistent level of wealth. The National Tax Agency publishes each year only the highest-ranking taxpayers. The list, however, includes those who have a temporarily high income for the reasons mentioned above. Data concerning tax payments can be an important resource for analysing the income pyramid but it is not completely reliable, since the system of taxation of salaried workers is different from that used for the self-employed.

The Administration and Co-operation Agency distinguishes 18 ranks of yearly income from a low of 999,999 yen or less to a high of 10 million yen and over. In 1986 the largest income group (8.8 percent) was 11th from the bottom (4 million – 4,999,999 yen); 41.4 percent of the population were in groups 9 to 13 (3 million – 5,499,999 yen) and 71.6 percent in groups 7 to 15 (2 million – 6,499,999 yen). The highest group contained 809 households, and the lowest just 38 households among the 10,000 sampled. We do not know the breakdown of the former, but it is certain that individuals with higher incomes are increasing and as a result the distance between the bottom and the top of the social pyramid is widening. It is usually the case that the lower classes in any society suffer most from adverse influences. These figures, however, do not entirely reflect the true vertical structure.

The 'money-game fever' and soaring land prices have given birth to many new billionaires as shown in the data of the National Tax Agency. The top individual income in 1986 was 1500 million yen, while the 50th in rank was paid 450 million yen. By contrast, at the bottom of society are the elderly vagabonds who have neither money nor family. They sleep in the open under corrugated cardboard even in winter. People receiving public assistance in Japan number 1.431 million. The average yearly income of assisted households was 312,965 yen in 1986, and the average household receiving assistance consisted of three members. Nevertheless, such dark sides are barely visible in the bright light of the affluent society.

Japanese society is highly organised in the sense that its social cohesion is strong. However, the structure of its business is less tightly organised. Highly organised big businesses are few in number. The Japanese economy is essentially based on numerous small businesses, the self-employed and family workers. In these categories are found many who work diligently and untiringly. Among the working population the proportion who are self-employed is 15.6 percent, though there has been a slight decrease in the long term. Unpaid family workers account for 9.3 percent of the labour force. The proportion of workers in these two categories is notably higher than in the advanced European countries. The Japanese economy and larger companies are actually supported by numerous small businesses. In order to understand the vertical structure of Japanese society, it is necessary to understand the discrepancy between big and small enterprises. The Japanese economy is, in fact, based on the latter. Factories with less than ten workers comprise 74.9 percent of the total, whereas those with more than 1000 employees are only 0.1 percent. The larger companies employ 13.5 percent of all workers, and their production accounts for 26.2 percent of the whole. The proportion of workers in middle-sized factories of 50–199 employees is 22.2 percent, and their production accounts for 21 percent of Japan's total output (see Table 8.10).

Generally speaking, the degree of modernisation and overall working conditions vary with the size of the company, at least in the manufacturing industries. The size of the company in which one is employed is therefore an important determinant of one's social status. Employees of the larger companies receive various fringe benefits along with their generally higher salaries. Consequently, ambitious university graduates seek employment in the larger corporations. The smaller and the larger business worlds reflect the duality of Japanese society, not only in economics but also in levels of education and sophistication. The larger enterprises recruit graduates from the higher-ranked universities, who are relatively westernised, while the employees of smaller businesses keep the traditional mentality, that is, the quasi-rural culture. However, in terms of human relations techniques, both large and small com-

Table 8.10   *Size of factory (Japan, 1984)*

| Number of workers in each factory | Factories Number | % | Workers Number (000) | % | Production 1000 (million yen) | % |
|---|---|---|---|---|---|---|
| 1–9 | 553,770 | 74.9 | 2107 | 18.5 | 15,748 | 6.2 |
| 10–19 | 86,454 | 11.7 | 1188 | 10.4 | 15,011 | 5.9 |
| 20–29 | 42,773 | 5.8 | 1045 | 9.2 | 15,044 | 5.9 |
| 30–49 | 22,280 | 3.6 | 866 | 7.6 | 14,740 | 5.8 |
| 50–99 | 19,286 | 2.6 | 1339 | 11.7 | 26,430 | 10.3 |
| 100–199 | 8776 | 1.2 | 1200 | 10.5 | 27,289 | 10.7 |
| 200–299 | 2578 | 0.3 | 622 | 5.5 | 17,423 | 6.8 |
| 300–499 | 1810 | 0.2 | 688 | 6.0 | 24,958 | 9.7 |
| 500–999 | 1185 | 0.2 | 806 | 7.1 | 32,080 | 12.7 |
| 1000– | 669 | 0.1 | 1531 | 13.5 | 67,288 | 26.2 |
| Total | 739,581 | 100.0 | 11,382 | 100.0 | 256,010 | 100.0 |

*Source:* Ministry of International Trade and Industry (1985) *Statistics of Industry.* Tokyo

panies are basically Japanese.

Compared with Western European nations, in Japan a higher proportion of people are engaged in commerce (22.9 percent), construction (9.1 percent), and agriculture, forestry and fisheries (8.5 percent). By contrast the proportions are lower in mining (0.1 percent), electricity, gas and water (0.5 percent), and public administration and services (28.2 percent). From 1980 to 1985 there was a marked increase in the proportion of employees in services (up by 15.8 percent), finance, insurance and real estate (11.1 percent), and wholesale and retail trade (5.7 percent). There were decreases (see Table 8.11) in forestry (15.9 percent), mining (12.2 percent) and agriculture (11.5 percent). During the same period there was a slight increase in professional and technical workers (8.6 to 10.5 percent) and clerical workers (16.5 to 18.4 percent).

Japanese official statistics distinguish five ranks of average monthly real income of the households of salaried employees, including white-collar and middle management. The average for 1986 was 452,942 yen for a 3.78-member household. The top-ranking income was 718,528 yen and the lowest was 250,540 yen. Although there is a tendency toward a widening of the gap, the inequalities in living standards among workers as a whole, including those in middle management, are not large. In 1986 the average real income of households in the highest rank was 2.87 times that of the average in the fifth rank, a slightly wider difference than in 1980 (2.65). Expenditure in the first rank was generally higher than in the

Table 8.11  *Number of employed persons by industry on basis of population census (15 years of age and over)*

|  | Number (000s) | | Increase & decrease (%) | |
|---|---|---|---|---|
|  | 1980 | 1985 | 1975–80 | 1980–85 |
| Primary industry | 6102 | 5419 | −16.9 | −11.2 |
| Agriculture | 5475 | 4845 | −18.2 | −11.5 |
| Forestry | 165 | 139 | −7.5 | −15.8 |
| Fisheries | 461 | 434 | −3.0 | −5.8 |
| Secondary industry | 18,737 | 19,206 | 3.5 | 2.5 |
| Mining | 108 | 95 | −18.0 | −12.2 |
| Construction | 5383 | 5300 | 13.8 | −1.6 |
| Manufacturing | 13,246 | 13,811 | 0.0 | 4.3 |
| Tertiary industry | 30,911 | 33,488 | 12.3 | −8.3 |
| Electricity, gas, water and steam | 349 | 322 | 8.8 | −7.7 |
| Transport and communications | 3504 | 3538 | 4.1 | 1.0 |
| Wholesale and retail trade | 12,731 | 13,453 | 12.0 | 5.7 |
| Finance, insurance and real estate | 2004 | 2227 | 14.2 | 11.1 |
| Services | 10,298 | 11,924 | 17.7 | 15.8 |
| Government | 2026 | 2015 | 3.4 | −0.6 |
| Unclassifiable | 62 | 105 |  |  |
| All industries | 55,811 | 58,218 | 5.0 | 4.3 |

*Source:* Bureau of Statistics, Management and Coordination Agency (1986)
*Population Census for 1985.* Toyko

fifth, especially on education, clothing and footwear, reading and recreation, transportation and communication, and furniture and household utensils (see Table 8.12).

Table 8.12  *Monthly living expenditure of workers' households (yearly average) (%)*

|  | 1970 | 1975 | 1980 | 1985 | 1986 |
|---|---|---|---|---|---|
| Food | 32.2 | 30.0 | 27.8 | 25.7 | 25.5 |
| Housing | 5.3 | 5.1 | 4.7 | 4.7 | 4.8 |
| Fuel, light and water charges | 4.1 | 4.1 | 5.3 | 5.9 | 5.8 |
| Clothing and footwear | 9.3 | 9.0 | 7.5 | 7.0 | 7.0 |
| Furniture and household utensils | 5.1 | 5.0 | 4.2 | 4.2 | 4.0 |
| Medical care | 2.6 | 2.4 | 2.4 | 2.4 | 2.4 |
| Transportation and communication | 5.5 | 6.6 | 8.5 | 9.7 | 9.8 |
| Education | 2.7 | 2.7 | 3.6 | 4.2 | 4.5 |
| Reading and recreation | 9.2 | 8.5 | 8.5 | 8.7 | 8.9 |
| Social expenses | 7.7 | 8.9 | 8.9 | 8.7 | 8.7 |
| Other | 16.3 | 17.7 | 18.6 | 18.8 | 18.6 |
| Total | 100.0 | 100.0 | 100.0 | 100.0 | 100.0 |

*Source:* As Table 8.9

The Economic Planning Agency provides statistics on ownership of household durables which reflect everyday life-styles. The spread of ownership in 1986 was almost equally high for washing machines (99.2 percent), colour TV sets (98.1 percent), vacuum cleaners (98.1 percent) and electric refrigerators (97.9 percent). On the other hand, differences between first-rank and fifth-rank households were relatively large in pianos (41/6.6 percent), video and cine-cameras (18.2/3.6 percent), personal computers (20.9/4.6 percent), furniture sets (26.2/6.5 percent), compact disc players (18.6/4.8 percent), and clothes dryers (18.7/5.8 percent). New recreational durable goods such as videos and compact disc players, which contributed most to the increase in expenditure (8.7 percent) over the previous year, are not yet found in the typical Japanese household.

Certainly a new elite class is growing in Japan. The rapidly rising 'soft industries' and the highly developed mass media as well as the 'money game' and rising land prices are contributing to the growth of the new rich. There are many young men who dream of making a fortune at a stroke and many adults who rush to public lotteries. Money provides a compensation for loneliness. Even elderly people and housewives play the stock market. Hedonism and the love of Mammon dominate Asian Rome. Severe class antagonism, however, does not exist in present-day Japan. In spite of differences in income, social divisions are mild compared with other countries because both the old and the new middle strata are relatively wide, and there is a tolerant attitude towards socioeconomic competition.

Although uses of leisure time have become remarkably diverse, a general equality of level prevails in leisure activities. Even the billionaires and Nobel prize-winners melt into Japanese mass society, watching the same television programmes, and reading the same newspaper columns as the average worker.

### Bread and circuses – politics and leisure

In present-day Japan politics does not exert a direct influence on leisure activities. It cannot be denied, however, that the blossoming of the leisure culture has been made possible by the prevailing liberal mood. There are no political hindrances to the full enjoyment of a variety of pleasures. Although the Japanese government often intervenes actively in the capitalist economy, it rarely interferes either positively or negatively in the leisure of the people. Economic development has been given priority to the neglect of a leisure policy. The government has no special ministry for sports or leisure in general. Sports are mainly regarded not as recreation but as a means of education. The Ministry of Education gives backing to several national athletic meetings which are principally competitions among representative teams from each prefecture. Until the end of the Second World War sport was expected to contribute to the breeding of strong soldiers. Consequently the martial arts (*budo*) were compulsory at school. Nowadays the Cultural Agency, under the direction of the Ministry of Education, gives formal support to artistic activities, but its expenditure on the arts is modest compared with those of Western countries. For instance, only 200 million yen is appropriated yearly for the purchase of pictures by the National Museum of Occidental Arts, an amount equal to only one-seventieth of the Paul Getty Foundation's annual budget.

Patterns of consumption in the nation are not so much guided as followed by the Economic Planning Agency and the Ministry of Welfare. The main policies of these organisations are directed towards economic development and the prevention of poverty rather than the improvement of leisure. National ministries and agencies contribute directly to leisure by the development and administration of public recreational facilities. Many such facilities also receive support from local governments. The most popular facilities are the national hostels, one or more of which can be found in each prefecture or large city. They are particularly convenient for family trips. The Japanese especially favour hostels located near hot spring resorts, which can be found in almost every part of the country.

Following the period of rapid economic growth the government has recently begun to pay more attention to leisure. The factors contributing to this new interest include increased pollution of the environment, increased stress in daily life, the economic need to increase consumption, and the need to neutralise aggressive impulses resulting from frustration. 'Bread and circuses' have been widely recognised as effective means of social control since the time of the Roman Empire. 'Empire, it is pleasure', said Napoleon III confronting his ideological opponents. Even Bismarck, controlling his nation by the stick, did not forget the carrot. Japanese prosperity has succeeded in spreading political apathy through every stratum. People can easily enjoy bread and circuses, the carrot without the stick, anywhere and at any time. Now, however, the Japanese government is having to cope with new difficulties, particularly how to expand the market for domestic consumption, lower the tariff wall, and promote trade, in an attempt to comply with requests from other countries. The government is also wondering how to provide support for declining industries, how to increase the free time of workers in more prosperous industries, and how to provide for more open space and greenery in the larger cities and control steeply rising land prices. Increasing domestic demand is the most crucial issue in foreign relations, whereas the price of land is the biggest problem in domestic politics.

### Epilogue

The Japanese have certainly been successful in establishing an economic 'great power', so it is inevitable that the envy or even anger of poor countries is aroused. Maybe I have described Japan too negatively or cynically in an effort to avoid accusations of chauvinism. Maybe an apology for the people is necessary. First, their standard of living is still lower than that of Europeans and Americans. It is material poverty that has led them to hard work. As a result, the scantiness of free time has made them lose freedom of spirit, which has led to a spiritual poverty. With few resources, they cannot choose but to eat even whales, regarding them simply as 'big fish', a permitted item in the diet of Buddhists. Secondly, the hard work of the Japanese has created a variety of relaxations and pleasures. They are not only working animals but also pleasure animals. The short song at the beginning of this chapter is one expression of this. Their diversions refresh the workers. The desire to enjoy life leads them to hard work, and this enlarges the leisure market. The uniqueness of Japan's richness of diversions can be explained fully neither by the country's politics nor by its economics, nor properly portrayed in the statistics.

If readers could live in Japan, most of them would surely be enchanted by the variety of pleasures, perhaps even including the most vulgar ones. Elegance and the arts coexist with indecency and coarse humour. The Japanese are able to contribute something to the world, not only by their quantity of free time but also by its quality. By their unique ways of enjoying human life, the Japanese will eventually, perhaps, influence other countries. With greater confidence, Japan could change from an economic leader to a cultural leader. But the time is probably not yet ripe. Part of the problem is that the Japanese do not yet know how to distribute their money and experiences to other parts of the world. Even so, at least they can offer a distinctive model of 'modernisation', whether negative or positive. For Japan itself, the 1980s is a time for reassessment; for determining exactly what has been gained, what has been lost, what might be recovered, and where to head in the future.

# 9

# France: Leisure Sociology in the 1980s

## Joffre Dumazedier

Leisure activities – amateur sport, television watching, travel, tourism, and so on – are well-established phenomena. Yet leisure itself is still a long way from being fully understood, at least in so far as it is a new social reality that is gradually being incorporated into people's overall life-styles in the technologically advanced societies. Just how widespread this kind of leisure has become poses a problem for sociology. Forms of leisure at the end of the day, the week, the year, and the working life, are not necessarily one and the same. Leisure's importance in the balance or imbalance within the free time which is a product of the chain of scientific revolutions which have reduced and transformed the nature of work, is still controversial (Reynaud and Grafmeyer, 1981; Mendras and Forse, 1983; Guillaume, 1986). Modern leisure is so difficult to define precisely that it is tempting to proscribe the term. However, I shall argue that sociology needs to grasp the nature of modern leisure in order to understand one of the major aspects of the long-term changes currently in process in the life-styles of all social classes. These changes are directly linked neither to spectacular political upheavals nor to cyclical economic crises. Modern leisure has appeared and developed in the wake of labour as if 'creeping in on tiptoe', to use Nietzsche's evocative phrase. In my opinion, only sociological analyses which incorporate a satisfactory conceptualisation of leisure will attenuate the blindness otherwise inflicted either by anachronistic moralisms of work or by utopian dreams of 'the end of work'. This will be the present chapter's central hypothesis, which will be demonstrated with reference to quantitative and qualitative evidence.

Most of this evidence is from empirical research carried out in France from the 1960s to the present (Boulin et al., 1982). This chapter draws extensively from the work of those researchers who met frequently on the Leisure Project, and on the cultural models which were developed from 1953 onwards at the CNRS (National Centre for Scientific Research) under the impetus of Georges Friedmann. However, the work of additional researchers, some of whom split from the original team, and others who never belonged to it, will also be used. Whenever it seems valuable, comparisons will be drawn between these results and the findings of empirical research in other societies.

I shall examine the two principal types of sociological or social theorisation which have tried to take this evidence into account, before concluding with a conceptualisation which in some respects is more conservative, but which is really much more pertinent, and better attuned, to the complex and transitory contemporary situation.

### More free time than working hours

It is well known that the sudden explosion of unemployment and short-time working from 1974 onwards came after a period of exceptional prosperity which has been described as the 30 glorious years. Long-term unemployment now affects approximately 10 percent of the working population – and probably twice this official figure if we are to be realistic – throughout most of Western Europe, with Switzerland as one of the few exceptions. It is less often noticed that the movement towards a reduction in working hours, so that more people can be employed, has gained momentum everywhere. When Karl Marx was preparing the Communist Manifesto, the amount of time worked annually by a typical urban worker, with no retirement limit, no holidays and often no Sunday off, was somewhere in the region of 4000 hours, with working weeks often 70 hours long if not longer, and working days of 12 hours in length. Today the French worker's lot has fallen to something like 1600 hours per annum, with retirement at 60, a two-day weekend, and a 6.5 hour working day. The working week, which averaged 46 hours in 1965, has since fallen to 39 hours, and the unions are now fighting for the 35-hour week. But more important, probably, in the long term is the fact that for those who work away from home, for those who work from home too, and for those who combine the two, free time now exceeds work time. What happened in the USA during the 1960s has happened from the 1970s onwards in France and other West European societies.

This spectacular change has been christened 'historical inversion' in the USA (Marcuse, 1963). This is an understandable term. One is tempted to put it to the test in France among those whose only perception of the dynamics of society is from the angle of social reproduction. Yet for the sociologist it is unsatisfactory to base talk of an historical inversion solely on a simple hour count in the evolution of time-budgets. We will see that a new kind of interaction of free time and labour began long before the preponderance of free hours. We also know that some people's outlooks and many social structures are still far removed from an historical inversion. The dead continue to dominate the thoughts of the quick, as was stated over 150 years ago by Auguste Comte, the founder of sociology. We can perceive now, at the dawning of the third technological revolution, that of information techonology, after those of steam and electricity, a slow and profound *re-evolution of social times* (Dumazedier, 1988). Let us first of all define the current state of free-time activities and the accompanying change of values in everyday life in our society.

We already know of the remarkable growth in activities offered by the leisure industries; by associations created to encourage physical, artistic, intellectual and social expression of all kinds, and by the public services of the state and borough councils with ever more prolific and ever more costly sporting and cultural facilities (Dumazedier and Imbert, 1967). In a society such as ours, where 58 percent of the workforce is now in tertiary industry as opposed to 7 percent in the agrarian sector and 31 percent in manufacturing, household spending on leisure outstrips spending on food. Leisure is the fastest growing spending area, along with health. Official sources say that leisure amounts only to 6 percent of the national budget. However, it has been estimated that, in reality, the true figure is at least 16 percent when one includes leisure spending in areas such as transport, hotels, restaurants, housing and entertaining at home (Dumazedier, 1974).

As a result of this, there are varied and ever-changing social activities which are not without their attendant problems. Above all, it is far and away most often during leisure time that major or minor acts of misbehaviour and prostitution are perpetrated. Since the 1960s there has been a steady rise in excessive consumption of alcohol, addiction to soft and hard narcotics, and in theft and other crimes. Outside of these increasing cases of social pathology which create a heightened sense of insecurity in the public mind, the free-time activities of the general population are passing ever more noticeably beyond the 'recuperation of the strength to work' which Karl Marx rightly insisted was the principal role of free time for the nineteenth-century labour force, crushed as it was by long, hard labour. The car now features in three-quarters of our households. Fifty-six percent of the French population goes on holiday. The majority of the 93 percent who have television watch it at least 15 hours a week. The average family uses other mass-produced leisure machines such as record-players, radios and tape-recorders for about five hours each day. About 60 percent watch feature films on television and a half go to the cinema at least once a year. Fifty-five percent play the Loto, the lottery or the PMU (pari mutuel urbain). However, only 17 percent watch plays on the television, and just 10 percent have been even once to see live theatre. Most of those who read, read fiction, but they comprise no more than 28 percent of the population, of whom only 20 percent go at least twice a year to libraries. It is said that nowadays 'everybody plays sport'. If the truth be told, 27 percent watch sport on TV, 17 percent regularly jog or go to keep-fit, and just 13 percent regularly play team sports. Half of the free time available is spent on all sorts of do-it-yourself, which is practised across the whole social spectrum, often as much for pleasure as for any practical use.

One quarter of the population in the major urban areas loses more than five hours per week travelling between home and work, with exceptional cases wasting three hours a day. These difficulties became even greater between 1973 and 1981. Account must also be taken of inequalities of financial conditions and social status. Newspaper games, cinema-going and DIY are fairly standardised with no great regard for class. But the underlying values are not always the same, and in other leisure activities there are huge distinctions, always to the detriment of the economically underprivileged classes, and to the benefit of those better equipped for individual sport, the theatre, cultural interaction and reading (Verret and Creusen, 1979; Verret, 1988). These distinctions would appear even more marked were we to separate the cultural habits of the 4 million underqualified immigrant workers and their families from North Africa, Spain and Portugal. Their leisure time is often interrupted by violent conflicts which occur much more frequently during their free time than when they are working.

### New values

Of still greater import than this unbalanced explosion of new social habits, is the force of underlying *collective preferences*. Be these conscious or unconscious, admitted or tacit, they reveal new value systems which are slowly changing the established equilibria of free time, and are beginning, to varying extents, to infiltrate all of daily life. These new equilibria are often at direct odds with still predominant social ethics. When ignored or repressed they produce increasing indifference, boredom and scepticism across an ever-broadening section of the population. And so, what of the development of what can be called *leisure values* in the lives of working men and women? We can compare the results of long-term studies of the French town of Annecy (1956–86) and 'Middletown'

(1920–80) in the USA. We can observe, occasionally differently formulated, more or less the same trends in the evolution of the relationships between self, society and nature. These trends appear initially within an innovating fraction of educated middle-class youth. They then spread gradually and unevenly through all classes and social categories to all age groups.

As the amount of time diminishes which is dedicated to work with all the constraints it imposes, there is a gradual liberation of desires and aspirations that had previously been contained and repressed. This does not herald the end of social control – which still exists to protect communal life and individual realisation – but the beginning of a new sort of control which, while being less regulatory and more liberating, often establishes and develops itself amidst misunderstanding and conflict. Part of what was once known as egoism is now paraded as dignity. A part of that service once imposed by a boss on his subordinates, by men on women, and by parents on their young, is now felt to be servitude. Social authority is now becoming more flexible so as to allow the individual freer expression.

Relations with others are also changing. On the one hand, the division of labour still encourages the reproduction of social relations needed for ever-greater productivity. The demands of family life still impose the sort of relations needed for the restoration of working energy and the continuation of the species. But the growth of free time in the forms of evenings out, weekends away, holidays and retirement has multiplied encounters, intimacies and attachments. The need to renew human exchange more freely in all its guises is felt more and more strongly. Repetition and routine are much less readily accepted. Boredom comes much more quickly. There is a growing need for more spontaneous and voluntary choice, which is necessitating a relaxation of social rules imposed by professional, family and educational institutions, and is bringing about a change towards greater freedom of individual choice which, in turn, often gives rise to new conflicts.

Finally, humanity's relationship with nature itself is changing. There is the famous saying of the nineteenth century: 'It is no longer a question of looking at nature, we must change it.' This statement remains applicable to economic affairs, but as the industrial sector gives way to service industry, there is a force of opinion, becoming stronger all the time, which insists that better nature conservation is required, along with better preservation of the atmosphere, water and wild fauna against the utilitarian pillaging of industry. The ecology movement is not simply a new political direction or an expression of contempt for industrial pollution; it is also an aspect of a new style of life which takes nature into consideration. The preservation of nature in all its beauty, its purity, the virginal splendour of its seas, mountains and plains can be appreciated in the reservations, the parks and their trails. An increasing number of urban workers of all classes turn first to nature for relaxation, and also for their pleasure. So a powerful collective desire has established itself at the heart of our free time to live more and more in symbiosis with the wild flora and fauna which are threatened by the excesses of utilitarian labour, as indeed they are by the profligacy of leisure.

In short, in this emergence of new values, of a freer lifestyle in one's relations to self, others and nature, lies the central, frequently hidden, significance of leisure which is the major source of the new space and 'time for living'. This is now a chief preoccupation of the French people: of 43 percent as opposed to the 27 percent who worry most about the need for money, and the 14 percent who are worried primarily by unemployment (COFREMCA, 1982).

It is hardly surprising if problems are posed by the assimilation of these values into the tourist and holiday trades. When these practices are taken into the rural communities of our own developed countries, or into the societies of Africa, Oceania, Latin America and Asia, they often conflict with the morals and the values of the indigenous populations. Nudity on the beaches, free sexual relations, and a lack of respect for the rest time of the working population can provoke serious confrontations with local religious and secular authorities. These liberated practices can undermine ethical structures in the host countries while replacing them with nothing more than love of money and pleasure. The influx of profit-makers can impede the expression by local artists and craftsmen of their own cultural values in authentic creations. These creations are replaced by mass products which tourists buy in huge quantities. Cultural tourism – that search for authentic creation inspired by traditional art – is reduced to the consumption of standardised objects and artificial spectacles which Picard (1986) has called 'tourist culture'. The uncontrolled influence of life-styles imported by urban tourists into the rural areas of developing nations can cause profound disturbances in the very identities of the local populations, whilst simultaneously being representative of a sought-after modernisation (Lanfant, 1980).

### Interactions

So what of voluntary socio-spiritual and socio-political involvements in this new environment? Engels predicted that the free time gained by the advance of the machine would encourage worker participation in 'civic affairs'. Frederic Le Play, in his biographical studies of carpenters, seemed to conclude that, with the lessening of work time, more time would be given over to religion. Neither of these predictions has come to pass. Each confused the desirable with the realistic. Even if half of the population watches television news from time to time, 80 percent never watch televised political debates, and 92 percent never go on street demonstrations or even to mass meetings. The degree of political indifference has risen since 1973: it is estimated that participation in political groups now runs at just over 2 percent (SOFRES, 1975), and that involvement in political trade union activity is about 15 percent (SOFRES, 1985). Despite a certain reawakening of religion and religious feeling in the climate of uncertainty inherent in a period of change, regular attendance at religious ceremonies in present-day France is only in the region of 17 percent (SOFRES, 1986). In all studies of time organisation since 1966 (Szalai, 1972), the quantity of free time given over to 'social organisation', which includes all political and trade union activity, has never been more than 5 percent, which is more or less the state of play for religion, whenever it has been considered. What is most surprising is that the figure of 5 percent involvement in political activity, broadly defined, varies little between French, German, American, Polish or even Soviet towns! Why should there be this similarity in the balance of spare time despite the differences in economic and political structures? Political sociology has never sufficiently taken into account that voluntary political involvement and activity are nowadays integral parts of free-time activity, and that in this free time they are competing with other leisure activities and are being transformed by the changes in values that leisure is placing at the core of modern daily life. Socio-political activities have an obvious influence on leisure activity. Politicians seek to increase this influence, but on the whole they are blind to the limits of this action and the conditions in which it can succeed. A voluntarist illusion prevents them from properly analysing the profound shifts in values at the heart of *all* free-time activity. This illusion precludes their inventing the forms of action and popular education necessary in a modern democracy. The leisure civilisation has still to be created. We live in a leisure society, but one that is still far away from the awareness which might create a balance in social time more attuned to the development of both the individual and society.

Socially constrained time, meaning professional and family work time, are also evolving. We have already remarked that the former is being even further reduced. The same goes for family work time, though to a lesser extent. According to the relevant studies, there are two reasons for the decline in family work time. The first is the spread of domestic gadget ownership. The second is a greater evaluation by everyone, but especially by women, of their own leisure time. Work has undoubtedly become a greater concern, with the recent spread of unemployment and fears of joblessness. But there is a simultaneous reduction in the number of employees for whom work is a major source of satisfaction. Three in four now find this outside of work (SOFRES, 1975). In 1976, in France, among those in the 15–25 age group, 14 percent found work their major source of satisfaction and 67 percent found this outside work, while 40 percent thought that work ought not to be obligatory. Figures from other societies, American and European, are roughly similar (Gallup International, 1976). Given this situation, businesses' outlooks are beginning to change. Flexitime is more in evidence (Chiesi, 1981; Grossin, 1987). Workers are striving to gain freedom for initiative and voluntary participation. A selective work time revolution has begun, despite initial strong resistance in the majority of businesses.

Work in the family, now shorter, more mechanised and better shared is declining in importance as a source of happiness, especially for women, contrary to what is still often assumed. A national cross-section of women was surveyed (SOFRES, 1982) to discover the areas of social time from which they derived most pleasure. Their answers put leisure first, child care second, marriage third, and work fourth. At the same time, faced with the uncertainties of social change, some sociologists have remarked on a revival in family relationships because nowadays these are more often voluntary than imposed (Segalen, 1981).

## Two incomplete theorisations

The emergence of social time to oneself, and the corresponding evolution of other forms of time, has created a new historical situation apparently beyond the bounds of dominant sociological theories. Many theoreticians of labour, especially those of a Marxist leaning, continue to proclaim, in abstract terms, the pre-eminence of work, and insist that it is still the chief need of the human being. In this outlook, free time remains essentially a means of recouping productive strength. Georges Friedmann (1964) conceived of leisure as either a 'complement' to or a 'compensation' for work, depending on whether or not the work was skilled. In all examples of this way of thinking, free time is seen as a by-product of work and remains subordinate to it. A theory of free time or leisure as such is inconceivable. For many labour theoreticians, it appears that there can *only* be a work theory (Prudenski, 1966; Naville, 1970). And there is still a work theory lurking behind attempts to analyse leisure as consumerism, because consumption, in the final analysis, is the mirror of production. Not all labour sociologists are of this reductionist standing, but it remains a widely accepted theorisation.

Admittedly, the theorisation seems to remain at least partially valid. It is especially interesting for its political applications. It places the origins of the production of free time in the workplace, and this process is driven by a permanent scientific revolution which enables workers to produce more in less time. The time which is thus generated, along with the wealth produced, is seen to be distributed according to the relative power of the different social classes. The dominating entrepreneurial class wishes to exploit the desire for leisure by the production and sale of goods and lucrative services, and its major rule is maximum profit. The masters of production tend to imbue work and consumption with values concordant with their own conservative interests. Today, however, this perspective bears little resemblance to social reality. Firstly, it over-simplifies the motivations of all the interested parties. Under the guise of objective analysis, it projects illusory certainties and imposes a dogmatic view of labour which has no basis in the reality of the lives of many present-day workers. This objectivistic illusion is shared and sustained by some workers' political parties, and has recently been invigorated by the Polish workers' movement. The politics inspired by this movement has probably become far removed from the real desires of those whom it initially involved. Next, this theory ignores the contribution by social movements other than labour movements to the winning of free time from social institutions. Examples include the feminist movements liberating women's time, youth movements, and those of the retired who often contribute to the creation of their own leisure time. The work theory does not allow for the historical establishment of new values with the growth in free time for *all* social classes. It is blind to the dynamics of the symbolic structure of free time, and to the relative decline in the old labour values and other institutional obligations. Or else it dogmatically places the coming of the 'enjoyment' of free time second to the long hoped for end of alienation at work (Naville, 1970). We can see how much misunderstanding of the working classes of the technologically advanced societies this theory is responsible for, despite the more realistic studies which have now been carried out (Verret, 1988).

Similar accusations may be levelled against family, educational, religious and political sociology, all of which have been affected by the emergence of mass leisure. But many sociologists have responded to this new reality either by ignoring it or by trying to incorporate it into their traditional theories. This results in a double consequence: on one hand they acknowledge the increased influence, be it good or bad, of new leisure activities on already constrained or dedicated social time. But partial integration into traditional theories is misleading, because this does not take proper account of the general dynamics of the new phenomenon. Thus, family sociology, when splitting family life into work and leisure, is all too ready to talk of the 'recreational function' of the family. There are even those who see this recreation as performing a major, integrative function (Scheuch, 1972; Stoetzel, 1983). But what of personal or collective leisure time beyond the limits of the family? This is of increasing importance in all age groups, for women and men. As for educational sociology, it still tends to reduce education to obligatory school-work, using methods which are more or less accessible to the initiative and knowledge of the pupils. Yet is not leisure itself a 'parallel school?' What of a young person's, or an adult's self-education brought about by lifelong voluntary enjoyment of free time? For, it is estimated, it is in this time that two-thirds of adult learning now occurs (Johnston and Rivera, 1955; Dumazedier and Samuel, 1976), along with all those types of collective and self-training which reinforce or destroy school-based concepts. Where religious sociology is concerned, given the ritual mixture of enjoyment and ceremony in its 'festivals', it sometimes directly or indirectly extends the festival concept to encompass the complex realities of leisure. But can one, in all seriousness, simply reduce to the concept of 'festival' the whole growth, throughout leisure time, the longest of social times, of physical, manual and artistic activities for participants and spectators? And finally, political sociology rarely gives political activity its proper, relative importance among free-time activities. As far as the politics of leisure is concerned, it is but a small and often forgotten chapter of political science (Sue, 1982).

Another set of theories swings to the opposite extreme. These theories are a response to the inability of labour, family, political, educational and religious institutions to come to terms with new values which draw ever further away from the attitudes prescribed and required by the institutions. These theories speak of individualism, narcissism and a Dionysiac spirit. They developed during the 1960s in the USA, and in Europe a decade later. Some proclaim 'the end of labour'. Marcuse (1956) prophesies the replacement of the myth of Prometheus with the myth of Narcissus, and Ivan Illich proclaims the end of school (deschooling society). He proposes a rehabilitation of the forgotten brother of Prometheus, and his complete opposite, Epimetheus the industrious. From Illich's viewpoint, labour ought to throw off the chains of productivism. Labour should be, first and foremost, a source of pleasure. It should take on the trappings of ideal leisure time and become interesting, creative and convivial. This dream is reminiscent of Fourier (1973), who believed, in the 1830s, that the day should have 13 working hours to be conceived as 13 hours of pleasure. In the 1970s, this vision inspired some young townspeople to seek artisan work in rural settings, doing what they desired, with those they loved, interrupting work for pleasant conversation or artistic, physical and convivial musical activities. This is humorously portrayed by Mendras (1979). Others, Gorz (1981, 1983) for instance, predict that the controlling time in life will be free time and that labour will move towards types of 'voluntary industrial or collective autoproduction'. Paul Yonnet (1985) sees the leisure revolution as the essence of modernity. The 'mass era' will follow on from the 'crowd era'. Individuation, depoliticisation and massification will become the 'road to democracy. . . a creation of individuals'.

What of the family as an institution in these perspectives, confronted with aspirations for a 'new world in love'? It will have to disappear, or so it is claimed, otherwise it will go on becoming an ever greater obstacle to the personal and social self-expression of the individual. The true revolution is no longer in the structures, but is said to be carried in the heart of each individual finally released from antiquated family restraints. Cooper (1971) predicted 'the end of the family'. The time was supposedly ripe for emotional and sexual liberation, according to Reich (1969), when there would no longer be any institutional barriers.

Even political thought has been influenced by similar concepts. For political activity to spread more easily into free time, it is argued that it must become more festive. The goals of political conquest and the exercise of power are said to be insufficient. The desire for political commitment, it is argued, can only arise from individual enjoyment. From this attitude the famous desire of the '68 Movement was supposedly born: 'to climax on the paving stones', or again, 'below the paving flags lies the beach'. These sentiments echo the political question of the situationalists: 'What have we achieved if, when we no longer die of hunger, we die of boredom instead?' (Vaneighem, 1967). Only in the 'depoliticised atmosphere' of a gala like SOS Racisme, a multi-cultural, non-political French anti-racist movement, does the May '68 spirit of a revolution within a revolution, lie, according to Yonnet (1985).

So what may one conclude from these theories? They take seriously and analyse deeply the values created by free time but, in my view, without accounting for the limitations imposed by their birthplace in the economy for the application of these values. They do not seem to recognise the fact that it is labour which, albeit by changing and becoming less intensive, has produced these values. These theories do not account for the institutional constraints needed by any society, whatever individual desires might be aroused. These theories are as unidimensional as those discussed previously. The first set are anachronistic, the second utopian.

### A neo-dialectic theorisation

At present, a theory of leisure time *production* is called for, which will simultaneously explain the corresponding *transformation* in the totality of social times. I will call this kind of theory *dialectical*, without allying it to any specific philosophy. Hubert, a friend of Durkheim, had already, at the beginning of the twentieth century, toyed with a sociology of social times by contrasting 'sacred' time with 'profane' time. In the 1930s, Maurice Halbwachs (1968) demonstrated that social time and collective memory vary according to institutional norms. In the 1940s George Gurvitch (1969), using political time as his starting point, attempted a sociology of active and static social times. Today we need to revive this kind of sociological analysis, but starting with the production by labour of that social time which has become the longest and most valued – leisure time. The issues at stake are absolutely fundamental, for in our changing society we are concerned with the limits and the breadth of the time assigned to autonomous individualistic expression, and with the ensuing new relationships between time to oneself (leisure time) and the socially occupied or socially constrained times which our society still needs.

We must avoid partial studies and analyses, which are often misleading. The totality of social times, as distinguished from both the psychological and the cosmic times which delimit them, operates as a finite system where the constituent parts evolve and interact in a dialectical manner: what one loses in scope and influence, another gains. We have already seen this in free time having become greater and more significant than constrained professional and family work time, and within free time leisure enjoys a 90 percent domination over spiritual and political commitments. It has taken the lion's share not only through its scope, diversity and ability to attract, but also through a combination of those values which it creates and combats. With its in-depth strata of values, ideologies, dreams and myths (Eliade, 1963), it exerts a profound and secret influence on all that produce it, including labour, and that set its limits. It is a sort of social and cultural iceberg unevenly present in all contemporary social classes and categories, and also nowadays in all age groups.

It is this new social situation, and the corresponding definition of the sociological problematics, which accounts for the change, in 1984, of the Leisure Team together with those cultural models developed 30 years previously at the CNRS, into a new team under the guidance of Nicole Samuel studying 'social times, age and cultural models'. In this new team, leisure sociologists are in regular working contact with labour, family and educational sociologists and, from time to time, with religious and political sociologists. In the same year, 1984, W. Grossin and N. Samuel launched a periodical *Les Temporalistes* which attempts to gather all social science studies dedicated to a greater empirical and theoretical understanding of social times in today's society.

Labour retains primary importance since it produces free time and the means to live. We will avoid talking of the ambiguous 'need' for labour. The majority of people would gladly do without it, if only they could (Gallup, 1986). We must seek to understand better the relationships in the life of the worker between work time and time outside work. What changes are caused by unemployment? New analyses are a necessity. For instance, the traditionally conceptualised 'work–leisure' couplet is increasingly inadequate. In this misleading grouping, 'leisure' is a global term in which there is a mixture of socially constrained time (family work), socially committed time (voluntary political activity), and time for oneself (leisure). There is a further problem: given the probability that unemployment will remain high throughout the current technological revolution, we must make a distinction between *unoccupied time* (un- or under-employment which springs from the inability of the economic machine to guarantee everyone a job), and *freed time* which springs from the machine which can produce more whilst requiring less commitment from the workforce. And yet we must not forget the interrelationship of these two types of time. This interrelationship is often ignored in political discourse on the 'shock of unemployment'. There will certainly be greater solidarity required between those with paid work and those without for as long as an international agreement on controlled economic expansion remains impossible, or for as long as production cannot be encumbered by a surfeit of workers who would be no more than the unemployed dressed up as employees. We must also ensure that this problem does not obscure another, of less immediate, but greater long-term, importance: why are those moments of unemployment imposed by the economic system of free enterprise not conceived more as moments that could be added to that time freed for the development of work at home, voluntary involvement in group activities, instruction or self-instruction in disciplines forgotten since school, or even amateur or semi-professional involvement in sport, craft or art? Investigation of such problems would probably bring into question both certain contents of the mass media, especially those engendered by the dominant logic of advertising, and the linking of education and schooling. Both of these ignore the growth, in the majority of the population, of the desire and the ability for self-instruction throughout all stages of life. Finally, beyond a certain level of guaranteed income the working population can find itself faced with a choice between greater wealth and more free time. There are further choices concerning the form that freed time should take: a shorter working day, or longer weekends and holidays, or earlier retirement. These issues have already been explored by public opinion testing organisations. Sociological study of the economic, social and cultural implications of such changes is just beginning.

Karl Marx (1973, 1980) foresaw the future importance of free time; 'Time saved can be seen as serving the production of a fixed capital, a fixed capital makes a man. . . to save on labour time is to increase free time – that is to say, that time which serves human development.' 'Serves', or 'is capable' of serving development? In fact the reality is more complicated. In our current social context, time set free has sometimes served man's degradation, sometimes his development. It can serve social conformism or creativity, and social involvement or avoidance. The same problems keep recurring for the sociologist. Are the contents of the mass media, subject as they are to the constraints of advertising logic, or political propaganda, the most suitable vehicles for encouraging creative choice in one's organisation of free time? Or again, do ten years obligatory schooling prepare the individual adequately for the free choices of instruction and self-instruction throughout his or her lifetime? Once again, we are faced with the need to confront the new problems of free time, and the problems of other social times, especially in the field of education.

We always come back to the interaction between the different types of social time. The multi-form expansion of free time forces a profound revision of the meaning not only of labour but also of other socially constrained and committed times. We cannot solve this problem simply by proclaiming the advent of individualism or narcissism, which are merely the expressions of an age-old yearning. We must analyse the emergence of a new societal function. The work of Dumedzil (1968) has acquainted us with three long-established features of Indo-European civilisations: religious, war, and productive activities. The first has always associated collective rejoicing with festivals controlled by religious authorities. The second imposes both external and internal political mobilisation in times of war and peace, under the aegis of the chiefs. The last imposes a well-organised, year-round division of labour on thoroughly stratified men and women (Dumont, 1966). In contemporary society a new function is establishing itself, a fourth function, manifest in the explosion of amateur activities in the free time which has become preponderant. These amateur activities do not depend on religious ceremony, are no longer imposed by political authority, and have escaped the controls of labour. They no longer totally subjugate the individual to institutional demands, but instead achieve the opposite. Indeed, institutional demands have been relaxed, freeing great expanses of time for oneself according to the rhythms of the day, the week, the year, and the working life, so that the individual may indulge his or her desires in whatever activities he or she wishes, in free, loving or friendly individual or collective relationships. It is, of course, true that choice is never absolutely free. It is conditioned by economic, social, political and cultural considerations. Yet today these afford degrees of freedom unheard of in centuries past. That time which was once the domain of researchers and artists for their discoveries and creations, has become potential time for amateur activities by the whole workforce, the stake being the quality of life itself. It is this new societal function, centred on the spread and the limits of individual social time produced by the logic of applied labour science, which we must analyse in conjunction with all other sociological disciplines. These are having difficulty in acknowledging the place of this new arrival, mass leisure.

### Epistemological revolution?

From this point of view, those questions thrown up by the preponderance of leisure are absolutely central. Since Veblen, sociology has often demonstrated how labour, consumerism, family and social class divisions contribute to the delimitation and conditioning of leisure. We still have a long way to go to understand how leisure can create a new person who is capable of changing slowly, or through violent ruptures, the balance between individual leisure time and socially dedicated or constrained time, as well as the symbolic structure of all social times. How can we use the ideas of the founders of sociology to understand the sources and character, through the slow rise of leisure to a predominant position, of the central problems of today's society? The founders' ideas are useful for analysing the anomie and alienation inherent in certain institutions, but how can we frame the problems posed by the development of a time of relative autonomisation of the individual, linked to a relative decline in the institutional norms imposed by work, family obligations, political and religious authority? This is, in fact, the exact *opposite* problem to the questions addressed by the founders of sociology.

Is it purely by chance that leisure sociology has, until now, enjoyed only marginal status compared with the dominant sociologies of labour, education, the family, religion and politics? Harold Wilensky began to raise this question at Berkeley in the 1960s. Most sociologists who once began to study our subject have subsequently abandoned it to pursue more 'serious' work, but some have persevered. This perseverance has slowly seen the build-up, throughout North and South America, Eastern and Western Europe, of a network of 'marginals', convinced that they are pioneering a new field in sociology which will become increasingly important as society moves to a post-industrial stage. It is true that many sociological undertakings in this field have remained on a purely descriptive level. So where might we find the concepts and theories which will really be of use to us? I have always been opposed to attempts at anachronistic theorisation about socially constrained and dedicated time dating from the last century, or utopian theorisations linked to more recent trends. The emergence of leisure time and the corresponding revolution in all social time demands, I believe, an *epistemological* revolution, able to offer new paradigms better adapted to the new situation. The general sociology of Georg Simmel (1971) might be of more use to us than any other. For him, the central problem was the production of 'individuality' by 'social forms', instituted and otherwise. 'Society', he wrote, 'forms the individuality as the sea produces waves.' He distinguished 'form', entirely determined by society, from 'content', the permanent battlefield of social norms and individual requirements. Indeed, this 'content' is the heart of 'individuality' and new identities. One can easily see the potential of such a general theorisation for leisure sociology. But this potential has not yet been realised. It must be said that Simmel himself was not much interested in the future of leisure; and his essays always seem somehow unfinished. He never laid out his 'rules of sociological method'. He often intermingled philosophical and literary thought with his sociology. Someone ought, some day, to confront the different aspects of his thought and the problems of our time posed by the autonomisation of 'individuality' in leisure, while remembering its interaction with the great questions posed by other founders of sociology – Marx, Durkheim and Weber.

While awaiting such a confrontation, it could be timely to turn to one of Simmel's own sources, to a philosopher of the production of 'individuality' by the 'individuum' itself against the major trends of society, namely, Friedrich Nietzsche. It was he more than any other who imagined what a society might be like which was organised to favour the free creation in each man, by every man, of the 'superman'. This is not Nietzsche the Antichrist, or Nietzsche the ambivalent herald of war, but Nietzsche the artist of the free creation of a work, or a life-style, in opposition to the empire of social conformism or 'flat hedonism', 'transmuting those values we received on our knees'. Nor did he consider that obligatory labour might lead us to such creation. In his *Aurora*, he was fiercely critical of the servility of enforced labour. In several of his works he stood against the 'pleasure merchants' who occasioned the loss of precious time. In *Ecce Homo*, his three conditions to facilitate the march to the 'superhuman' were good nourishment, natural surroundings and time for recreation. Which nineteenth-century sociologist could have made such remarks, giving such central importance to recreational time in a society of individual creation?

The great work of Nietzsche's maturity, *Thus spake Zarathustra*, begins with a parable of great interest in questioning the predominance in everyone's life of the new leisure time, subject as it is to conditioning and social conformism of all types. It is the fable of the camel, the lion and the child. 'I will tell you of three changes of the spirit: how the spirit changes to a camel, the camel to a lion, and the lion to a child.' The camel kneels to pick up the heaviest of loads, then goes about its work in the desert. The spirit which likes to be burdened is just like the camel which, once loaded, hurries to the desert it has to cross. But at the end of the desert, the spirit becomes a lion, 'wanting to gain his freedom and rule his own desert', one which he longs to create. 'You must', is replaced by 'I want', to create new values. The lion himself is not yet able, but his strength can gain the freedom for new creation; 'the strength one must have to free oneself from the dragon of custom, servility, and dominant conformisms'. Yet what can the child do that the lion could not? And why must the 'ferocious lion' become a child? It is because we must strive for a child's innocence and gain its permanent ability to play, so that the 'game of creation' might give a greater sense of living in a society.

It is of course true that a fable is no corpus of scientific hypothesis. But is it not possible that Nietzsche's thought might inspire some part of sociology? And why not? The sociological investigation of what Gurvitch (1969) called the heterogeneity of social times stands only to benefit from an open union of the thought of the founders of sociology, especially Marx, with the thought of Nietzsche. It would thus become easier to analyse the new balance of time to oneself, and socially committed or constrained times in today's society. I feel that this union lies at the heart of the problems of general sociology at the close of the twentieth century. We must hope that an advance by leisure sociology in the study of the cultural revolution of social time will take us into the twenty-first century with better adapted sociological concepts.

## References

Boulin, J.V., J.P. Huilbant, J. Loos and P. Rosanvallon (1982) *Survey des Recherches Portant sur l'articulation du Temps de Travail et Temps Libre en Europe*. Paris Université de Paris IX-Dauphine/Centre de Recherche Travail et Société.

Chiesi, A.M. (1981) *Il Sistema degli Orari, l'organizzazione del Tempo di Lavoro nella Grande Città*. Milan: Angeli.

Cooper, D. (1971) *The Death of the Family*. London: Allen Lane.

Dumazedier, J. (1974) *Sociologie Empirique du Loisir*. Paris: Seuil. *Sociology of Leisure*. Amsterdam: Elsevier.

Dumazedier, J. (1988) *La Révolution Culturelle du Temps Libre, de 1968 à 1988*. Paris: Librairie des Meridiens.

Dumazedier, J. and M. Imbert (1967) *Espace et Loisir*, 2 vols. Paris: Centre de Recherche d'Urbanisme.

Dumazedier, J. and N. Samuel (1976) *Société Educative et Pouvoir Culturel*. Paris: Seuil.

Dumedzil, G. (1968) *Mythe et Epopée – L'idéologie des trois functions dans les Epopées des Peuples Indo-Europeens*. Paris: Gallimard.

Dumont, L. (1966) *Homo Hierarchicus*. Paris: Gallimard.

Eliade, M. (1963) *Aspects du Mythe*. Paris: Gallimard.

Fourier, C. (1973) *Le Nouveau Monde Industriel et Sociétaire*. Paris: Flammarion.

Friedmann, G. (1964) *Le Travail en Miettes*. Paris: Gallimard.

Gorz, A. (1981) *Adieux au Prolétariat*. Paris: Seuil.

Gorz, A. (1983) *Les Chemins du Paradis*. Paris: Galilee.

Grossin, W. (1987) 'Pour une Ecologie Temporelle', *Echange et Projets*, 49: 33–40.

Guillaume, M. (1986) *L'état des Sciences Sociales en France*. Paris: La Découverte.

Gurvitch, G. (1969) *La Vocation Actuelle de la Sociologie, Antecedents et Perspectives*. Paris: Presses Universitaires de France.

Halbwachs, M. (1968) *La Mémoire Collective*. Paris: Presses Universitaires de France.

Illich, I. (1970) *Deschooling Society*. New York: Harper and Row.

Johnston, J.W.C. and R. J. Rivera (1955) *Volunteers for Learning*. Chicago: Aldine.

Lanfant, M.F. (1980) 'Le Tourisme International dans le Processus d'Internalisation', *Revue Internationale des Sciences Sociales*, 1: 14–45.

Marcuse, H. (1956) *Eros and Civilisation*. London: Routledge.

Marx, K. (1973) *Grundrisse. Foundations of the Critique of Political Economy*. Harmondsworth: Penguin. (First published Moscow, 1939).

Marx, K. (1980) *Voyage au Pays de L'Utopie Rustique*. La Paradou, 13125 France: Actes Sud.

Mendras, M. and M. Forse (1983) *Le Changement Social*. Paris: Colin.

Naville, P. (1970) *Le Nouveau Leviathan. 1: De l'aliénation à la Jouissance*. Paris: Anthropos.

Picard, M. (1986) 'La Vision Balinaise du Defi Touristique', *Sociétés*, 8: 21–3.

Prudenski, G.A. (1966) *On the Methods of Time Budget Research*. Novosibirsk, USSR: Academy of Science.

Reich, W. (1969) *The Sexual Revolution*. London: Vision Press.

Reynaud, J.D. and Y. Grafmeyer (1981) *Français Qui Etes Vous?* Paris: Documentation Français.

Scheuch, E. (1972) *Soziologie der Freizeit*. Cologne: Kiepenheur and Witsch.

Segalen, M. (1981) *Sociologie de la Famille*. Paris: Colin.

Simmel, G. (1971) *On Individuality and Social Forms*. Chicago: University of Chicago Press.

Stoetzel, J. (1983) *Les Valeurs du Temps Présent*. Paris: Presses Universitaires de France.

Sue, R. (1982) *Vers une Société du Temps Libre*. Paris: Presses Universitaires de France.

Szalai, A. et al. (1972) *The Use of Time*. The Hague: Mouton.

Vaneighem, R. (1967) *Traité de Savoir-Vivre a l'Usage des Jeunes Générations*. Paris: Gallimard.

Verret, M. (1988) *La Culture Ouvrière*. Saint-Sebastien, 44230, France: ACL Edition.

Verret, M. and J. Creusen (1979) *L'Ouvrier Français*. Paris: Colin.

Yonnet, P. (1985) *Jeux, Modes et Masses, 1945–1985*. Paris: Gallimard.

# 10

# The USA: Modern Times and the New Solidarity

## Phillip Bosserman

### Modern times

The Charlie Chaplin film, *Modern Times*, remains a biting commentary on modern work in advanced industrial society. Charlie at one point is caught in the cogs of a large wheel which threatens to grind him into pieces. His situation seems hopeless, a condition possibly felt by more people than ever in the 1980s. A recent Louis Harris poll found that 70 percent of a national sample sensed a disturbing amount of stress in their lives (Harris, 1987:35).

Social scientists in the United States and elsewhere have studied the impact of the assembly line on the personal and social lives of factory workers. During the 1930s, Elton Mayo organised a team of researchers from Harvard University to observe in depth a group of workers at a General Electric Company plant. That research produced a widely read book, *The Social Problems of an Industrial Civilisation* (1945) which subsequently influenced how work was organised. In France, Georges Friedmann's studies of production workers resulted in several seminal volumes, *Où va le travail humain?* (1954), *Machine et humanisme: problèmes humains du machinisme industriel* (1946) and *Travail en miettes* (1953). Friedmann proposed in the latter book that the only hope for modern workers lay in their leisure: that leisure would have to compensate for dissatisfying, debilitating work. Clearly Charlie Chaplin's relief from his entrapment in modern work would come in his play and recreation after paid work was over. Thus, what is leisure in the USA today? I will consider it first of all as social time.

### Social time and modern times

The concept of social time has a rich sociological heritage. Emile Durkheim observed in *The Elementary Forms of Religious Life* (1915), that time is one of the fundamental categories of human life. Drawing from Immanuel Kant, Durkheim underlined how individual and social life find their framework within primordial dimensions of time and space. Both of these elements are social constructions of group life. Durkheim's student, Halbwachs, expanded on this notion in his seminal work, *La mémoire collective* (1950). He posited that each society has multiple time frames according to various groups' experiences of their everyday lives. George Gurvitch expanded and refined these ideas of Durkheim and Halbwachs in his *La multiplicité des temps sociaux* (1962), translated into English as *The Spectrum of Social Time* (1964). He was the first sociologist to attempt to place the study of time as a social construct at the centre of sociological theory. He recognised that 'every society must attempt to unify, even if only relatively, [the] multiple manifestations of time and attempt to arrange them in a hierarchy' (Gurvitch, 1964: 13). More recently Georges Balandier (1963), Jean Ziegler (1971), and Edward Hall (1969) have added to our understanding of social time in their studies of perceptions and social constructions of time in the different cultures of Africa and Latin America. Edward Tiryakian (1981) has expanded our comprehension of the concept in applying it to the uprooted, the refugees within present-day modernity (see Robert Lauer (1981)). The most recent refinement of the concept is in the work of members of the research team at the CNRS, previously headed by Joffre Dumazedier and now by Nicole Samuel. This team has made probably the most systematic and fruitful study of free time and leisure that any group or individual in the world has been able to accomplish over the last 25 years. Samuel's book, *Le temps libre: un temps social* (1984), written with the assistance of Madelaine Romer, makes the point that free time is a complex of multiple social times. Within these, new social relationships and values are emerging. The outcomes include new life-styles and new dimensions to social life that we are just now beginning to comprehend and appreciate.

Specifically, we may now detail what we mean by social time. It has to do with the rhythms, cadences or periodicities which people interacting within groups create as part of the structure and ordering of their group life. More than this, these social times are 'institutionalised by the culture patterns of a civilisation within periods of history' (Samuel and Romer, 1984: 9). Within each society, among the different subgroups and subcultures, one finds distinctive social times common to their members. There is a multiplicity and heterogeneity among these various social times, as both Gurvitch and Halbwachs previously noted.

So what are some important types of modern social times? Samuel and Romer first point to *work time* including the time it takes to get to and from the job. Because education is most frequently tied to occupational careers, school time can be treated as a part of work time. However, great changes are under way in this institutional sector. A second type of time is what people allocate for family obligations. A third type is the free time from both paid work and family obligations. This multifaceted time includes religious practices, political obligations, whether for a political party or a voluntary association, and leisure. Each of these times is separate and distinct. Reflecting the debt they owe to Joffre Dumazedier, Samuel and Romer define leisure as that part of free time which is oriented towards personal fulfilment. A person chooses to do a certain thing because 'this interests me'. There is no utilitarian goal, no hidden agenda, but simply a desire to do this because of the satisfaction and pleasure it, in and of itself, gives.

## A new solidarity

Having outlined what we mean by social time I now want to describe exactly what free time, as a multiplicity of social times, is creating in modern society. Nearly ten years ago I had the privilege of being part of a summer seminar organised and led by Edward Tiryakian at Duke University. During that summer we reread some important works of Emile Durkheim. I was able to reconsider Durkheim's *La division du travail social* (1893). Durkheim followed the lead of the founder of sociology, St Simon, as the latter had tried to come to grips with the immense, far-reaching, dual social forces of the French and industrial revolutions. St Simon had pleaded for a sociology of modernity and, indeed, saw its birth in the crucible of the wrenching revolutionary changes. Durkheim likewise saw this modernity in the maturation of the industrial revolution in France. French society was then struggling to establish a democratic government within the Third Republic. Durkheim defined his own *raison d'être* to establish sociology as a bona fide subject at university level. At the same time, he was heavily involved in trying to make the Third Republic work. To establish sociology at the university level, Durkheim had to combat the entrenched attitudes which reduced explanations of human behaviour to psychological and biological causes. Durkheim emphasised in a systematic way the influence of social forces on human behaviour. He argued that these forces had a reality which allowed them to be studied concretely and scientifically, and posited that a new type of social order had emerged as a result of industrialisation and urbanisation. This new type of social arrangement was the result of the way in which people related to one another within an industrialising and urbanising environment. He called social order *solidarity*, and specified that modernity's solidarity was *organic*. The key to this organic solidarity was the division of labour.

Durkheim's description of the division of labour went beyond that of economists. The latter saw it as the source of more efficient production. Durkheim sought to expose the underlying moral or normative basis of any society, especially modern society. Every society must ultimately rest on a moral order, a solidarity, and for Durkheim the key question was how to explain what holds modern society together. His conclusion was that the division of *social* labour keeps the social body intact, making co-operation become an imperative for all who participate in the society. In order that each individual may function in his or her role, that individual co-operates with others who are performing different, essential functions. By virtue of this interdependence, each individual gains greater autonomy, thus opening up the system, providing for expansion and creativity with increased efficiency. To quote Durkheim:

> Whereas [mechanical solidarity] implies that individuals resemble each other, this type [organic] preserves their difference. The first is possible only in so far as the individual personality is absorbed into the collective personality; the second is possible only if each one has a sphere of action which is peculiar to him; that is, a personality. It is necessary, then, that the collective conscience leave open a part of the individual conscience in order that special functions may be established there, functions which it cannot regulate. The more the region is extended, the stronger is the cohesion which results from this solidarity. . . the activity of each is as much more personal as it is more specialised. . . .Society becomes more capable of collective movement, at the same time that each of its elements has more freedom of movement. (Durkheim, 1933: 131)

Durkheim stated that individual freedom expands with the division of labour. The organic solidarity of modern society provides a moral order because of the interdependence of the participants, the parts, in the organic whole. The direction of this process is evident, the outcome is positive. To long for the good old days is to overlook the potential good which the increasing division of social labour can make possible.

It is not self-evident that Durkheim's optimism has been justified by subsequent developments. Many people today are not experiencing greater individual freedom and autonomy as a result of the increasing division of social labour. On the contrary, large-scale bureaucratic organisations have tended to stifle autonomy (see Gurvitch, 1957: 220). Durkheim did realise that people could be caught increasingly in anomie, a state of normlessness, because they lacked integration into a group – almost a contradiction in terms for Durkheim. In the celebrated preface to the second edition of *The Division of Labour in Society* (1933) he called for a reworking of the old 'corporation' which had functioned so well in the Middle Ages and earlier in Rome.

> Instead of being limited only to the workers of a city, it must enlarge in such a way as to include all the members of the occupation scattered over the territory, for in whatever region they are found, whether they live in the city or the country, they are all solidary, and participate in a common life. (1933: 24)

Though Durkheim was an evolutionary theorist in many ways, I would argue that societal discontinuity was what he mainly saw. He believed that a new type of social order was emerging, which he named organic solidarity. Today, in the 1980s, we seem to be travelling through a similar system break in which another new type of solidarity is hoving into sight, and indeed may already be upon us. Periods of time away from paid employment and family duties have increased enormously over the past few decades. This fact is one of the deeply hidden dimensions of present-day modernity. Time without work has increased to such an extent that the major proportion of the average citizen's waking hours is now in these time zones. New values, norms of behaviour redefining life-styles, life courses and life foci are emerging, to such an extent that sociology and the other social sciences are required to take this sector seriously. Historical discontinuity in present-day societies is resulting in another new type of solidarity, one which I shall call *personal communalism*. In this new phase of modernity several contradictory, dialectical movements are visible. First, the advanced type of capitalism which predominates in post-industrial societies requires high levels of consumption to remain viable. Consumption requires time. One reason for giving workers time off from their jobs, such as a full Saturday with pay, was always to leave them this essential time to consume. The systematic elimination of the Blue Laws, as they were known in the United States, which required stores to be closed on Sundays, has added another day for convenient consumption. Second, a de-structuration and corresponding restructuration of the organisation of employment has taken place during recent decades. Durkheim distinguished between technical and social labour. Technical labour is divided into a series of simple movements each of which is accomplished by a different worker. The net social result of such a division of labour is that the worker is further and further removed from a sense of being involved in a whole creative process. The division of social labour comprises all other aspects of work, organising it into specialised groups which eventually become occupations. The division of social labour's most remarkable effect is not that it increases the output of the divided functions, but *it renders them solidary*. Through it individuals are linked to one another. Without it they would be independent. Instead of developing separately, they pool their efforts, they are solidary, but it is a solidarity which is not merely a question of the short time in which services are exchanged, but one which extends much further. (Durkheim, 1933: 60–1).

Nowadays new technologies are reducing the amount of time that human workers need to spend producing goods. The workforce has been rapidly shifting into services. This in turn has affected rhythmic patterns of work. Those workers remaining in manufacturing have seen their work time decrease dramatically. Greater flexibility in work scheduling is also a spin-off. Workers can more easily choose what hours they will work at paid employment each day, week, month, year and even throughout their lifetimes (Best, 1980). Presumably if not as many workers are labouring at jobs, and if the jobs themselves take fewer hours because of automation, then the environment, physical resources and personal energy are saved. Technological displacement does create severe dislocations and much pain for those employees laid off. Hardest hit are categories such as the aged, ethnic minorities, youth, and single female heads of households and their children.

At the same time as the workforce shifts into the service sector of the economy, there is a corresponding increase in the social division of labour. Greater specialisation is occurring in the services, leading to the separation of work from free time. Monica Suber's research on professional workers forcefully shows that 'there is little support for the contention that leisure identity compensates or is generalised from work identity'. Leisure has its own intrinsic rewards, social integration and self-identity, and is not simply a response to the work situation (Suber, 1983: 448). The services organise their work time frames differently. Moreover, worker demand is for extending the block periods of free time from paid work. Longer weekends, vacations, sabbaticals, later entry into the workforce, earlier retirement and greater longevity are new phenomena prompting a reassessment of societal goals and norms. De-structuration of employment time leads to a general questioning of such matters as full employment, the workload, the length of the paid work day, week, year and life, and the centrality of employment. Does the work ethic encompass non-work time and, if so, what happens to the distinction between employment and non-employment? These seemingly contradictory movements produce a fascinating result. Time is increasingly becoming free from paid work because:

1. The economy requires consumption, and free time is necessary for people to consume.
2. Technological innovation liberates people from work by reducing paid work time while forcing others into unemployment.
3. The increased specialisation of employment in the services, and a concomitant rationalisation of this creates pressures for freeing time in larger and larger blocks.

Paid employment as an activity central to one's being is decreasingly important to people. It is a means to other goals which are now primary. Using Durkheim as a guide, I can say that just as the social division of work is that which makes up the major part of work in all its ramifications, so the social division of free time or leisure time makes up the major aspect of this social time complex of modernity. And because of its sheer size and presence in modern society we are witnessing the formation of a new type of solidarity. My task now is to spell out the features of this solidarity which I call *personal communalism*.

### The contours of personal communalism as a new solidarity

Before I describe this new social solidarity, I want to add a final element to the explanation of why we have now reached a global turning point. Pitirim A. Sorokin stated in his *Social and Cultural Dynamics* (1937) that there is

> the *existence of limits* in the linear direction of most social processes. . .
> that sooner or later the trend reaches its limit, and then the process turns
> aside into a new path. This means the denial of the existence of a
> perpetual main linear trend in history and most of the social processes.
> (1937: 187)

The evidence I have given thus far concerning the mutation in the present social times, in their rhythmic patterning and framework, is a good example of Sorokin's *principle of limitation*. There are a number of such indicators that throw light on the path of current social processes which are leading in new directions. Edward Tiryakian (1967) has catalogued other indicators based on his study of revolutionary periods, especially the crucial decades just before violent political uprising. He notes:

1. The dislocation and change in size of populations.
2. The appearance of new religious movements.
3. Marked change in the sexual habits of a population in which old norms no longer hold.
4. The appearance of radically new forms of artistic expression.

All of these represent, then, a change in direction of the social order, and arrival at a new boundary or limit. In a broader context we can see that our world is in a general crisis which indicates that such limits have been reached. First, we have reached the end of any reliance on war as a means of resolving conflicts. The nuclear bomb and the ever-increasing miniaturisation of tactical nuclear weapons make warfare an impossible option. Second, the ecological order is in serious trouble. Maximum economic growth is no longer a viable goal. Third, the new technologies already referred to are freeing us from toil, and causing vast dislocations of people from jobs. New life cycles must be the order of the day. Finally, the injustice and lack of dignity for persons of colour, the old and very young, women, and those who hold certain unorthodox beliefs are so great that a reversal is necessary. Each one of these makes it imperative that the world choose another direction or sink into chaos. That other direction is what I would like now to describe. This direction leads to a different social order, what Durkheim was wont to call a solidarity. What are its contours?

### As a global society

I begin this schema of a new solidarity by turning to my mentor at the University of Paris who had a very good idea of what the future might hold. Georges Gurvitch (1964) described several types of what he called global society. The type I want to introduce here is a global society which Gurvitch concluded had not existed, and as yet did not exist, anywhere on the globe. However, hints of what it will be like have begun to appear. He called this new type a *planned, decentralised, pluralistic and collectivist society*. The concept of collectivism seems out of place with the other attributes. I prefer to emphasise a global society which is decentralist, pluralistic, planned, personal and communal.

Gurvitch saw this global society having a 'we-ness' which emphasised community and communion as the key types of social relationship. I would characterise these as primary, face-to-face, *gemeinschaftlich*, and folk in nature. Kai Erikson in his now classic study of a group of Appalachian villages wiped out by a devastating flood (Erikson, 1976: 187) calls this type of relationship 'communality'. The relationships are like those of a family. Persons in the community are 'neighbour people'. They have what Herbert Gans calls a 'person orientation'. Gurvitch went on to describe how the global social structure would be small scale, centring on local groupings in which factories, schools and utilities would be owned and operated by local groups in co-operation with larger governmental units. The state would be decentralised. Planning would be based on free consensus, free expression of ideas; the whole would be open to the creative and innovative, in both ideas and persons in unforeseen and imaginative roles, embedded in open and diverse voluntary associations. Knowledge would be free of ideology and open to everyone both to create and to learn; artistic expression and consumption would be one means of social control; a creative morality based on virtue and responsibility would be the other means that would dominate. An emerging new culture would give to persons and groups every means necessary to dominate techniques and instruments of that culture rather than these dominating human beings (see Henry, 1963).

The types of social time that will rule in this new society will be explosive and creative. The gap will close between the structural arrangements – institutions, in current sociological parlance, a concept which Gurvitch detested – and real, everyday lives played out in what Gurvitch called *the total social phenomena*. The extraordinary thing about Gurvitch's scenario is that he sketched it out in the early 1960s. This global type of society had not then come into being, but he saw hints of its arrival. Yugoslavia was a particularly important experiment to examine according to Gurvitch. Aspects of Israeli society and the northern European countries, especially the Danish experiment with rural co-operatives, learning and service, were also worth noting.

### A decentralised future?

As Gurvitch viewed the future he sketched a decentralised, communalist global society. This was his conception of what I have been calling the new solidarity. Durkheim's dichotomy of mechanical and organic solidarities, the former being those which fit pre-industrial or small-scale societies, and the latter appropriate for industrial societies, is now over 100 years old. The industrial era has given way to a new post-industrial type. I am aware of all the shortcomings of this appellation. However, something has happened. 'Everything tied down is comin' loose', to quote Gabriel in Marc Connelly's *Green Pastures*. The present industrial, organic or *Gesellschaft* type of society has reached its limits. It is now taking a different direction. That direction is as Gurvitch presumed and Sorokin suggested. The latter saw three possible types of value system: ideational, sensate and idealistic. He strongly hinted that the next direction would be towards the ideational, a system based upon the reality principle of a supersensory and super-rational deity, spiritual force or presence. The last period of this type in

Western history was the Middle Ages. 'A basically similar major premise respecting the super-rational and supersensory reality underlay also the integrated culture of Brahmanic India, the Buddhist and Taoist cultures, Greek culture from the eighth to the end of the sixth century BC, and some other cultures' (Sorokin, 1941: 19). Theodore Roszak projects somewhat the same future in his *Where the Wasteland Ends*. He writes:

> My argument has been that the single vision, the ruling sensibility of the scientific worldview, has become the boundary condition of human consciousness within urban industrial culture, the reigning Reality Principle, the whole meaning of sanity. On that Reality Principle and on the artificial environment which is its social expression, the technocracy has been raised as a benevolent despotism of elitist expertise. Whatever else we must do to supplant the technocracy, we must, indispensably, throw off the psychic stole from which it draws its strength. This is necessary not only if democracy is to be preserved, but also if we are to be healed of the death-in-life alienation, which is the psychic price of single vision. . . Nothing less, I think, than that we should undertake to repeal urban-industrialism not in a spirit of grim sacrifice, but in the conviction that the reality we want most to reside in lies beyond the artificial environment. And so we should move freely and in delight toward the true post-industrialism: as a world awakened from its sick infatuation with power, growth, efficiency, progress as if from a nightmare. (Roszak, 1973: 379–80)

No doubt Roszak saw that the so-called advanced societies had arrived at the boundary line of urban industrialism. Society could not afford to go any further. We have cashed in our chips and must turn in a different direction. That direction, for Roszak, is the following:

> The real solution to the urban problem is massive deurbanisation. We must find ways out of the city for those who want to leave. Well-developed rural and village life, autonomous small towns must become a live option, a necessary kind of variety. And I am not referring to villages and towns that are characterless metropolitan satellites. Ideally, as in ancient Attica, the country round about should be regionally integrated with the opportunities of an accessible, humanly scaled polis. The gates of Athens respired rural dwellers in and out of the city in a regular rhythm; that was one of the secrets of its vitality. (1973: 384)

Roszak essentially is returning to Sorokin's ideational reality principle and Gurvitch's future global society. I think Gurvitch thought of it as a *necessary* future. This reading of a new social solidarity is taken up by another social critic, Richard Louv, who visited a number of places in the United States in which Americans were seeking some alternative living arrangements from urban industrialism. He wandered about these enclaves and came away sensing that the inhabitants were still a part of the problem. To seek private shelter from the realities of the social world about oneself is, like the ostrich, to hide one's head in the sand. Louv conceives of a 'Third Vision' which is neither the old urban-industrial model, nor an escapist dream of some who have fled urban blight and pressures.

> This third vision would encourage the resettling of America, if done with a sense of stewardship for the land, if done not just for a few of the lucky, but also for those pushed out of the old cities and old industries. It would encourage small farms and part-time farms and the gradual growth of small towns, while discouraging buckshot development and environmental destruction. It would encourage the trend, so far more wishful thinking than reality, toward urban villages within the anticities – not just for a privileged few, but for a mixture of economic and racial groups. It would discourage the privatisation of the public responsibility. (Louv, 1983: 301)

In essence Louv's vision of the new solidarity required for the post-industrial period recognises that a balance must be struck between the private and the public spheres, the individual and the communal. In America we have so overemphasised the individual to the neglect of the community that both communal bonding and personal responsibility have little meaning. The crisis of public morality among our elected officials at the highest levels of government is a powerful testimony to this fact. The new solidarity will require decentralised urban centres where people are closer to their elected representatives and where the qualities of *Gemeinschaft* personal and economic relationships obtain, where an understanding of what the stewardship of the earth means has a chance to permeate citizens' lives, where *small is beautiful* and large-scale social structures and environments are ugly, where the peaceful ways of gentleness and compassion predominate because the society encourages what Sam Keen suggests, namely, 'touch, sensuality, aesthetic appreciation and caring sexuality' (Satin, 1987: 1). All of these qualities are at the core of the new solidarity required for the post-industrial era. We either choose these alternatives or we continue on a road which will lead to the eventual decline in the quality of our physical and spiritual lives.

### Entre-temps

Meanwhile, we have the time to accomplish this turn-around. I am envisaging and proposing a radical, revolutionary change in the core values of our industrial societies. This revolutionary change is one for survival. Each social solidarity has central core values, what Talcott Parsons called its 'cybernetic control lever' (Parsons et al., 1961: 61). Harking back to the mutation in time allocation which is a major structural feature of post-industrial society, the resultant free time dominates the waking hours of our average lifetimes. Modern industrial societies have advanced the opportunity for education among their citizens. Well-educated citizens thus represent an increasingly critical mass. They are critical in the sense of their size, and in that they have both the mental equipment and the time to look critically at their societies and at their individual and collective lives, to make judgements about what they want their future to be. Each society needs to encourage its citizens to assess their situations critically, and to envisage creatively what they collectively desire for the future. The types of social times Gurvitch noted for his projected global society included creative time and that of 'pushing forward'. He saw this society as fraught with contradictions and conflicts. Hence, either the type of time which alternates between advance and delay, or the time that lags behind rather than looks ahead could be favoured. Laws and rules to make sure of a certain level of equality emphasise these types of time, and such will necessarily be the case in the decentralised, pluralistic, social solidarity that Gurvitch projected. The boundaries of the present system are being stretched to breaking point. A turning in the direction of decentralisation is thus imperative.

Another aspect of this turning is towards simplicity. Generally speaking, life has become overly complicated, overloaded with too many sensors and stressors making life nearly unbearable. Kai Erikson, from whom I quoted earlier, described in his book, *Everything In Its Path*, the destruction of 14 communities by a terrible flood which was the result of a coal-mining company's neglect. He went on to assert that in many respects modern life itself is a disaster. By this he meant that the daily grind is a chronic disaster for many people:

> One does not need to visit the homes of the wretched to find symptoms of trauma, for there are ample indications that modern life itself can become a principal cause of traumatic reaction. One of the long-term effects of modernisation as we know it has been to distance people from primary associations and to separate them from the nourishing roots of community, and the costs of population. (1976: 256)

Erikson goes on to say that the neuroses infecting the modern population are those brought on by first, an increasing relativism 'in which people come to feel the lack of fixed moral landmarks and established orthodoxies. . . . How will people develop a secure sense of self in the midst of relativity that threatens to encompass everything?' Second, by an age of impotence

> in which fewer and fewer people are able to derive meaningful satisfaction from the act of producing something that is both sanctioned and needed by the rest of the community – goods, offspring, or something else – and come to the conclusion that their presence on the planet does not make very much difference to anyone. (1976: 257)

Third, an age of sensory overload is upon us

> in which there is so much diverging information to absorb, so many moralities competing for one's attention, so many contradictory sensations to respond to, that people without the right kind of insulation run the risk of developing scar tissue from ear to ear. One result of all this is apt to be a flattening of affect, a sheer anaesthetisation of the moral and cognitive sense, as if one were suffering from a kind of 'psychological concussion'. (1976: 258)

No wonder the ringing cry of Thoreau penetrates our psyches: simplify, simplify, simplify!

So it is that a movement calling for *voluntary simplicity* has become significant to a growing number of people in the United States. Duane Elgin, in his book *Voluntary Simplicity* (1981), describes in detail this movement towards a 'way of life that is outwardly simple and inwardly rich'. What does this life-style mean? Richard Gregg puts it this way:

> Voluntary simplicity involves both an inner and outer condition. It means singleness of purpose, sincerity and honesty within, as well as avoidance of exterior clutter, of many possessions irrelevant to the chief purpose of life. It means an ordering and guiding of our energy and our desires, a partial restraint in some directions in order to secure greater abundance of life in other directions. It involves a deliberate organisation of life for a purpose. (quoted in Elgin, 1981: 31)

Voluntary simplicity is a manner of living that makes a 'deliberate choice to live with less in the belief that more of life will be returned to us in the process. . . a paring back of the superficial aspects of our lives so as to allow more time and energy to develop the heartfelt aspects of our lives' (Elgin, 1981: 33). Voluntary simplicity is not at all simple. Elgin suggests that 'to integrate and maintain a skilful balance between the inner and outer aspects of our lives is an enormously challenging and continuously changing process' (1981: 33). Elgin provides some valuable insights into just how we may live more voluntarily simple lives. There are both written and living 'manuals' or guides to such a way of life. These include whole communities such as the inner-city communes in places like San Francisco, Boston and Baltimore. I think of the Jonah House community, whose director is Philip Berrigan, as a case in point. The members of this community live outwardly simple, but inwardly abundant and expressive lives. They are dedicated to a peaceful world and to a just society. Their whole endeavour as a community is centred on these purposes. They find great satisfaction in what they are doing. *New Options* (Satin, 1987), *The New Age Journal* (Graves), *The Futurist* (Cornish) and *Mother Earth News*, are good sources of ideas for alternative modes of living. It is important to underline that no one way describes voluntary simplicity. It is contextual and situational to each individual and group.

## Conclusion

In this chapter I have tried to sketch out why I think we are experiencing the emergence of a new type of social solidarity in the USA in the 1980s. We saw in the work of Emile Durkheim how this same kind of thinking was applied to the coming of industrial society. Following his lead, it can be argued that we are now seeing the breakdown of modern society. Hence the need to extrapolate the appearance of another new social solidarity which I have called personal communalism. All social systems have boundaries, and drawing from Pitirim Sorokin's insightful work, it can be posited that the boundaries of modern, industrial society have now been reached. We, by necessity, must now make a radical turn in a different direction or face certain ruin as a people and a planet. The very size and density of our modern life pleads for decentralisation in which small is beautiful and less is more.

This calls for a new value structure. A contemporary social movement called *voluntary simplicity* represents such a turning, involving a new set of core values which drives a society. The transformation required is both internal to the individual and the collective minds, and external in terms of the behaviour of both. This chapter began by describing a structural transformation of immense importance that has taken place within modern societies, which is the radical change in social times. The subsequent creation of free time, a multiple collection of social times, means that citizens of contemporary societies have the available time from paid work to address the crisis of our age. For this free time is chosen time, discretionary time. To be sure there are enormous social forces and constraints upon this time, particularly from the economy, based as it still is on growth and the subsequent need for citizens to consume more and more. But this very growth is one of the factors producing the crisis we sense. We have reached the boundary of an economy dependent on consumerism. Crude material wealth does not bring fulfilment. There is a profound poverty in our abundance of things. Indeed less is more, and voluntary simplicity is ultimately gratifying.

Another dimension to this crisis lies in the very size of our institutions, our cities, and the complexity of modern, technocratic, expert-centred, fragmented life. Small is beautiful; decentralised, de-urbanised communality is the structural rearrangement which can rescue personal relationships from the anomic despair now plaguing their survival. Too much of modern life is a disaster. Again, the time to choose, create and plan for a global society which is decentralist, pluralist, personal and communalist is here. Whether the people of modernity will choose to put into place this new social solidarity is unknown. Yet the limits are upon modern society and a turning around, a radical redirection is required. I think the evidence points to such a redirection. Can we really believe that human beings will be so stupid as to march like lemmings into the sea? I think not. For within the context of free time there are surely enough people who will plan a truly human future.

## References

Balandier, G. (ed.) (1963) *Le Temps et la Montre en Afrique.* Bienne: Fédération Horlogière Suisse.

Best, F. (1980) *Flexible Life Scheduling.* New York: Macmillan.

Cornish, E. (ed.) *The Futurist*, 4916 Saint Elmo Ave, Bethesda, Maryland.

Durkheim, E. (1893) *De la Division du Travail Social: Étude sur l'organisation des Sociétés Supérieurs.* Paris: Alcan.

Durkheim, E. (1915) *The Elementary Forms of Religious Life.* London: Allen and Unwin. (First published Paris: Alcan, 1912).

Durkheim, E. (1933) *The Division of Labor in Society.* New York: Macmillan.

Elgin, D. (1981) *Voluntary Simplicity.* New York: William Morrow.

Erikson, K. (1976) *Everything In Its Path.* New York: Simon and Schuster.

Friedmann, G. (1946) *Machine et Humanisme: Problèmes Humains du Machinisme Industriel.* Paris: Gallimard.

Friedmann, G. (1953) *Le Travail en Miettes.* Paris: Gallimard.

Friedmann, G. (1954) *Où Va le Travail Humain?* Paris: Gallimard.

Graves, F. (ed.) *The New Age Journal.* PO Box 853, Farmingdale, New York.

Gurvitch, G. (1957) *La Vocation Actuelle de la Sociologie,* Vol. 1. Paris: Presses Universitaires de France.

Gurvitch, G. (1962) *La Multiplicité des Temps Sociaux.* Paris: Centre de Documentation Universitaire.

Gurvitch, G. (1964) *The Spectrum of Social Time.* Dordrecht: D. Reidel.

Halbwachs, M. (1950) *La Mémoire Collective.* Paris: Presses Universitaires de France.

Hall, E. (1969) *The Hidden Dimension.* New York: Anchor Books.

Harris, L. (1987) *Inside America.* New York: Vintage.

Henry, J. (1963) *Culture Against Man.* New York: Random House.

Lauer, Robert (1981) *Temporal Man.* New York: Praeger.

Louv, R. (1983) *America II*. New York: Penguin.

*Mother Earth News*, PO Box 70, Hendersonville, N. Carolina.

Parsons, T., E. Shils, K.D. Naegele and J.R. Pitts (eds) (1961) *Theories of Society*. New York: The Free Press.

Roszak, T. (1973) *Where the Wasteland Ends*. New York: Anchor Books.

Samuel, N. and M. Romer (1984) *Le Temps Libre: un Temps Social*. Paris: Librairie de Meridiens.

Satin, M. (ed.) (1987) *New Options*, 2005 Massachusetts Ave, Washington DC.

Sorokin, P. (1937) *Social and Cultural Dynamics*, Vol. 1. New York: Bedminster Press.

Sorokin, P. (1941) *The Crisis of Our Age*. New York: E.P. Dutton.

Suber, M. (1983) 'Work and Leisure: the Problem of Identity among Professional Workers', *Loisir et Société*, 6: 429–56.

Tiryakian, E. (1967) 'A Model of Societal Change and its Lead Indicators', in S. Kalusner (ed.), *The Study of Total Societies*. New York: Praeger.

Tiryakian, E. (1981) *Sociological Determinisms of Uprootedness*. Durham: Centre for International Studies, Duke University.

Ziegler, Jean (1971) *Le Pouvoir Africain*. Paris: Editions du Seuil.

# 11

# International Tourism Resists the Crisis

## *Marie-Françoise Lanfant*

### Always growing?

In 1950 40 million tourists crossed national borders. By 1963 there were 93 million, and 310 million in 1985 when the World Tourist Organisation predicted between 460 and 480 million in the 1990s.

It is generally believed that modern tourism began in England at the beginning of the seventeenth century with the so-called Grand Tour, a cultural practice which became widespread among young aristocrats who, before making their entrance to the adult world, completed their education by travelling on the continent. The nineteenth and twentieth centuries saw an extension of these practices to other social classes, but mass tourism commenced only in the 1920s, firstly in the USA, when millions of cars began pouring off production lines and enlarging the leisure opportunities of urban and suburban populations as did the introduction of paid holidays during the 1930s. In Europe tourism became a mass phenomenon only after the Second World War. There was then talk of an explosion, a tidal wave, a rush, an ant-hill gone mad. At that time, mass tourism was seen as the democratic fulfilment of individuals' demand for holidays. Then came the spread of international tourism, which was seen as a step beyond the boundaries of domestic holiday-making. The entire phenomenon of tourism and its worldwide expansion were explained by individuals' demands for holidays and leisure, born out of industrial society.

It is more difficult to explain the subsequent apparently unstoppable rise in international tourism purely in these terms. The uninterrupted increase during the past few decades has impressed all observers. All obstacles have been overcome. The fears of those who, from time to time, have imagined that tourist activity was severely threatened have proved mistaken. During 1968–9, the period of student riots in Europe and America, there was a decline in the growth rate of international tourism, but only for a year. The 1974 fuel crisis led to an actual decline in tourism, but this downturn lasted only for one summer. In 1975 growth picked up again and reached a record rate of 11.8 percent in 1977, which led experts to conclude that people did not want to do without their holidays. Growth continued at an average annual rate of 8 percent until 1980 when the world was hit by a new energy crisis. In 1982 there was zero growth in international tourism and some forecasts were again downwards, but not for long, because in the following year the upward movement was resumed. At each of these junctures the impending crises were checked because the tourist industry was able to react quickly in response to depressing trends, strengthening its ability to control demand and the market.

Crisis is a scare word, a way of calling for unceasing vigilance. It appears necessary to react quickly so that the usual customers' desire for travel is not blunted. Crises must be foreseen, anticipated even, and preparations made in advance. Measures are prepared to alleviate the effects of panic which an untimely rumour spread through the media might cause. The tourist industry has learnt how to thrive on crises. Edgar Morin's (1981) observation seems particularly apt: 'We are in a time when crisis is no longer an accident in our societies but their way of life'. Alain Minc (1982) has also argued that, 'Capitalism thrives on permanent imbalance; it is its nourishment, its fountain of youth'.

During the years when industrialised societies experienced high rates of economic growth, the steep rise in international tourism was impressive, but could be easily explained in terms of the increased average incomes of working populations. Since the mid-1970s, however, with pockets of poverty becoming deeply embedded in even the most prosperous societies, this explanation has seemed less plausible. Some commentators have argued that tourism has developed a resistance, an immunity, to the depressions that have afflicted developed economies. One observes that 'Its recent rate of increase has been double the average rate of growth of total consumption in the countries concerned' (Moussis, 1986). Some citizens today appear prepared to accept restrictions in areas previously considered vital in order to continue to travel. What drives them on?

**The marketing of tourism**

In part, at least, it is the tourist industry that now drives the tourists. The growth of tourism has become increasingly supply driven. Tourism first came to be regarded as an industry in the 1930s, a period of economic protectionism. Under threat of the great crisis, governments strove to keep their trade in surplus, and began treating and regulating movements of people just like movements of goods and other assets. Tourists were likened to goods, and their travels to import–export movements. Since then the economic factor has gradually taken precedence over social and cultural factors in the growth and regulation of international tourism. Great interests operate in tourism today. Everywhere in the world we are seeing an abundance of initiatives to create tourist products and to become involved in a flourishing business. New practices in the marketing of tourism find ways to link supply and demand ever more closely by defining groups of customers and networks of consumption. Governments exalt the idea of tourism, and make it a priority in their economic strategies.

In 1963 the United Nations solemnly proclaimed the importance of tourism's contribution to the economies of developing countries. At the instigation of the World Bank, many underdeveloped countries have subsequently striven to realise the value of their land and to create attractive tourist products. Thus, within these countries, vast enclaves have been formed which are cut off from centres of population and aim at attracting hundreds of thousands of foreigners, particularly from rich countries. The tourist areas are empty for much of the year, and during the tourist season some are completely sealed off and forbidden to natives. The Maldives are an extreme case. This vast area of some 100,000 square kilometres, made up of more than 1200 islands which extend for 800 kilometres through the Indian Ocean, has over the years been turned into a string of island resorts, each with its own complex of hotels and services for tourists. Throughout the world we are seeing the creation of similar tourist resorts and services reserved exclusively for holiday-makers. We see rising up, in areas which not long ago were undeveloped or on the way to becoming deserted, beautiful architectural constructions. But to achieve this, the land is cleared of native populations, communities are broken up, tribes of nomads with no fixed dwelling who for years crossed these lands where they found water, food and temporary resting places, are driven out. Landscapes are being remodelled, shore-lines enlarged, and villages and whole regions transformed into resorts. Tourist developments are multiplying with a luxury and display of amazing inventiveness. Today almost all nations are trying to gain the benefits of a tourist trade which can produce so much profit, a '*sopra piu*' as Troisi (1940) would have said. This situation can arouse fierce rivalries, with more and more countries forever entering into competition to attract the maximum number of tourists, the new golden hordes, the bearers of foreign currency.

During the 1980s, with affluent societies themselves experiencing an economic crisis, tourist activity has become an even more attractive proposition. Once considered merely supplementary by most industrialised countries, tourism is now regarded by many as a major economic activity of the future. So we now see these countries adopting postures and practices which, in the past, they assigned to poorer nations. Tourism has become a major factor in the economic development programmes of post-industrial societies. Tourist activity is believed to bring considerable benefits: creation of employment, and a multiplier effect on growth. In the 1980s it has been seized on as a remedy, in some cases the only apparent remedy, for the unemployment which has risen on the old continent. Tourism has the capacity to reduce foreign debt, which makes it attractive at a time when some great industrial nations are experiencing severe balance of payments deficits. Furthermore, as a result of tourism's expansion, these countries expect to lessen the effects of the ups and downs in their domestic economies. So, more and more societies have become more and more involved in the process of generating tourism.

Nothing illustrates this better than the changes in tourist policy in European countries over the last decade. Within the European Economic Community there is now an acute awareness of the economic potential of international tourism. This activity was estimated to represent 8 percent of private consumption in the countries which comprised the Community in 1982. The income that Spain and Greece derived from tourism was an argument used to justify their membership of the EEC. In 1983 a resolution adopted by the European Parliament read:

> The promotion of tourism in Europe brings about a tightening of links between citizens, it enhances mutual understanding and contributes to a better understanding of each other's cultures and special qualities, which is in line with the aim written into the preamble to the Treaty of Rome, to build the foundations of an ever closer union between European peoples.

In 1984 a special commission was established within the EEC to formulate a common policy for member states.

When examining tourism today we find ourselves dealing with a phenomenon which arises from a whole range of factors of a political, economic, geographic, technical, socio-cultural and symbolic nature. This phenomenon is currently leading to changes in virtually every area of collective life, in institutions, and in mentality. The idea, therefore, that tourism concerns only certain geographical regions where tourists come and go is false. To limit our perspective to the places where tourists journey from and to would restrict our ability to understand tourism's present-day multi-dimensional significance. Tourism does not exist only where there are tourists!

### Tourist company networks in the world economy

Over the years the tourist industry has created a production mechanism which is now one of the most powerful levers in the entire world economy. The economic agents are not independent firms, each working according to its own individual logic. Operators in the countries which receive and despatch tourists have progressively become multinationals through amalgamations, leading to horizontal and vertical integration. These multinationals have networks of agents in ostensibly separate business sectors. The tourist production mechanism has operated as a prototype for the transnational corporation in the world economy. All the main characteristics of the emergent world economic system are already well developed in the tourist industry – displacement of the unit of production, delocalisation of raw materials from their places of origin and producers, organisation of free export zones, and enclaves of production and consumption run directly by the firms sometimes to the detriment of the customs and practices of the host countries. Many decisions which concern regions and, indeed, whole countries are now taken at the international level by transnational corporations. The so-called partners, the countries or the regional or local authorities, may be unable to intervene or even enter the discussions. Competition between firms is often annulled by preliminary agreements.

The decision to build Eurodisneyland outside Paris illustrates perfectly the leading role now being played by the tourist industry in the creation of a global economic system. A US company which first specialised in the creation of leisure parks has become an international network of firms, creating a host of products for a global market. The new town of Marne-la-Vallée near Paris was chosen for Eurodisneyland, and is expected to welcome 10 million visitors annually. This site is aimed not only at stimulating tourism and earning foreign currency, but also forms part of an ambitious plan of land restructuring and regional development intended to place Paris and the Ile-de-France in a pivotal position in a communications network radiating through Europe to the rest of the world. Marne-la-Vallée will soon offer a concentration of new industries sponsored by the Walt Disney Company, which over the last ten years has successfully diversified its activities. This firm unites into one industrial whole the development of leisure parks, a cable communications network for press and television, the manufacture of pictures, models and all the apparatus essential to the creation of illusion. This new industry incorporates the most up-to-date scientific discoveries in communications, and is marshalling all the knowledge required to create a *planetary culture* of universal influence.

An interesting point in all this is the deliberate invention of reality which the promoters are often achieving. Eurodisneyland is the materialisation of a humanist philosophy. By means of theatre it broadcasts what sociologists have identified as values central to American society: the desire to belong to an interdependent community akin to a large family, to enjoy a fun atmosphere, and to display at all times a smiling and cheerful appearance. 'Visiting a leisure park should give one a feeling of well-being. Our challenge', says R. Beards, 'is to make this feeling come alive for the billions of people who live on this earth. . . what we must do is transform our country, to constantly improve it and after that we will transform the world. It is a vast project but while others are lost in idle words we will accomplish the task which will shape the future' (Beards, 1988).

In Manila in 1980 the World Tourist Organisation declared:

> Tourism. . . is the moral and intellectual basis of mutual understanding and interdependence among nations. . . equipped to bring in a new economic order which will help to reduce the gulf between developed and underdeveloped countries. . . a means of reducing international tension and developing co-operation in a spirit of friendship, of respect for the rights of man and of mutual understanding. . . in an equality of destiny of societies and nations, and of the unique character of each culture. . . .(OMT, 1985)

Dann (1986) has analysed some 4000 samples of tourist advertising. In the brochures the tourist is shown in childlike postures, in the form of an adult but with the mind of a child, subjected to natural desires which seek immediate gratification constrained only by the pleasure principle. Dann also explores how the theme of Mother Nature is presented. He explains how the brochures show images reminiscent of a mother's breast, suggesting luxuriant virgin landscapes, enchanted hills, mysterious valleys, torrential rivers, lakes beneath a smiling sun which caresses and massages us, and gives its beneficial warmth to beautiful, bronzed, healthy children who surrender in total innocence. These themes, to be truthful, are not new. In Veblen's (1899) theory, the leisured class is compelled by the need to satisfy primitive instincts. Kurt Krapf (1952), an economist, in his contribution to the theory of tourist consumption, did not hesitate to refer to Jungian theories of the unconscious in explaining the mysteries of tourist demand. Thus, he constructed a concept of the tourist in search of an archetypal origin common to the savage and civilised man. Edgar Morin (1962), in his turn, perceived a planetary culture 'as a way of understanding which responds to a cosmopolitan aspiration upheld by the idea that all civilisations are born of the same common tree. . . referring to the emotional predispositions of an imaginary universal man who is like the child and the archaic, but always present in the *homo faber*. . .'

However, in the specific case of Eurodisneyland we are not in the realm of pure illusion. The scenes and characters are not all fictional: many are drawn from history. In many cases they are people in the *collective memory* and arouse feelings of national, regional or local identity. How will as eccentric a culture as the American be received in France? This question has preoccupied the creators of the Eurodisneyland project who have carried out study after study to analyse the mentality of future visitors. The French are inclined to a deep-rooted chauvinism, being very proud of their historic values and cultural heritage. The problem is further complicated because Eurodisneyland is not exclusively aimed at French visitors. It hopes to attract millions from all over Europe and elsewhere, people who so often in the past have waged fratricidal wars against each other. In this context, the worldwide ambitions of the promoters of the operation become contradictory. For the time being, they are adopting a policy suited to the present situation. Their problem is how to internationalise the spirit of Disney, and to this end they are not hesitating to revive his original name, Isigny. They are internationalising man himself, 'this truly unique citizen. . . this citizen of the world'.

Scores of similar initiatives are being launched. Ethnic and linguistic minorities in every continent are making their voices heard. In Europe, inspired by the prospect of the Act of Union, regional identities are asserting themselves forcefully in new strategies and demands for increased powers. Regions are claiming superiority for their unusual characteristics and distinctions, which are being packaged as tourist products. Throughout the history of the creation of nation states, local communities and regions have progressively been stripped of their powers. With international tourism, however, they are finding a new way to regain their former status. In the process of the reconstruction of Europe, provinces are promoting a conception of a Europe of Regions. Local communities, in their turn, are arguing for a Europe of Peoples. There are abundant possibilities for conflict.

## Post-modern culture and tourist neo-culture

Tourism divides, but simultaneously lays the foundations for a new unity. Touristification provokes a dialogue which crosses, tears and divides cultural systems. The processes of this dialogue overlap, confuse and contradict each other. What we see at local level, rather than a conforming and unifying process, is a cohabitation of many strategies which in principle run contrary to each other. For example, a firm attachment to traditional values often coexists with resolutely forward-looking practices.

In France the growth in the number of second homes during the recent decades has led to the construction of some very grand, architecturally daring schemes in coastal, mountain and rural areas. But at the same time, and often side by side, we see an almost manic infatuation with restoring deserted villages, châteaux, priories, old country cottages and prehistoric caves. Residential tourism has given birth to a whole new building industry which uses the most modern technological advances and mixes them with the traditional skills of rural artisans. For example, developers try to preserve intact mountain villages with traditional chalets, while building alongside them ski centres with mechanised lifts and artificial slopes, and powdered snow for summer use. The tourist industry is also seeking out picturesque fishing villages and building pleasure ports into urban developments where boats can be moored at the entrance to buildings, as at the palace doors in Venice. Sand is being imported to the rocky Mediterranean coast to create unique bathing resorts. And in the heart of great urban centres there are schemes to re-create tropical nature with lagoons and coconut palms. We are creating centres for science, engineering and the arts where visitors, with guides, can imagine themselves to be cosmonauts, deep-sea divers, or pot-holers.

The international cuisine which has become the norm in top tourist resorts is a good example of the combination of the raw and the cooked, the natural and the artificial. This new art has little to do with that science of taste which inspired the great culinary masters of the past who built the reputations of their regions. International cuisine unashamedly mixes the ingredients of various regional specialities. Its peak is the mixed salad served on a decorated plate. Something similar applies to clothes. The female tourist is just as happy with a piece of material bought from a flea market, or a ready-to-wear garment of synthetic material, or a heavy costume, hand-embroidered on damask, provided they can all be prettily draped around a body free from imperfections thanks to the daily consumption of factory-processed 'natural' mineral water.

But it is in the field of tourist entertainment that this kind of coexistence is perhaps most vivid. The combination of diverse symbols is not simply born of amateurish enthusiasm or a taste for show. It reflects the cultural muddle in which kitsch societies take so much pleasure. These hybrid cultures are revolutionary. The archaic becomes post-modern, the classic becomes baroque, proponents of the avant-garde draw their inspiration from primitive art, and the shock of the future collides with the shock of the past. By clever twists and turns, cultural tourism comes to be fed by a tourist culture, a truly two-sided entity which can fulfil the related expectations of visitors and the societies that welcome them. One might be tempted to say that it is Western civilisation, whatever that may be, which imposes its norms. However, there are numerous examples of cultural exchanges in the opposite direction. Bali and Java have revived their cultural displays and artistic traditions, even those designed for their own gods. Innovators from technically advanced countries often look to traditional societies for inspiration. Tourism, which at first seems to belong unmistakably to modernity since it derives from industrial society, turns its back on the sophistication of that society and assimilates tradition, relics and even obsolescence into its design. Tourism thus attempts the reconciliation of that which was contradictory. Such efforts are called post-modern by some philosophers.

However, tourism is not in opposition to the values of modernity but operates in conjunction with them. The transmutation of values it permits is not akin to the works of certain avant-garde artists in the 1920s who rejected anything that was already highly valued. The post-modern culture is created by the integration of species and kinds in a coiled movement which produces the type of universality which Morin (1962) believes to be characteristic of a new planetary culture.

### The production of tourist attractions

In response to the demand for tourist products to market, much historical research has been carried out to recreate scenes and events from the past with a view to their reconstruction and display. Efforts to preserve cultures, to restore heritage, to conserve works of art, to re-create outstanding events, and to develop museums and archaeology are multiplying year by year. We see buildings and objects, which only a short time ago seemed destined for scrap, becoming heritage or collectable works. Thanks to tourism many of these relics are now on the way to becoming profitable. Demand is so strong that we are turning into history even things which are still in use today. Everywhere in Europe and on other continents we encounter this same process. As soon as the traditional activities that gave a region its vitality are at risk, solutions are sought which involve tourism taking their place. Whether or not there is any initial tourist attraction seems to matter not a bit. The tourist industry constantly invents new sites and sights. Folklore which never existed is discovered. The scope of archaeology is widened to include the present. Thus the notion of natural advantages, through which economists believe they can explain the special characteristics of a region which make it a tourist area, becomes irrelevant. Even within the United States this process of touristification is in motion. As soon as agricultural land is allocated to a new use, archaeologists, ethnologists and touristologists quickly flock, as elsewhere, reinventing ethnic groups, the culture and the society that once existed. They are even crossing the frozen plains of the North, and despatching scouts to mark out some remarkable journeys, before selling them, at exorbitant rates, to create Christmasses full of magic.

We should not imagine that only the relics of ethnic cultures are profitable. While exporting its expertise abroad, the Walt Disney Company is gathering towards its geographical centre avant-garde productions on which to base some future commercial enterprise. A cathedral of modern painting is to be built and filled with totally original works. Some believe that we are now seeing efforts to create a new and universal reservoir of memories in response to trends which are destroying national, regional and local identities, together with former attachments to native lands and cultures. Heritage, native land and ancestry find suitable modern homes within international tourism whose mission, essential function and duty appears to be to hold on to or unveil all evidence of human and animal life since the beginning of time. This evidence, dutifully preserved, bears witness to the transmission, without apparent break, of original creation. Herein lies the source of the quasi-religious compulsion to travel in order to discover new things.

All conservationists soon confront strategies which seem to be pulling in different directions. One looks to the past and tries to preserve the integrity of monuments, sites and heritage. The other preaches that they should be appropriated and brought to life in schemes of cultural development linked to tourism. Reconstruction of the past satisfies the criteria of historical research only when undertaken by historians with scruples about the verification of sources and facts. The presentation of the past in places which become tourist attractions obeys rather different rules. Not everything can be said and shown. The industry insists that sites be attractive, but this is not the real problem. Sites must satisfy the tourists' demand for authenticity. Guarantees of authenticity are expected. This sometimes means that the spectacles must be more real than reality. Delicate problems arise when it is necessary to respect foreigners' sensitivities. Today's hosts and visitors were often enemies yesterday. People expect tourism to be a peacemaker, so the tourist industry believes that it is best to avoid anything which might stir old hostilities. This may lead to ignoring whole areas of history, or denying events which still linger cruelly in some people's memories. It is an often misinterpreted and sometimes gilded history that is offered to tourists. Conversely, tourism is sometimes used to revive or nourish national or regional sentiments, and even to declare, in the view of guests, resistance to some domestic or foreign repression. Given the many and varied contradictions, the often asked question of whether the intrusion of tourism leads to the degeneration of cultures or contributes to their renaissance seems rather naive. Any movement towards the genuine preservation of cultures seems doomed once it engages with the processes of tourism which change, weaken, destroy and consume to excess. The two case studies which follow illustrate the complex tangle of economic and symbolic transformations involved in creating a tourist product.

### The manufacture of a cultural heritage

Let us examine the case of a bourgeois family who, on the death of a parent, inherited a dilapidated forge dating back to the Middle Ages (Bazin, 1987). Up to the time of its closure in 1975 this forge was subject to all manner of changes in line with the technical advances of the day. The building was well constructed of attractive old bricks and situated in a lush valley in a rural area. Its owners obtained a public subsidy to restore the forge to an earlier appearance, made the building into a mini-museum, then transferred the site to public ownership. Eminent local and regional officials, and representatives from the central government, then entered into dispute about its guardianship. With the change of purpose the building assumed entirely new meanings, which varied according to the beholders. The place which for the family was an inheritance, a link with their hard-working forebears, was taken out of their care and ownership. What was a harsh workplace for generations of peasant workers assumed a cultural value. Suddenly the formerly oppressed workers were expected to become willing artisans. What was for the region and the commune a little workshop of no great importance became an Arts and Crafts Museum which began to attract historians, sociologists, ethnologists and archaeologists who then set about adding to the collections and reconstructing the past of the region, thus transforming the site into a cultural heritage. For the state authorities the place became, first and foremost, a tourist attraction to be marketed as a useful image in promoting the region. Thus, in the course of its reconversion, the forge, formerly private property and a family inheritance, became a tourist asset. Entrepreneurs, government agencies and the working class now stand together at the altar of international tourism to pass their heritage down to future generations.

**The display and the foreigner**

Edward Bruner, an ethnologist by training, studied at first hand an encounter between visitors and those visited, hosts and guests, by joining a group of Americans travelling to Africa to discover a primitive society, as the tourist brochure had promised (Bruner, 1986, 1987). Bruner approached the tourist encounter as if he had been going to the theatre to see a previously unperformed work. The spectacle that he witnessed demonstrates how the local actors, the natives of the place, in the flesh, had been taught how to offer their public a cultural display corresponding to the tourists' expectations. This performance assumes particular significance when we realise that we are talking about the Masai, an invincible warlike people who have preserved their identity within the state of Kenya which has now embraced international tourism as a means of enhancing its economic independence and recognition. The encounter took place in the Mayers' territory. The Mayers are the descendants of former European settlers who, at the time of independence, adopted Kenyan citizenship. To improve their lot, they had the idea of turning part of their land, which was close to native villages, into a kind of ethnic reserve. They reached an agreement with the village chief that a model village, especially aimed at welcoming tourists, should be built on the Mayers' land. Thus every day between 50 and 150 visitors, accompanied by interpreter-guides, began disembarking from coaches to be greeted personally by the Mayers.

Thus we continue the visit with our ethnologist, a tourist for the time being, armed with his camera. We can observe the African way of life and scenes typical of daily existence. We are shown the materials which come from their looms, and the decorated weapons which have made the Masai famous throughout the world. We see their elementary tools, and even mix with the villagers and eventually speak to them. As the culmination of this visit we take our places on specially made rows of stepped seats to watch a 'wild and sensual' war dance. The Mayers also play their parts in the tableau. They are the real link between guests and hosts. They show each group how they should conduct themselves to fulfil the expectations each has of the other. All evidence of outside influence which would remind us of technically advanced civilisation has to be removed: plastic watches, radio aerials, jeans and T-shirts. The visitors are made to understand that they must avoid looking blasé or disappointed. We understand that the ethnologist who watches these displays with some emotion may feel somewhat troubled when confronted with these new links which are being formed, through international tourism, between societies of ethnological interest and their guests coming from afar especially to discover some basic truth. This poses the question of the role of ethnology in the tableau, in exotic societies confronted with the sophistication of the modern.

It would be wrong to imagine that the process of offering to tourism one's daily life, packaged as a display, is peculiar to archaic, far-flung, backward societies. This same process can be seen in the hearts of great European cities which not only conserve, restore and faithfully rebuild their oldest remnants, but also insist that the inhabitants contribute to the re-creation of neighbourhoods as they were in the past. And it is not only when preparing for special festivals that these well-intentioned local people join in. It becomes an everyday practice to display old customs for the pleasure of sightseers. To varying extents we have all become actors in a 'quest' for culture which involves tearing down while at the same time conserving, and finding originality without even trying to discover it. We are all inventors!

### Elementary structure of society in the system of tourist attractions

MacCannell (1976) has offered a neo-Durkheimian interpretation of tourism as a constraint which the modern-day individual cannot escape. Visiting a monument is like a sacred rite which must be performed in the course of one's travels. The trip acquires a sense of commemoration as did, and still does, the journey of the pilgrim to the place of his spiritual fulfilment. In order to be included in a journey, a site must be marked by some distinguishing characteristic which makes it uniquely worthy of attention. MacCannell deliber-ately uses a vocabulary borrowed from religious culture to make us understand that almost any object can be turned into a tourist attraction and become that 'something' which must not be missed at any price. To elevate 'something' into such an attraction we frame it, raise it up, light it, enshrine it and put it under spotlights. Thus, when displayed, the attraction appears set apart from the base world of everyday objects. It thereby becomes in some way sacred.

The tourist who travels from place to place becomes engaged, without even knowing it, in the fulfilment of a ritual celebration and permanent homage to the works, remnants and relics of the civilisations of our forebears. He participates as the final link in the chain of tourist production and consumption to which so many international organisations are now dedicated. The 1980s have seen many serious meetings called by these organisations instructing governments, and those involved in the preservation of sites and monuments, to take account of the spiritual value of tourism. In Mexico, in 1982, the French Minister of Culture, no doubt with good intentions, proposed that every country should become involved in cataloguing cultures to be included in a Common Fund of Universal Heritage. Even sociology, with its schemes for classifying cultures, is threatened by the embrace of the tourist industry. Sociology and tourist culture have, perhaps surprisingly, similar objectives – the gathering together of all the individual cultures which cover the planet into one universal whole (Lévi-Strauss, 1962). Hence, perhaps, the profound culture shock which encountering international tourism leads sociologists to experience.

## Note

This chapter is a shortened and edited translation of the original French text.

## References

Affergan, F. (1987) *Exotisme et Altérité*. Paris: Presses Universitaires de France.

AIF: Association Internationale Futuribles (1985) *Dossier de Synthèse Documentaire sur l'avenir de la Fonction Touristique*. Paris.

Ascher, F. (1986) 'Tourisme', *Sociétés*, 2: 5–6.

Balandier, G. (1960) 'Dynamique des Relations Extérieures des Sociétés Archaïques', in G. Gurvitch (ed.), *Traité de Sociologie*. Paris: Presses Universitaires de France.

Bazin, C. (1987) 'Capital Industriel, Patrimoine Culturel: vers un Capital Touristique?', *Problems of Tourism*, 10: 63–75.

Beards, R. (1988) *Creating the New World of Tomorrow*. Paris: Epcot.

Boyer, M. (1980) 'Evolution Sociologique du Tourisme – Continuité du Touriste Rare au Touriste de Masse et Rupture Contemporaine', *Loisir et Société*, 3: 49–81.

Bruner, E.M. (1986) 'Experience and its Expressions', in V.W. Turner and E.M.

Bruner (eds.), *The Anthropology of Experience*. Chicago: University of Illinois Press.

Bruner, E.M. (1987) 'Mayers' Ranch and the Kedong Masai Manyatta', *Problems of Tourism*, 10: 25–9.

Dann, G. (1986) 'The Tourist as a Child', paper presented to XI Congrès Mondial de Sociologie, New Delhi. August 1986.

European Parliament (1983) *Document du Parlement Européen*, PE 83: 993.

Gee, C. and C. Gain (1986) 'Coping with the Crisis', *Economist*, June: 3–12.

Institut Européen des Hautes Etudes Internationales (1986) *Développement Touristique et Identités Régionales*. Nice: Presses de l'Europe.

Krapf, K. (1952) *La Consommation Touristique: une Contribution à une Théorie de la Consommation*. Aix-en-Provence: Centre d'Etudes du Tourisme.

Krapf, K. (1961) 'Les Pays en Voie de Développement face au Tourisme: Introduction Méthodologique', *Revue de Tourisme*, 3: 82–9.

Krapf, K. (1963) *Tourism as a Factor in Economic Development*. Rome: United Nations Conference on International Travel and Tourism.

*International Social Science*. 32: 141–3.

Lanfant, M.F. (1980) 'Tourism in the Process of Internationalization', *International Social Science*. 32: 141–3

Lanfant, M.F. (1987) 'L'impact Social et Culturel du Tourisme International', *Poblems of Tourism*, 10: 3–20.

Lanfant, M.F., C. Bazin, M. Picard and J. de Weerdt (1988) *Les Problematiques de l'impact Social et Culturel du Tourisme International*. Paris: URESTI–CNRS.

Lanquar, R. (1984) 'Nouveaux Patrimoines, Nouveau Tourisme', *Revue de Tourisme*, 4: 12–16.

Lévi-Strauss, C. (1962) *La Pensée Sauvage*. Paris: Plon.

Lipovetsky, G. (1983) *L'ère du Vide: Essais sur l'individualisme Contemporain*. Paris: Gallimard.

MacCannell, D. (1976) *The Tourist: a New Theory of the Leisure Class*. New York: Schocken Books.

Maffesoli, M. and C. Rivière (1985) *Une Anthropologie des Turbulences: Hommages à Georges Balandier*. Paris: Berg.

Malempre, G. (1982) 'Le Tourisme comme Industrie Culturelle', *Revue de Tourisme*, 1: 2–5.

Michalet, C.A. (1976) *Le Capitalisme Mondial*. Paris: Presses Universitaires de France.

Minc, A. (1982) *L'après-crise est Commencé*. Paris: Gallimard.

Morin, E. (1962) *L'esprit du Temps: Essai sur la Culture de Masse*. Paris: Grasset.

Morin, E. (1981) *Pour Sortir du Vingtième Siècle*. Paris: Nathan.

Moussis, N. (1986) 'Communication', in *Le Tourisme: Facteur de Développement en Europe*. Brussels: Colloque ASEDIFRES.

OECD: Organisation for Economic Co-operation and Development (1984) *Politique du Tourisme et Tourisme International dans les Pays de L'OCDE*. Paris.

Perroux, F. (1982) *Dialogue des Monopoles et des Nations: Equilibre des Unités Actives*. Grenoble: Presses Universitaires.

Picard, M. (1984) *Tourisme Culturel et Culture Touristique: Rite et Divertissement dans les Arts du Spectacle à Bali*, PhD thesis, EHESS, Paris.

Pluss, C. (1987) 'Le Tourisme aux Maldives: un Cas Extrême, un Cas Exemplaire?', *Problems of Tourism*, 10: 76–82.

Ritchie, J.R.B. and C.R. Goeldner (eds) (1987) *Travel, Tourism and Hospitality*

*Research: a Handbook for Managers and Researchers*. New York: Wiley.

Urbain, J.-D. (1978) *La Société de Conservation*. Paris: Payot.

Veblen, T. (1949) *The Theory of the Leisure Class*. London: Allen and Unwin. (First published 1912).

WTO (1979) *Etude sur la Contribution du Tourisme à l'Échange des Valeurs Spirituelles et à une Meilleure Comprehension entre les Peuples*. Madrid.

WTO (1980) *Déclaration de Manille sur le Tourisme Mondial*. Madrid.

WTO (1985) *Rôle de l'Etat dans la Sauvegarde et la Promotion de la Culture comme Facteur de Développement Touristique et dans la Mise en Valeur du Patrimoine Nationale de Sites et de Monuments à des Fins Touristiques*. Madrid.

# Index

*Index compiled by Fiona Barr, Society of Indexers*